Penguin Handbooks

# The Penguin Money Book

Eamonn Fingleton was born at Malin, Co. Donegal, in 1948.
He won a scholarship to Trinity College Dublin, where he read
economics and mathematics. He joined the *Irish Independent*
as a reporter when he graduated in 1970. He has worked as a City
reporter for the *Daily Mirror*, money editor and columnist for
the *Sun* and savings editor for the *Financial Times*. He is now a
financial writer for *Now!* magazine. He is widowed.

Tom Tickell, who is thirty-seven, has been family finance editor of the
*Guardian* for almost eight years, and has broadcast extensively about
finance. He was educated at Westminster School and Oxford and
claims that he understands people's blocks on finance because he
himself managed to fail O-level maths on five separate occasions. His
career in journalism began as a scriptwriter for Independent Television
News and he spent two years as a general feature writer for the
*Economist*, before joining the *Guardian* in 1970. He is married, lives in
north London and his hobbies are politics and mimicry.

Eamonn Fingleton and Tom Tickell

# The Penguin Money Book

Penguin Books

Penguin Books Ltd, Harmondsworth, Middesex, England
Penguin Books, 625 Madison Avenue, New York, New York 10022, U.S.A.
Penguin Books Australia Ltd, Ringwood, Victoria, Australia
Penguin Books Canada Ltd, 2801 John Street, Markham,
Ontario, Canada L3R 1B4
Penguin Books (N.Z.) Ltd, 182–190 Wairau Road,
Auckland 10, New Zealand

First published 1981

Made and printed in Great Britain by
Richard Clay (The Chaucer Press) Ltd, Bungay, Suffolk
Filmset in Times New Roman

# Contents

# Acknowledgements

We have both had enormous help in writing this book, and would like to thank everyone who has been through our copy both checking and making suggestions. We are particularly grateful to Mark Daniel of Equitable Life for advice on a whole range of subjects. Roy Randall of Royal Insurance, Richard Sleight of Legal & General, and Albert Hallam of Barclays Insurance Services helped on insurance matters. Mavis Moulin of Moulin Sargent, Patrick Lewis of the Inland Revenue, Clare Leeming of NatWest, and David Major of Godwins all helped on tax points.

Our thanks go too to John Fairbairn of M & G Securities, Tony Arnaud of Touche Remnant and Bert Morris of Lloyds Bank Unit Trust Managers for help with the chapter on risk investments; John Orr of the Department of Social Security and Mike Brown of the Company Pensions Information Centre (retirement chapter); John Fry of the Abbey National and Joe Bradley of the Nationwide (saving and house-purchase chapters); Charles Scanlon of Simmonds & Simmonds and Clare Dyer of the Law Society for help on wills (Chapter 11); Kate Nash; and Geoffrey Kelly of Barclays and Glen Emmanuel of NatWest (banking chapter).

Anne Tickell gave us great encouragement, and help in typing and correcting, and we would like to thank our editors at Penguin, first Jill Norman and then Peter Wright, for a lot of patience and support.

E. F.
T. T.

# 1. Making the Most of Your Money

Many people are terrified by finance, and all the ramifications of mortgages, insurance, bank and hire-purchase loans and so on. They feel not only that the whole subject is dreary, but that it is incomprehensible to anyone who is not a professional. They are wrong on both counts. The difficulty is that there are armies of specialists in each subject, each of which has developed its own jargon so that it all sounds more complex than it is. Sometimes this language is a form of shorthand, no doubt, but jargon can also be used to sell you some ingenious, flashy insurance or investment scheme that you do not want. The first rule for coping with your finances is to make people explain themselves, and never to commit yourself to any plan immediately. You usually need time to mull it over and get a second opinion.

Your financial needs change in the course of your life – as you grow older, start to pay tax, have to think about buying a house, and begin insuring your possessions and yourself too. You shift from saving to borrowing and back to saving again in the course of a lifetime, at the end of which comes retirement.

Most young people should start planning to buy a home of their own as soon as they leave school. The huge profits people have made from home ownership over the last decade are not an accident: they result from a mass of subsidies for home ownership. State incentives to buy your own home have been under attack from economists for years, as a distortion of the market in determining how the nation's resources should be used. But both main political parties remain committed to home ownership and home owners' privileges look certain to survive more or less intact for years to come.

The cheapest way to buy a house is usually with a building-society loan. Normally you need to have saved with a society for many months before it will consider you for a loan. As Chapter 5 points out, building societies vary widely in their lending rules, so it is worth making sure the society you start saving with is happy to make the sort of loan you have in mind. Home buyers are coming under increasing pressure to take out mortgages linked to endowment policies, but experts consider that the ordinary 'repayment' type of mortgage is still the best buy for most basic-rate taxpayers. It is considerably cheaper than even the cheapest of the endowment methods in the early years, when not only is money more valuable but home buyers are most stretched.

If you do buy an endowment life-insurance policy, a few hours shopping around for the right company will probably pay big dividends. Anyone who simply accepts the first policy offered to him may well later discover that the insurance broker had not done his homework – or had his own reasons for suggesting something that turns out to be an unsuitable choice. The stakes are high. A recent survey by *Money Management* magazine showed that for twenty-five-year endowment policies maturing in 1980, the best companies paid out more than half as much again as the worst. A man aged twenty-nine at the start who had invested £10 a month before tax relief in a policy with the Norwich Union would have collected £9,022 – the highest pay-out in the survey. The worst pay-out was only £5,209, from the Federation Mutual. The average for all companies was £7,201.

Even more important than shopping around for the best company is to question whether you need an endowment policy in the first place. Every year thousands of single young people sign up for endowment policies almost as soon as they start earning, without questioning what their real financial priorities are. Later, they often find that they want to buy a house and need to raise a deposit. The money invested in the endowment policy would have built up to a tidy sum if it had gone into a building-society account. But an endowment policy is a long-term plan and has little or no cash-in value in the early years. Many savers caught in this trap find they lose out in two ways: they cannot afford to continue to pay premiums on the endowment policy while they accumulate the house deposit, but by cashing in they wave goodbye to most of the hard-earned premium money they have so far paid.

These are just two examples from the dozens of pitfalls that await those who do not think out their financial priorities early in life. This book's main aim is to give you the information and advice you need to work out a strategy for your finances.

It is particularly important to get life insurance into perspective, because life-insurance salesmen can be hard to resist and the amount you commit to a life policy can add up to a staggering figure over the years. Struggling young family men are often pushed into taking out endowment policies as a way of buying life cover to protect their widow should they die early. In fact, as Chapter 2 points out, little-known 'family income benefit' policies are by far the best way of buying simple life cover. A family-income-benefit policy can give a thirty-year-old man as much as £50,000 of immediate life cover for less than £25 a year. If you wanted an endowment policy with £50,000 of initial cover you would have to pay more than £2,000 a year. Of course, an endowment policy offers much more than simple life cover – and family-income-benefit policies have the drawback that the total amount of cover declines as each year passes.

The difference between endowment and family-income-benefit policies is the difference between Rolls-Royces and Minis. But by scaling down the amount of cover you buy, you can have an endowment policy to fit your pocket. Who would buy the back axle of a Rolls-Royce if they could have a whole Mini for the same price?

And what if you have a family?

Children are not likely to pay tax, unless the income arises from an investment provided by their parents. So if you want to save on their behalf, the best way to do it and to be able to use it for instant money is usually through a bank deposit account. Building-society interest may come tax-paid, but children get no benefit from this if they do not pay tax.

Parents can help students by a tax covenant, which uses the tax system to provide them with extra funds, on top of what the parents have given. We look into this in Chapter 8. A holiday job is another source of income for students, and there are ways of ensuring that they do not have to pay tax each week, if they do not come within the general net. Students are just the people banks try to entice in as customers, with special offers of various kinds. For all the advertising, there is not much difference in what they offer.

You can get by without a bank account – nearly half of Britain's work-force still do. But, as Chapter 3 shows, managing your money is easier if you have a cheque-book account with a bank. For a start, saving is less painful if you do not have cash burning a hole in your wallet or purse. Bank standing orders which automatically settle regular bills are almost essential for anyone with monthly mortgage payments or insurance premiums to pay. But the most valuable single perk you get from a bank account is the chance to borrow at reasonable interest rates. The lending rates of the big banks are usually several percentage points lower than those of finance companies. Also their lending is more flexible – if you are a good customer, a telephone call may be all that is needed to arrange an overdraft to tide you over a minor financial crisis.

Banks are constantly changing their scales of charges for cheques and standing orders, but overall there is usually little to choose between them. The Post Office's National Girobank lacks some of the more sophisticated services of the big banks, but can be a convenient and cheap alternative for anyone who needs just a basic current-account service.

If you have spare cash available, what do you do with it? The traditional answer is to save it. Certainly a cushion of money to tide you over emergencies is useful. If you want to put away funds for longer, you should go for the contracts which have a lifeline, allowing you to take out your funds early if you need it, even if they impose an interest penalty for doing it. To get the most from your saving you need to invest in ways to suit your tax position, and you need to be clear on how long you can afford to tie up your money. For non-taxpayers investing a lump sum, the best bets are likely to be government securities, local-authority loans or bank deposit accounts (see Chapter 7, 'Short-term Saving'). Generally, the longer you tie up your money, the higher the interest rate. For people paying tax at the basic rate, building-society 'term' shares are a good bet. National Savings Certificates pay tax-free returns, so are particularly suitable for high-rate taxpayers, but are also often a useful choice for basic-rate taxpayers. Regular savers get a good tax-paid return combined with maximum flexibility in building-society 'subscription shares'. If you can be sure of staying the course for four years, building-society insurance-linked plans are a little-known but highly lucrative alternative. The National Savings inflation-proofed Save As You Earn scheme is an excellent bet if you can save for five years, particularly if you are a high-rate taxpayer.

If tax is deducted from your pay at source through the PAYE system, there is often little you can do to cut the Inland Revenue's take except make the most of allowances for home loans, pensions and life insurance. But as Chapter 8 explains, covenants are an under-used way of earning tax relief on money you give to relatives or to charity.

Where a married couple both have well-paid jobs, they should watch for the point at which it may make sense for them to renounce married status for tax purposes and opt to be taxed as single people. In the 1980–81 tax year, this might be worth while when joint earnings exceed £16,000 (if there are allowances for mortgage interest or pension payments, the threshold would be correspondingly higher).

The self-employed have considerable scope for cutting their tax bills by careful planning, but usually their position is so complicated that they need the advice of an accountant. A crucial point that anyone setting up in business should note is that you give yourself maximum scope legitimately to delay paying your tax bills if you choose your financial year to end shortly after the beginning of the tax year. Would-be entrepreneurs should also remember that thanks to recent Budget changes it is now usually wiser to start as self-employed rather than operate through a limited company: you can use start-up losses to claim rebates of PAYE tax you paid in previous years.

The earliest most people can afford the luxury of an endowment policy is probably in their thirties. But even then an endowment policy still may not be the best answer. Most people who stop to think about it will probably find they need to save mainly for their old age. As Chapter 9 explains, pension-oriented saving earns more tax subsidies than life insurance and provides dramatically better returns over the long run. The best-known methods of boosting your pension are restricted to the self-employed and others not in full-scale company pension schemes. But company-pension-scheme members may also have attractive opportunities that they are not aware of. All the same, remember that you cannot cash in a pension contract.

Retirement brings a change in the tax rules, so it is worth checking that you are not going to be hit by problems with the age allowance. It can make keeping your savings in a building society less attractive, for instance. Index-linked Savings Certificates, whose inflation-proofed returns are tax-free, are overwhelmingly attractive for the over-sixties.

If you own your home, Chapter 9 shows you how to get an income from it.

Most people put off making a will until late in life, although this is running the risk of trouble if you die young. As Chapter 11 points out, life for a bereaved husband or wife is a little easier in the months after you die if you have left a will, otherwise there may be family rows about who gets what and there may be delay before your affairs are tidied up. A hidden bonus from making your will is that it may alert you to a long-term financial problem looming on the horizon: capital-transfer tax, the gifts tax which has replaced death duties. At the rates applying in 1980–81, if you have net assets of more than £50,000 you are likely to face a capital-transfer-tax problem sooner or later, but you can reduce your liability by planning ahead.

You generally get what you pay for when you insure your possessions. Many people make the mistake of not insuring their home and its contents for their full value, so there is a row with the insurance company if they have a claim. 'Inflation-proofed new-for-old' cover, explained in Chapter 6, is what most people probably need – and if they economize by going for lesser cover they may be badly out of pocket on claims.

You can cut the cost of car insurance by shopping around for the lowest quotation, but many small companies offering cut-price insurance often turn out to be unsympathetic and tardy about paying claims. The 'excess' principle, by which you are covered for the amount of a claim above a certain figure (often

£100), can be useful in cutting premium costs. Insurance companies can afford to give a good discount because an excess cuts out a mass of administratively costly claims for small amounts.

Risk investments like shares, unit trusts and equity bonds are mainly for people who have something left over after they have made the most of tax-advantaged investments like pensions and endowment policies. Playing the stock market can be an interesting pastime, but, as Chapter 10 points out, it is a luxury for most people and the amount of money devoted to it should be strictly controlled.

Where should you go for financial advice? No one expert covers the whole range of personal finance and you can end up with conflicting advice depending on whether you consult an insurance broker, solicitor, bank manager, stockbroker or accountant. Partly, the explanation is that the experts will naturally recommend a course of action in the field they know best – and they may well be unaware of opportunities outside their speciality. Commercial pressures such as those produced by the practice of paying insurance commission may also distort an adviser's view. It is a good practice, when comparing alternative courses of action, to ask how much commission is involved.

It is always useful to get a second opinion before taking an adviser's recommendation, but where advisers' views conflict you have to fall back on your own understanding of the subject and your judgement of people.

Newspapers are becoming an increasingly informed source of independent advice. The *Daily Telegraph*, with its Saturday 'Money-Go-Round' section, and the *Daily Mail*, with 'Money Mail' on Wednesdays, have pioneered the trend and their coverage is still among the most comprehensive. The Saturday editions of *The Times*, the *Financial Times*, the *Guardian* and the *Daily Express* also devote considerable space to expert comment. The *Daily Mirror* has a long-standing reputation for responsible coverage in its money column, which appears on Tuesdays, Wednesdays and Fridays. It makes a particular point of checking the credentials of financial organizations advertising for money – and its policy of turning away advertisements from unproven insurance and finance companies was dramatically vindicated when several advertisers on its black-list collapsed in the 1973–74 crash. The *Sun* has a money column on Tuesdays and is similarly alert to readers' financial needs. Among the Sunday newspapers, the best coverage is in the *Sunday Times*, the *Observer* and the *Sunday Telegraph*. The *Financial Weekly* devotes a page each week to personal finance and the *Investors' Chronicle* has a useful personal finance supplement every quarter.

Most general readers will probably find the specialist magazines, *Planned Savings* and *Money Management*, heavy going, but they are invaluable for the experts, particularly for performance comparisons of insurance policies and other investments. *Money Which?*, issued quarterly with *Which?* magazine, is a model of clarity and attention to detail; its annual tax guide alone makes the subscription worth while. For subscription information, write to the Consumers' Association, Caxton Hill, Hertford sG13 7lz.

On the air, Radio 4's *Money Box* programme on Saturdays is the best source of regular advice, and for television viewers there is Thames Television's *Money-Go-Round* programme and BBC 2's *Money Programme*.

# 2. Life Insurance

Life insurance[1] is nothing new. A Roman legion, based in Algeria, had its own life-insurance club in the second century AD, where each man paid money into a fund which would provide 500 denarii for his widow if he died, as well as contributing towards the expenses he would run up if he were posted elsewhere.

It is a vast industry nowadays. Ironically it has been growing rapidly recently just when the economic arguments are against it. Inflation has been running above 10 per cent for much of the last decade. In theory most forms of life insurance are a bad buy in those conditions. You are committing money for at least ten years and in many cases for fifteen or twenty just when its value is falling. Scottish Widows, one of the most respected insurance groups, revealed in the middle seventies, before heavy inflation had set in, that someone cashing in a twenty-year endowment policy at that time would only have received a return of 2 per cent overall, if you left inflation out of the picture. Even so, taking out some kind of policy still makes sense. Insurance may prove an inadequate shelter from financial storms, but that is better than no shelter at all. At the same time inflation works both ways. It cuts the real cost of the premiums you pay year by year, just as it will erode the value of what you are going to receive. Finally, the policies which combine insurance with savings are always useful if you want to borrow money from a bank by providing some security on which the manager can base his loan.

1. Life insurance, by the way, is just the same as life assurance. People in the business claim that *insurance* is about disasters which may or may not happen to you – fire, burglaries and so on – while *assurance* covers death, which is inevitable for everyone and where the only uncertainty is on timing. The word 'assurance' is now going out of use.

Where there has been a shift is in the kind of insurance people take out. Very wisely, they have started to move away from the long-term savings plans towards the original purpose of insurance – which is to protect families from the economic consequences of someone's death.

The industry is subject to a mass of controls and restrictions. Some of the earliest, which put strict limits on who insured whom, appeared in the eighteenth century. They were to ensure that people did not take out insurance on the life of some stranger or acquaintance and thus acquire a financial interest in his death.

What are the rules? You can insure yourself – and your wife's (or husband's) life. More generally, if you have lent someone money, you can insure him for the size of the debt – but no more. There are any number of policies you can choose, though, and the industry's language is often confusing. But whatever contract you take there will usually be government help on the premiums or annual instalments you pay towards it.

## Tax Relief

Government help – through tax relief– is not automatic, for you will need insurance which meets a series of conditions. It must be designed to last for at least ten years, and you must pay for it not in one lump sum, but in a series of regular payments. They may rise gradually (though this is rare), but no one premium must be more than twice another. If your policy complies – and almost certainly it will – you can claim relief at $17\frac{1}{2}$ per cent at least, in the year up to 5 April 1981. From then on, the relief will come at 15 per cent, which is half the present basic tax rate.

Until recently, you had to pay over the full cost of the premiums and then get relief back through the tax system. Now the payments you make each month have been adjusted downwards to allow for the tax relief. The government makes a direct payment to insurance companies to cover the income which the relief used to give them directly. This help on tax does not extend indefinitely. It only applies to the first £1,500 you spend on it – at least if you have an income of under £9,000 a year. If you get more, you are limited to one-sixth of your income going on life insurance. The rules are to prevent rich people from using the system to avoid tax.

## With-Profits or Without-Profits?

Insurance which suits one person will not necessarily be good for another. On the conventional contracts you will have to choose between a with- or without-profits policy. Without-profits is very simple. Your contract lays down that you – or your heirs – will receive so many pounds when the insurance is over, and that is what arrives. This guaranteed figure is higher than the minimum sum you would get on a with-profits policy, but for most people, it is not as good a buy.

Conventional with-profits insurance builds up in layers. At the base is that minimum sum which the company is bound to pay you; in most cases it comes to roughly the same as what you would pay if you provided your contributions towards it right up until it ended. The company then announces bonuses, once a year or once every three years depending on its habit, and though in strict law it does not have to do so, skipping the bonus is unknown. Once it has been declared, the bonus becomes part of your policy and cannot be withdrawn. Since the war the interest which the companies have given through these bonuses has drifted upwards as interest rates have risen generally. Most of the gains have been illusory because higher rates simply reflected higher inflation. None the less they have been a big selling point. Until recently it seemed a point of honour that the next bonus should be at least as high, if not higher than the last one. But a 3 per cent rate is far more useful when prices are rising at 5 per cent than one of $4\frac{1}{2}$ per cent when inflation is running at 10 per cent.

Most insurers will also give you a final layer, when the policy expires. This terminal bonus, which first appeared eight or ten years ago, is designed to give people whose policies become payable in any one year some of the investment profits that the group has made in the previous twelve months. Its size will depend on conditions at the time (though some insurers try to even out the benefits a bit); it could give you anything from 5 to 25 per cent of what you have accumulated already – and it may not appear at all.

Commercial Union, for instance, never pays these 'terminal bonuses'.

The kinds of policy you can choose come in a spectrum, with straight protection at one end, and investment with insurance trimmings at the other.

## Types of Policies

*Term insurance* is basic protection. It lays down that if you die within a period of perhaps ten or fifteen years, there will be a substantial payout for your family. One risk that term insurance does not cover is the onset of some serious long-term illness, or perhaps an injury while the policy is running. If you have one of the ordinary term policies, and are unlucky enough to be affected in this way, you would find it very hard, and perhaps impossible, to get new insurance after the first lot has expired. *Convertible-term* cover takes care of that risk, though it will cost between 10 and 12 per cent more in the first place. It guarantees that, whatever your medical state, you will be allowed to take out life cover of any kind with the same company on the same terms as someone of your age who is in perfect health when your first insurance expires. But you must decide to make your move while the first policy is still running, rather than leaving it until the end.

Most term policies are for a fixed sum, so inflation will erode their value. One company, Legal & General, has introduced an inflation-proofed version, where the potential pay-out rises with the Retail Price Index each year. You then raise the premiums you pay at the end of the year, so that in effect you have had some inflation-proofing on tick. In theory you take out a new contract each year, so you are not automatically committed to the increase. If the company has to pay out, because you die, the sums rise at a flat rate of 10 per cent a year. *Decreasing term* is a variant on the term theme and is a useful way of ensuring that some debt like a mortgage or a bank loan will be paid off if you die before it is settled. The insurance covers exactly what you owe, and as your debt goes down, so does your insurance.

Who does best out of term insurance? It can be ideal if you are a young man in your twenties, married, with perhaps a couple of children, and want a policy which costs relatively little, but will provide your wife with enough to bring up the children if you are not there to help her. In the same way, a term policy may be useful for her too. Decreasing-term cover may be relatively well known. The other two forms of term insurance are not, though they form part of the standard insurance package which most people have in the United States.

If you are in your forties you should generally look for an alternative, at least for the main part of your life insurance. Getting a savings contract to build up money for your retirement is going to be very expensive in your fifties when the average forty-year-old's term contract might expire. Whole-of-life insurance, defined below, is one possibility if you just want to protect your family. But endowment contracts which give you a chance of benefiting yourself are always attractive.

*Family-income benefit* is also from the term-insurance stable, but comes in a rather different form. It is designed to provide not a lump sum, but an income for a fixed period of time. If you take out a ten-year contract, and die after five, your family will get an income for the remaining five years. Most plans provide a fixed income, but there is also an index-linked variant which raises – in line with prices each month – the sum on which any income would be calculated. Again, you pay for the proofing in the following year's premiums. If you die, the income will go up but this time by a fixed 10 per cent.

Family-income-benefit policies probably fit just the same people who do well out of the other forms of term insurance. Considering its cost, family-income benefit should be an addition to your insurance package rather than an alternative. A widow getting an income can always commute part of the income – which means turning it into ready money.

There is one way of getting these policies more cheaply. But you can only do it if you are self-employed, or work for a company where pensions are 'contracted in' to the government's scheme, and do not offer any extras on top. If that applies in your case, you can go for what is known as a 226A scheme, and get tax relief in full. If you pay tax at 60 per cent, there is a 60 per cent saving, and not relief at $17\frac{1}{2}$ or 15 per cent. But there are limits to what you can contribute, and it is worth taking a long look at the conditions before you commit yourself.

*Whole-of-life* (or *whole-life*) *policies*, like term insurance, only pay out money when you as the holder have died. But this time they will do so whenever that happens, and not just if you die within a particular time-span. They probably make most sense if you are elderly and want to leave your family a substantial sum. If you are relatively young, you probably will not want to close all your options in this way and could find a term policy a better buy.

Traditionally a whole-of-life without-profits policy was what every young man should avoid, but what he was likely to be sold. Hambro Life, one of the more adventurous companies, recently produced a smartened-up variant on the old theme. The guaranteed pay-out the group provides on death is more attractive than those of its rivals. But Hambro keeps the right to raise the premiums you pay, after ten years, if the yields from investments, on which it based its original figures, prove too optimistic. Independent auditors will check the figures before any increase to see it is fair. Subject to the same conditions, Hambro Life could raise your premiums again at five-yearly intervals. The plan is ingenious, for if inflation continues the real cost of the premiums would have fallen back after ten years anyway. Even so, whole-of-life no-profits is very rarely the right kind of policy for someone who is relatively young.

*Endowment insurance* at least gives you yourself a chance of gaining. If you take out a twenty-year endowment and die before the time is up, your family will collect the proceeds. If you survive, they will go to you and – what is more – be larger. If you had died after fifteen years, there would have been five years' bonuses missing.

Over the last decade, there has been a move away from the fixed- and long-term policies of the past, partly because inflation has shortened everyone's horizons. Now more flexible arrangements, which come under names like Ten Year Plus and Flexi-dowment, have emerged. You certainly have to hold them for the full ten years, to get their rewards, but you are usually free to cash them in then or to leave it for a year or another five years, or indeed until you retire. In some ways, the tax relief makes them more attractive than the longer-term endowment contracts which last for twenty-five years. Assume you contribute £100 a year to your insurance. After twelve months, the policy just contains the £100 you put in, and so tax relief (using the 1980/81 figure for relief) covers 17½ per cent of the value of the contract. After four years the contract may have grown to £500. But the relief is still on your £100 contribution and not on the £500. So the value of the relief dies away.

One of the most usual ways of using endowment insurance is by combining it with a mortgage as a way of buying a house. The pros and cons of doing that are discussed in Chapter 5.

'Industrial' policies, where the Man from the Pru – or the Pearl or the Britannic for that matter – collects your premiums from the door, usually provide a form of with-profit endowment policy, though it can be a whole-of-life insurance. But remember that whatever the cover you have got in industrial insurance, you pay for the privilege of having it collected. The company's costs are much higher and the returns are lower than if you pay for your contract through a bank.

## Unit-Linked Insurance

Unit-linked insurance has just begun to make inroads on the working-class market of the industrial policy. Its big impact so far has been among middle-class buyers. The unit-linked schemes provide very few of the traditional guarantees. If you buy unit-linked insurance, your policy is directly tied to some investment like a unit trust, which can only put its money into shares, or more occasionally a fund buying a combination of shares, property and government stock. Most of your money in the first year goes into the cost of setting up the policy, but premiums after that buy units in the fund. Assume it is a unit trust, whose cash is invested across a whole range of shares. The value of your insurance depends on how those shares perform and (very slightly) on the interest that the group is earning on any spare cash it is holding outside. If you want to know what your policy is worth at any time, you can look it up in the *Financial Times* each day, multiplying the number of units you hold by the offer price which is shown there.

Insurance whose value will fluctuate should not be the first line of protection for anyone. Some, though not all, of the unit-linked plans promise to give you or your heirs the value of all the money you have invested if the price of the units comes to less than that when the policy ends. But with inflation in double figures, that is a remarkably flimsy guarantee. That life-jacket should only be a worry if you die before your insurance is due to end or you need the money at some particular time like retirement. Most unit-linked contracts last for a fixed time and then allow you to cash in any time after that.

Insurance salesmen can make times when share prices are low look attractive, suggesting, paradoxically, that you as a saver do best in those conditions. The great catch-phrase you are likely to hear is 'pound cost averaging'. If economic conditions are gloomy, each premium you pay buys you more units, because share prices are cheap. So your insurance is gathering seed-corn for the moment of recovery. When the *Financial Times* index of share prices starts rising again, there will be all the more to gain from the increase. That is true as far as it goes, but the principle works both ways. When confidence is high, each premium you contribute will buy relatively few units, whose value will fall when the pendulum moves in the other direction. Overall you should gain, admittedly. Share prices at the top of each Stock Exchange peak have tended to be higher than those at the previous summit, at least in money terms, if not in terms of value. But it is not an automatic and overwhelming advantage all the same.

The broad headings dealt with above may be the main branches of the life-insurance tree, but specialized forms of cover exist in plenty. If you want to send your son or daughter to a fee-paying school, school-fees insurance can guarantee that funds will be available to settle at least part of the bill. Several companies have arrangements where the premiums you pay go to a series of separate policies, designed to mature one after another so that some income is there when needed year after year. Alternatively, if you can afford the school fees, you can insure against the risk that you might die while the children are at school – and not leave enough funds behind to continue their education – by a policy designed to cover the financial gap for those five or ten years.

Older people often want to protect their families from the impact that capital-transfer tax (see Chapter 8) will have on their estates when they die. Companies have designed policies based on whole-of-life insurance to settle part of the bill which will appear when that happens.

## Cashing In and Paying Up

Insurance-company figures tend to project what has happened in the last twenty years into the next twenty years. If you are going to get the full gains of any insurance policy you will have to carry on right until the day when your policy is due to end. Often it does not happen. One very big group claims that four out of ten people who start a life-insurance policy cash it in within five years. It is a very bad move. If you have any doubts about whether you can keep up the payments on a particular form of cover you should probably go for something cheaper. The law now gives you the right to cancel any policy, without penalties, if you do so within ten days of taking it out.

The returns of cashing in or surrendering the policy are poor. You may expect to get some money back but, if you do so within two years of taking it out, you will probably get nothing at all. All the expenses for setting up the insurance come at the front and so do the company's payments to whoever recommended it and set up the arrangements for you. Just to add to your woes, your tax office will take back part of the tax relief you have had on your premiums if you cash in your policy within four years. There are no guarantees, at least from British companies, on what you will get if you cash in the policy after that, and the rates they pay have moved several times in the last five years. But very broadly you could expect to receive no more than what you had paid into the company – without interest – if you surrendered it half-way through its life.

If you are covered by a Canadian company, like Canada Life or Imperial Life of Canada, the general rules do not apply. The companies provide guaranteed cash-in values which are fixed before you even start. The first one may appear in some cases when the insurance has been running for only twelve months, though more usually it is two years. On top of that, most of the Canadians will top up their basic figure, though they do not promise to do it. These guaranteed values are a big selling point, but they have their price. What you gain on the surrender values, you lose on the overall investment. The Canadian companies have to hold some of their premiums back to allow for the cash-in applications which come in each year, so that in the end the overall returns are often poorer than those from their British counterparts. (If cashing in a policy makes no sense, except occasionally in the case of whole-of-life industrial contracts, borrowing may be the answer – see Chapter 4.)

What do you get if you cash in an insurance policy? It depends on the type of contract but, whatever the firm, you will be very unlikely to get anything if you cash in a term policy. At the same time, you will receive less if you surrender some whole-of-life contract than you would on insurance endowment.

There is another option, which is to leave your money where it is, but just to stop making any further payments. Making the policy 'paid-up', as this arrangement is known, does not necessarily give you half the benefits if you do it after ten years of a twenty-year contract. Companies will usually scale down more than proportionately the guaranteed sum on which they are making payments. They will go on paying bonuses, based on this scaled-down figure, usually at a lower rate than that for everyone else. If you are going through what looks like a temporary bad patch, you can always make up the payments you have missed later on.

## Who Insures You and the Guarantees

There are two main types of life office, as the groups are known. If you take out a policy with a mutual company – like Norwich Union, Standard Life or Equitable Life, for instance – you become one of the company's owners along with many thousands of other people. All the money these groups accumulate in their life funds is available to pay out in the form of bonuses, or to go into building up reserves for the future. Others, including Legal & General, Commercial Union and Eagle Star, are companies in the usual sense, which just happen to sell insurance. Shareholders are liable to receive a dividend, but that is no instant disadvantage, for it means that outsiders are present to monitor how the company is doing. A rule of thumb suggesting that one lot are going to give you better terms than the other does not exist.

Either group will take you in, whatever your job, though if you are in certain occupations you could find that you have to pay slightly more than other people. Airline pilots and deep-sea divers will probably face a loading of this kind, while journalists and publicans occasionally can have similar trouble. Both the latter come near the top of the alcoholism charts. One or two specialist insurers will not take you on at all, though, unless you work in a particular profession. Medical Sickness, for instance, caters only for doctors and dentists – though it will provide health as well as life insurance, while the Royal Pension Fund for Nurses only covers nurses, offering life insurance as well as pensions.

Then come the friendly societies, which are owned by their members. There are several names to roll around the tongue, like the Independent Order of Oddfellows, Manchester Unity and the better-known Independent Order of Foresters. Like the groups with more prosaic titles – Hearts of Oak, for instance – they grew up in the nineteenth-century tradition of self-help. Friendly societies often specialize in industrial door-to-door life insurance and have tax advantages, at least on the small policies they offer. Unlike other insurers most do not pay tax on the interest which rolls up for people whose life cover has a basic value of £1,000 or less. They can also provide policies with a guaranteed maximum value of up to £15,500, but there are problems if they do, for the tax relief is worth less.

The industry's central body is the Life Offices Association, which works from Aldermary House in Queen Street, London EC4. One or two groups, most prominently Equity & Law, do not belong to it – and nor do most friendly societies.

You are protected if the firm which has insured your life goes bust. An official body, the Policyholders' Protection Board, can demand a levy from all groups in the industry, if it happens. At the very least you will get 90 per cent of the benefits to which you are entitled, when the insurance runs out. More probably, your company and your insurance policy with it would be taken over by another group, so that it continued under a different name. Ironically, these rules only apply if you happen to pay your own insurance bills directly, rather than, as with an industrial policy, to a collector who picks up your premiums. But if a big industrial office collapsed, the same would happen in practice. Industrial insurance comes under the Registrar of Friendly Societies, not the Department of Trade.

## The Sellers

You can always go direct to a company to buy the insurance that you want, but there is no discount for cutting out the middle man, and the odds are that there is someone else in the market with better terms. The first move is to try a broker, though in practice it usually works the other way round. The industry claims, probably rightly, that few people want to buy insurance. They have it sold to them.

Agents may approach you, though they may work for one or perhaps two companies and cannot offer you any choice. They may deliver a speech which they have learned by heart, often attempt to blind you with insurance jargon and are usually adept at making you feel ashamed by refusing to take out whatever it is they are offering. So you should be on your guard. The chairman of one big unit-linked insurance company recently claimed that his salesmen never sold a policy which was not needed because they all had a course in ethics before they started. But as they have to live entirely on the commission they make on sales, it seems unlikely that he was right.

Insurance brokers are, or should be, different, providing an independent judgement on what suits you best, for your particular age and circumstances. Their advice is free, for the money they receive comes from the insurer to whom they introduce you.

How do you know whether your particular broker is good at his job? You cannot tell, but at least the word 'broker' should mean something. Until recently anyone who wanted to be a broker could stick up a sign outside his shop or office announcing that he was one. A new law now lays down that anyone who wants to be a broker will first have to be accepted by a new body, the Insurance Brokers Registration Council. Britain is now half-way between the old rules and the new and the regulations restricting the term 'broker' to someone with some recognized knowledge of what he is doing may come into effect in 1981. The new brokers will have to show that they have experience in their business by having worked in the field for at least five years, though if they have professional qualifications, the period goes down to three. The council is going to set up a general indemnity fund to ensure that, if some rogue broker runs off with your premium money, you will not lose by the fact, and it has also set up a professional code of conduct.

After they have been accepted, most brokers will probably belong to the new trade association, the British Insurance Brokers' Association, known as BIBA. But it is not compulsory. Eventually the people running every broking company should be professionally qualified, but that will take a very long time. Even when it happens, you will not know that the particular person in the office who answers your question is an expert.

Banks often give insurance advice. If you are looking for unit-linked cover they may be tempted to recommend their own funds, though with the exception of Barclays Unicorn, bank trusts have not done particularly well. Accountants often come into the picture and there are a mass of people claiming to be insurance advisers, insurance specialists or insurance consultants. The titles may sound impressive, but they have no legal meaning at all. Whoever organizes the insurance, the terms of commission are the same, at least for companies which belong to the Life Offices Association. They do not necessarily affect people's judgement, but it is as well to know what they are.

The longer the commitment you make and the more you pay in premiums the more commission the seller will make. There is one important qualification. The old bias in favour of whole-of-life policies has weakened, for people now earn no more on them than they do on a twenty-five-year endowment policy. Term insurance, though particularly good for young people, provides very little for whoever sells it. Most of the money the sellers receive comes when you take out the policy. There is also a very small 'renewal commission' year by year, as you continue.

Two of the best-respected companies in the business – Equitable Life and London Life – do not pay commission, so that brokers will rarely mention them. At the other end, one company, Equity & Law, which does not belong to the Life Offices Association, pays over the usual rate.

If you want to check the conventional policies (those which are not tied to a unit trust and offer a guaranteed figure), it may not be as easy as it looks. Logically, a bonus rate of 5 per cent should always be better than one of 4 per cent, but it is not always so. Some insurers work on the compound-interest principle, paying bonuses on bonuses as well as on the original sum. If your 4 per cent interest is based on that principle, it will swiftly offer you more than one which pays 5 per cent on the basic sum at the bottom of the insurance, but nothing on your bonuses. So you have to ignore those calculations and go for the tables published by specialist papers like *Money Management* and *Planned Savings*, which show what you get back for every hundred pounds you pay – on past form. There is no absolute guarantee that companies which have done well in the past will do so in the future. On the conventional side of life insurance, though, firms with good records tend to stay at the top of the performance charts, as Standard Life and Equitable Life have done, for instance. The figures from *Planned Savings* (see Table 1) show the top performers for two separate years, 1978 and 1980.

This pattern of stability does not appear on the unit-linked side, where last year's loser is sometimes this year's best performer.

## Life Insurance If You are Ill

If you are not in good health when you want to take out the policy, you will do worse than Table 1 suggests. Insurers can either make you pay over the odds for the cover you get or, indeed, turn you down altogether. If your application has been rejected, your name will go down on a central file as a difficult case. Every policy form you will ever see asks if you have been refused life insurance in the past. Insurers swear that being on their central register will not prevent you from taking out life cover with a more lenient firm – like Sun Life, for instance. But at the very least it will not help.

If you have diabetes, epilepsy or a history of heart trouble, you should go through brokers – preferably well-established ones – to ensure that you do not meet that first refusal. Things are easier than they were. Companies take on more people because they have established 'pools' where they reinsure risks jointly which they probably would not take on separately.

Table 1 **Insurance Top Ten Performers**

Returns for a man of thirty investing £100 a year (before tax) for fifteen years, whose policy matured in April 1978 or June 1980

| Company | Guaranteed sum | Reversionary bonus | Terminal bonus | Total |
|---|---|---|---|---|
| *Policy Maturing in April 1978* | | | | |
| 1 Clerical Medical & General | £1,416 | £1,311 | £318 | £3,045 |
| 2 Equitable Life | £1,412 | £1,191 | £260 | £2,863 |
| 3 London Life | £1,428 | £1,025 | £358 | £2,811 |
| 4 Friends Provident | £1,416 | £1,042 | £260 | £2,718 |
| 5 Standard Life | £1,421 | £936 | £330 | £2,687 |
| 6 Provident Mutual | £1,450 | £814 | £422 | £2,686 |
| 7 Guardian Royal Exchange | £1,422 | £930 | £325 | £2,677 |
| 8 Crusader | £1,365 | £962 | £349 | £2,676 |
| 9 Scottish Provident | £1,410 | £1,168 | £71 | £2,649 |
| 10 Royal London Mutal | £1,391 | £849 | £403 | £2,643 |
| *Policy Maturing in June 1980* | | | | |
| 1 London Life | £1,440 | £1,131 | £475 | £3,046 |
| 2 Norwich Union | £1,422 | £1,195 | £412 | £3,029 |
| 3 Equitable Life | £1,412 | £1,277 | £336 | £3,025 |
| 4 Clerical Medical & General | £1,369 | £1,262 | £359 | £2,990 |
| 5 Scottish Amicable | £1,383 | £1,091 | £450 | £2,924 |
| 6 UK Provident Institution | £1,405 | £1,192 | £324 | £2,921 |
| 7 Royal London Mutal | £1,391 | £881 | £626 | £2,898 |
| 8 Standard Life | £1,421 | £1,036 | £431 | £2,888 |
| 9 Friends Provident | £1,416 | £1,109 | £333 | £2,858 |
| 10 Legal & General | £1,401 | £1,087 | £326 | £2,814 |

NB. The table does not contain results for any group whose policies are not generally available, e.g. the Royal Pension Fund for Nurses.
*Source: Planned Savings Magazine.*

The first pool for diabetes appeared in the thirties. Since then, as the industry has developed more experience, the rates for diabetics have become lower. If you have emerged from hospital with a heart attack, you will not get a policy immediately. But if there has been no trouble after three or four years, you will get your insurance – at a price.

## Summing Up

Most people need some kind of life insurance, even if it is not automatically the one which sellers want them to buy. The problem is that there is no single answer to what it should be, for everything depends on individual needs and circumstances. But in general terms the rules go as follows. If you are young and want to give your family as much protection as possible against the risk that you may die or be killed in the five- or ten-year period when expenses with children are at their highest, term insurance is the best answer. If you add in family-income benefit, to provide an income, so much the better.

Whole-of-life insurance can be a useful way of doing the same thing if you are in your fifties, and want the cover to be in force whenever you happen to die. But whole-of-life is very rarely suitable for younger people. If you are offered it, the point to remember is that it offers a lot of commission to the people selling it.

Next comes looking after your own interests. Conventional with-profits endowments guarantee that face value will not fall. They may not do as well as the unit-linked alternative, but they provide more certainties, which are probably worth having. Unit-linked contracts may provide better figures. After all, companies do not have to worry about the risk that conditions in the future may not be as good as they are now – and put aside money to cope with that risk. Putting away seed-corn for policies which mature in the future means that there is less for those whose contracts are payable now.

There is always the risk that your policy may mature just when times are hard and the stock market depressed. However, in most unit-linked contracts you do not have to cash in, you can wait until things improve and the unit price moves up.

That is all very well in theory. But if you cannot postpone your retirement and want the money, you have no flexibility. At the same time you will get no help deciding when conditions are right to cash in. Cynics suggest, very rightly, that it is only when the sky seems the limit and everyone believes you are mad to sell your units, that you should do so.

The conventional with-profits policy should provide the basic cushion of savings in most cases, with any unit-linked insurance providing the second tier. But everything depends on how each individual weighs stability against the prospect of a more valuable policy which carries more risks.

# 3. Running a Bank Account

Where should you keep your money? In one sense this is a silly question, for everything depends on how much is involved and how far you want to spread it to limit your risks. This chapter is about the funds you need to survive, day by day, and to pay the bills that appear, which limits the number of answers if only because you need a place that is not only secure but instantly accessible.

You could always choose to keep your cash somewhere in the house, under the mattress perhaps, or in one of those endless places which thieves are always supposed to miss and never do. That is the worst idea. If the money is stolen you have no recompense and cash cannot be traced. Choice two is to keep a lump sum in a savings account on which you can draw as you need – like the National Savings Bank or a building society, or perhaps a bank deposit account. If you do this you have to draw out money before you go shopping and so carry considerable cash with you. The National Savings Bank will limit you to taking out £30 a day. If you want more, you can draw up to £100 over the counter, but your bank book has to go up to headquarters, and it will take up to a week to return. Some building societies too will usually provide no more than £100 in cash. Sometimes the limit is higher.

The advantage in all three cases is that you can collect interest. The National Savings Bank and building societies will pay at least one or two regular bills each month – perhaps for the rates or on subscription – though they are not keen to advertise the service. Banks do not do it from bank deposit accounts.

Opening hours are good. The National Savings Bank operates through Post Offices, which are open for shop hours, as are most building-society branches. Neither is stuck with a six-hour day beginning at 9.30 and ending at 3.30 with permanent Saturday closure as the banks are. Even so, about half the adults in Britain have a current account in one of the clearing banks, such as National Westminster and Barclays, which have branches in almost every high street. They can provide far more than the savings accounts can do – through cheques, standing orders and so on – and can also lend you money for a whole range of goods more cheaply than anyone else.

## Bank Services

*Cheques* are the most useful service of all. They provide a simple way of telling your bank to transfer money from your account to another account, though it is becoming increasingly difficult to use them on their own. Most shops and restaurants now insist on a cheque guarantee card to back cheques they take. The card ensures that if the signature on the cheque matches the one on the card, and the assistant writes down the card number on the back of the cheque, the bank will pay the bill – on sums up to £50 – whatever the state of your account. But that is the limit. If you are buying something for £100, the rules do not allow you to make out two cheques and then use your card to back them both. Shops will sometimes bend them, though

You can always keep a record of what you have paid, for cheque-books have a space at the front or a stub on which you can record the details. If your cheques and cheque card are stolen, you should not suffer. Banks will cope with fraud of that kind provided you let them know about the loss immediately and they have no reason to think you helped them disappear.

Cheque cards have one big disadvantage. In the past, if you paid a bill by cheque and then found that you were not happy with what you had bought, you could 'stop' the cheque so that the bank did not pay it, at least until you had given them the go-ahead. If you back them with a cheque card that is not possible, because banks are bound to pay cheques guaranteed in this way. However, you still have your right to take up any complaint with the shop concerned, which is legally responsible for the quality of what it sells.

Barclays is the one bank not to issue a separate cheque card. Its customers use a Barclaycard, which doubles up as a cheque guarantee card – at least in Britain, though in its role as a credit card it will work in most countries round the world.

Cheque cards do not come automatically and managers can always withdraw them.

Managers can 'bounce' cheques if they are not guaranteed and you have not enough money in your account to meet them. They will give you ample warning first. If the branch is firing a shot across your bows, the cheque will come back to the person paying it in with the words, 'RD – Please re-present.' 'RD' stands for refer to drawer – for you, as the person who signed the cheque, are the drawer. It means that your creditor must ask you and not the bank why it has not been met. Financial etiquette lays down that the bank cannot discuss its customers' affairs.

'Please re-present' softens the blow for it implies that the creditor may get his money after putting the cheque through the system a couple of times. But a cheque marked in that way does your reputation no good. A straight RD is worse still. Your payee – to use the disgusting legal terminology – can always ask you, but in practice, he will know the answer perfectly well already.

Most cheques come 'crossed' with two lines across the middle. It means that they can only be paid into another account and so provides some protection against theft. But if you want to give a cheque to someone who has not got an account, the only way you can ensure they get cash across the counter is to give them an open cheque which has nothing across it. But the banks are not enthusiastic about open cheques because they present a larger risk.

The great point about cheques is that you do not have to go into your own branch, or indeed your own bank, to take out or pay in money. You can draw out up to £50 on a cheque from any branch of any bank. If you have not got a cheque card, you can ask your branch to make 'drawing arrangements' with a branch of the bank – or any other for that matter – close to your work. You are then free to draw up to a certain sum there each day of each week, depending on what you have agreed.

The process of transferring money is relatively fast. If you pay in a cheque drawn on a National Westminster account into a Lloyds bank to go into your own account in the Midland, the process should not take more than three working days.

*Cashcards* get round some of the problems of banking hours, for they allow you to take out money at the drop of a computer number in a terminal. The original versions provided you with £10, but with the more modern machines you have your own credit limit per charge. So you could take out perhaps £40 or £50 a day as well as ordering a cheque-book, discovering the state of your bank balance, and ordering a bank statement.

Lloyds has put some of its terminals inside the branch, so that you cannot use them outside bank hours.

*Standing orders* are instructions to your bank to pay regular fixed bills like insurance payments or the mortgage automatically each month. If costs or charges rise to change the bill, you have to cancel one order and take out another for the higher sum. Companies will be swift to let you know when it is necessary.

*Direct debits* settle regular bills, but in a different way. You set them up, but in doing so you give your local council or whoever else you are paying the right to demand more funds if charges go up – without consulting you. Technically, this is known as a variable debit: but most of them take this form.

The process is not only useful in times of high inflation. It also makes sense for bills which will vary from time to time, like those for gas and electricity, and of course makes life administratively easier for big businesses. All the same, direct debits are not a complete blessing. It is far harder to query a bill after you have paid it than before, so the system is worth treating cautiously. In the past, bank branches have been known to change standing orders to direct debits on their own initiative, claiming that it will help everyone. That is now forbidden and any organization which is changing its charges, and so taking more money from your account, has to let you know that it is doing so.

*Bank statements* will appear once a month, once every three months, or indeed how often you want them. Each item is numbered and you can match the particular number with the number on the cheque stubs so that you have a list showing to whom the payment has gone. Girobank does more still. It will send you a slip after every single credit paying money into the account or every ten debits taking funds from it.

The *Eurocheque* system allows you to use the standard cheque card to draw out money from banks in most European countries – up to £100 a day in local currency. All the main tourist centres contain at least a couple of banks providing the service. They display the Eurocard logo – the letters EC in red and blue on a white background. Greece, Turkey and several states in Eastern Europe belong to the scheme. There are banks in Morocco and Tunisia which will take the cards – and even the Soviet Union has banks which will accept them, in Moscow and Leningrad.

One problem comes with Barclaycards, which will not act as cheque cards abroad as they do at home. Holders have to collect a separate piece of plastic – Barclays Eurocheque Encashment Card – from their local branch, giving a couple of weeks notice that they want it. Of course, they can use Barclaycard as a credit card while they are away, just as they can use Access. Eurocheque cards – of the Barclays or the other variety – will only do their stuff in a bank.

*Traveller's cheques* are far more flexible, for many hotels, restaurants and shops will take them, though you will get the best exchange rate at a bank. The high-street banks and Girobank are not the only groups to produce them, for Thomas Cook and American Express are both big issuers – and so are many others. Whoever provides them will reimburse you if they are lost or stolen, though they will want you to inform the local police. If disaster strikes, having the cheque numbers speeds things up considerably, so you should always keep them separate from the cheques themselves. You go to a local bank and telex your branch, which should advise the overseas group to advance you at least part of the money immediately.

Barclays has a series of repayment centres in most European states, and American Express allows you to collect up to $100 (note dollars) from branches of Avis, the car-hire firm. Both companies offer their own cheques in several currencies. You can get cheques made out in dollars, D-marks or yen from other banks, if you want to protect yourself from some sudden sterling crisis while you are away. But they come from 'correspondent banks' in each country, so that if you want travellers cheques in D-marks from Lloyds or NatWest then your cheques may be issued by the Dresdner Bank, for instance. The problem can come on loss. Overseas banks will certainly return your funds eventually, but you will not get them quickly.

One or two companies which only deal in bank notes recommend that you should take all your money in cash and insure its value separately – avoiding a 1 per cent issuing and paying charge as you do. The advice should be ignored.

*Budget accounts* are a service many people ignore, though they can be useful. They can ease the strain of a spate of big bills which come bunched together and push your account firmly into the red. Fuel and light bills are always higher in winter for instance, and there is often a matching summer peak when you pay for holidays.

The budget accounts should ensure that you spend the same sum month by month. You start by estimating your spending on big items that come perhaps every six months or a year – holidays, insurance and so on – and those which will vary like fuel charges. You then add a margin of perhaps 15 to 20 per cent to allow for the next twelve months' inflation and finally come up with a total. The bank then transfers one-twelfth of that figure month by month to a budget account. Meanwhile you have a separate budget-account cheque-book which you use for payments. The balance in the account should then swing from black to red and back again over the year. If your figures work as they should, the end of the year should find the account empty but not in debt.

There is always a catch. The bank will either demand a straight fee for its work or charge you interest – on the normal over-draft terms – when you owe on the account. But you certainly do not get any corresponding interest when the account is in your favour. A new Cashflow scheme by Lloyds is the one exception.

*Trustee and executor departments* take over responsibility for administering wills and ensuring that bequests are paid properly.

Bank managers, meanwhile, can always advise you on basic financial problems, but it is worth remembering that they will have a certain bias and may try to steer you towards using the bank's own services in each field – like their own unit trusts, for example. If you want help on more sophisticated investment, they will obtain advice from stockbrokers and pass it on to you. But they will not be responsible for it. So if you want to take some big financial step, you should get advice from two or three different people – an accountant and perhaps an insurance broker – remembering, as you do, that each has a particular financial axe to grind.

## Which Bank?

There are five giant banks – National Westminster, Barclays, Midland, Lloyds and Williams & Glyn's in descending order of size – which dominate banking in England and Wales. There are plenty of others, including the chain of Trustee Savings Banks. The latter used to be little more than private versions of the National Savings movement, but they have changed dramatically in the last ten years. Now more than 2 million people have current accounts with them, though there are still many more savers. The TSBs offer the full range of bank services, though for the moment, anyway, they are more cautious on lending than the others. You can cash their cheques in any of the high-street banks, and incidentally, if you have an account with NatWest, Barclays or any of the others, you can use a Trustee Savings Bank to do the same.

Then come the specialist banks. Coutts, for instance, has held the royal account ever since Mr Coutt played a fourth hand at cards with the Prince Regent and won royal favour by losing gracefully. Its staff are dressed in frock coats, you need a considerable minimum balance to remain in favour and all statements come with the name of the person or company to whom you made the payment. The Co-operative Bank, at the other end of the scale, has relatively few branches, but customers can cash cheques for their personal use in most large Co-op stores up and down the country. At the same time, they can use branches of other banks to do so too. Finally come the regional banks like the Yorkshire. The diversity is a bit of a charade for, apart from the Co-op, the smaller banks are owned by the larger ones.

In Scotland, meanwhile, three big banks predominate: the Clydesdale, the Bank of Scotland, and the Royal Bank of Scotland. They work just like the others except for the fact that they have the right to produce their own banknotes.

*Girobank*, run by a government corporation, is completely national. It does not depend on banks but on over 22,000 Post Office branches in Britain which work shop and not bank hours. All transactions go through the system's giant computer at Bootle. The payment you make through Giro depends on your creditor. If he has a Giro account, you can pay him by a Giro transfer form, but otherwise you make out a Girocheque. Both will take three working days to go through – the same time as a cheque from the high-street banks. The system also provides a cheque-card and personal-loan service. The old distinction between the 'goodies' who had their salaries paid into Girobank and the others who did not has been abolished.

The three main differences with the banks is that Giro will not handle work as an executor, it cannot provide you with financial advice, and it is more restrictive on overdraft lending then the others. More detail on that last point comes in the next chapter.

*Choosing a bank* is not easy, but once people have committed themselves they usually stay with the same bank for life. The lethargy factor partly explains why banks are so anxious to attract students, providing rewards in the form of gift vouchers, pens and so on. Surveys in the Consumers' Association magazine *Which?* tend to show that smaller banks are more popular than the giants. But generalizations are not easy. What matters is what the particular branch and branch manager are like, and no one can forecast that in advance.

In general terms, it is worth staying where you begin unless conditions become very difficult. The longer you have been a customer, or at least one with a reasonable record for answering letters and keeping the branch informed, the more helpful they will be providing you with loans. One way of making yourself popular is to make a point of asking for permission to run slightly into the red before you do it. The move may seem unnecessary, but it makes a lot of difference to your reputation in the bank.

## The Cost of an Account

Bank charges vary slightly from bank to bank, as Table 2 shows, though the banks use the same system. They will not demand money from you if you keep a fixed minimum sum in your account over their accounting period. If you fail that test, you may pass another and still avoid charges. The bank works out what it could have earned with the money in your account – assessing notional interest, it is called – and then sets off charges for cheques and anything else which takes money out of the account against the notional interest. If the interest comes to more

Table 2 **Bank Charges (September 1980)**

|  | Minimum balance (£) | Charge per debit (p) | Notional interest |
| --- | --- | --- | --- |
| National Westminster | 50 | 15 | ½ per cent below deposit |
| Barclays | 50 | 13 | 1 per cent below deposit |
| Lloyds | 100 | 17½ * | 1 per cent below deposit |
| Williams & Glyn's | 50 | 15 † | 10 per cent |
| Trustee Savings Bank | 50 | 5 | None |
| Midland | 50 | 15 | 11½ per cent |
| Girobank | 0 | 10 ‡ | None |
| Clydesdale | 0 | 9 | 1 per cent below deposit |
| Bank of Scotland | 50 | 12 | 2 per cent below deposit |
| Royal Bank of Scotland | 50 | 12 | 1 per cent below deposit |
| Co-operative Bank | 0 | 12 | None |

* Cash dispensers 12½p.
† Standing orders and direct debits 7½p.
‡ Standing orders 18p.

than the cost of the debit, you avoid charges. You do not collect interest yourself. If the debits come to more than the interest, you pay the difference between them in bank charges. One bank, the Co-op, makes no charge at all for personal accounts kept in credit, whatever the number of transactions.

The period over which they do their calculations varies from one bank to another. National Westminster, Lloyds, Barclays and Williams & Glyn's do them once every three months while the Co-op, TSB and Midland assess them twice a year. Table 2 shows the minimum charges – and the cost of pushing a cheque or standing order through the system. If you want to work out your own figures, they may take some time. You have to allow for all the various complications, like Lloyds' habit of charging differently for cheques, and the cost of withdrawals you make by using a cash card.

The obvious answer to bank charges is to cut down the number of cheques you issue, which is not as difficult as it sounds because the banks themselves have devised a way in which you can do it. *Bank Giro* is its name, and it is completely different, incidentally, from Girobank. Most big firms include a bank giro on their bills which allows you to pay money directly into your bank rather than sending the cheque to them, saving postage in the process. Better still, you can wait until a series of big bills appear with their own bank giro forms. You fill them all in, and present them with one covering cheque to your own branch – and not any other. The staff cope with them, but charge you for one cheque not six.

*Free banking*. Banks often claim that if you do not pay charges, you are getting 'free banking'. Banking is free if cheques, standing orders and all the rest cost you nothing – unless you are in the red. That is the system which the Co-op Bank operates and it also applies in Girobank, though in that case there is no offsetting notional interest if you do slip into overdraft. The others always claim that if you do slip into the red the Co-op Bank will cost you more overall.

If you have to keep £100 in the account to avoid charges, the banking charges are not free. The banks use the balances they have in their accounts to lend to industry and to provide overdrafts, personal loans and so on. So they use your money to get interest. Assume that a building society was holding the minimum £100 balance you need to avoid charges (at least on the first test) in Barclays. You would collect a return yourself. So what you do not pay in charges, you provide to the bank through the interest which it can earn and which you do not get.

# 4. Borrowing

## How to Do It

Borrowing, like alcohol, produces extreme reactions. At one end are the financial teetotallers who will never borrow money, except perhaps on a mortgage, for fear that they will lose control if they do. At the other extreme stand the 'loanoholics' who regularly get themselves loaded with debt, and have enormous trouble in paying it off. Some even reach the stage at which they bluff their way into yet another loan to pay off the instalments on what they have borrowed already. In between come the great majority of people, who can borrow sensibly. If you plan to take out a loan, the crucial question is whether you can afford the repayments each month without any trouble. If you are spending more than a quarter of your take-home pay on your instalments, the simple answer is that it will be difficult to manage – particularly if you have a young family in the background.

It is all too easy to assume that you will be able to cope. If you want a loan, you should work out just what effect repayments will have on the family budget and what you will cut out to afford them. It may seem obvious, but most people do not do it. If you pass all those tests, you should think about what the money is going to cost you – not in terms of pounds and pence each week, but in terms of the interest you have to pay. If trailing round shops looking for bargains makes sense, then it is all the more important when you borrow. Far more money is likely to be involved.

The Consumer Credit Act, which governs the law on borrowing, lays down that everyone offering to lend money must show their charges on the same basis: they cannot tack on hidden extras like commission fees and arrangement surcharges. The detailed provisions making this change of the law effective were to come into force by the end of 1980. However you borrow, there is always the chance that you may run into difficulties with repayment, perhaps because you lose a job or your family circumstances change. If that happens, you should tell the lenders immediately. Companies have met the problem before and will be sympathetic, rescheduling the debt so that you pay it over a longer time or perhaps even agreeing to forgo the instalments completely for two or three months while you sort yourself out. What is fatal is to stop payments completely in the hope that no one notices. Invariably they do.

The firm will produce plenty of threats and legal reminders before taking you to court. But if you develop a reputation for being awkward you may well find it difficult to get another loan even if you are never actually summonsed.

If there is nothing like that in your background, you have lived in the same house for a while, and yet your applications for loans are regularly turned down, you should ask the reason. Companies often use credit reference agencies which keep records of all court judgements on debt for the previous five years and details on bankruptcies, too, to check on people. Some agencies also store details of regular bad payers who only produce the money at the last moment before they are summonsed.

The two biggest groups are Credit Data, based in Manchester, and the United Association for the Protection of Trade, which lives in Croydon. If your name is on their lists, or indeed any other credit group's list, you have a legal right to know it. If you send them a request for information and a fee of 25p, they have a legal duty to let you know if your name is on their files. If the details are inaccurate, the group will correct them. Even if they are not, you can write a twenty-five- or thirty-word explanation of just why you got into trouble, which they will read out when someone makes an inquiry about you. Shops sometimes claim that credit agencies forbid them to lend to particular people, but it is not true. All the agencies do is pass on information.

Banks will only provide money to customers who do not need it, or so goes the old gag. There is a grain of truth in it. Like everyone else, bankers want to be sure that you will repay what you borrow and the more security you can offer the better they will like it. But developing a reputation for knowing how to handle money by ensuring that your current account does not judder in and out of the red is probably more important still.

But when you want to borrow money there are any number of suppliers – and arrangements.

*Overdrafts* come cheapest, though they are often for temporary borrowing – perhaps for a couple of months. You can draw out funds as you need them up to a certain limit. Charges fluctuate. All the banks have a central base rate which they use to calculate all their interest charges at any one time. These base rates themselves fluctuate in line with other interest rates round the world. If you get an overdraft as a personal customer, the odds are that you will be charged somewhere between 3 and 5 per cent over the base rate operating at the time – and when the base rate moves, so, too, will the cost of your borrowing.

The bank may insist that your overdraft is 'secured', so that you have to put, perhaps, a life-insurance policy or the deeds of your house in their keeping to protect them against default. If you have some financial windfall like a legacy in the pipeline, you could well get an overdraft. The bank manager can always demand that you pay off the overdraft at any time, but in practice he will give you some notice when they want their funds returned.

Girobank customers can get overdrafts, but on restricted terms. If your salary is paid into Girobank, you can overdraw by £70 or so at a time. If it is not, any overdraft will be limited to around £40. Either way, your next salary cheque or big credit must bring you into the black again.

*Personal loans* are very different. Those from the banks last for one to three years, though some for home improvements will stretch to five years and, incidentally, bring tax relief with them if the improvements are going to be permanent. Other personal loans – for cars, washing machines, or anything else – do not offer tax relief of any kind. Everything is arranged in advance. You borrow a fixed total for a fixed time and at a fixed interest rate and pay it back in equal instalments each month.

At the moment you start a personal loan it will almost always be more expensive than a new overdraft. But if interest rates rise, the positions can occasionally be reversed. The loans themselves are usually for reasonably large sums of money, ranging from about £500 to £3,000. When interest rates are very high, it is no time to commit yourself to a personal loan. Your interest rate will remain fixed at its original level even if all other interest rates are coming down.

Loans within the family are always possible – and the forms they can take are endless. The one golden rule is to get all the details written down, and agreed – with both borrower and lender having copies. Disagreements on the terms after the loan has started can cause immense family bitterness.

*Life-insurance loans* – borrowing from the group with which you have insured your life – are one way of getting money relatively cheaply. Most conventional policies (explained in Chapter 2) have a surrender value for which you can cash them in if they have been running for a while. It is on the security of this cash-in value that the group will lend you funds. If you have an endowment or whole-life policy taking this form, borrowing should be possible.

The company will lend you between 75 and 80 per cent of the cash-in value of the policy, often at a fixed rate of interest. There is usually no need to pay back the money within a particular time span. The insurers will wait to deduct both what they have lent and the interest on it from the proceeds of the policy when it finally becomes payable.

Surrender values grow very slowly so that the move will provide you with relatively little money unless the insurance has existed for some time. Sometimes you can borrow against the strength of a unit-linked policy, but not always. Save & Prosper, for instance, will allow you to borrow up to the value of the contract, though the group will want regular repayments so that you pay back the money within five years. Other companies, like Hambro Life, will not do it at all.

Whether borrowing in this way makes sense depends on circumstances. If the insurance is designed to provide you with a large sum, so that the contract is more investment than insurance, there may be a case for it. But if it is designed to protect your family from the financial problems your death might create and thus is a form of protection, then it does not make sense.

*Finance houses* is the technical term for what most people still call the H P companies, though hire purchase is only one of many forms in which they lend money. The one common characteristic

of all their loans – for cars, washing machines or any other goods –
is that they will always cost more than money from a bank. You
can always ask the finance house for money direct, but if you are
buying a freezer or a refrigerator, the shop will often act as
intermediary for you. The same goes for most motor dealers.

Government regulations ensure that you cannot borrow the
full cost of what you want. If you are buying a freezer, for
instance, you generally have to put down 20 per cent of the price
as a deposit and repay the rest within thirty months. Admittedly,
the law allows you to cut down the deposit to 10 per cent of the
total, but if you take that course, you have to settle the rest of the
bill within nine months.

The rules on cars are more stringent still: the deposit must
amount to at least one-third of the price and you must repay the
rest of the money within two years. The lenders also have their
own quirks. The older the vehicle and the less money you want to
borrow, the higher the interest rate you often have to pay. The
dealer who organizes a loan for you will collect commission from
the finance house for doing it, so that taking a loan which he has
organized has given him a bigger profit margin. It could be worth
trying to get slightly more for any old car you are trading in or
attempting to find a slight discount on the new one to allow for the
fact.

Most finance-house credit divides into five types:

*Hire purchase* is still the standard way of borrowing, at least if you
are buying a car. The goods which you have bought on HP do not
fully belong to you until you have paid the last instalment. In
essence you are hiring the car, refrigerator, or anything else
until you have bought it. Indeed you always have the right to
reject what you have bought, at the last minute, if you want. But
it will cost you dear to be that quixotic for you will get considerably less than half of what you have paid returned to you.

One proviso covers defaults. If you have paid more than one-
third of the total, the company cannot take back the goods
without getting a court order.

*Conditional sale* is very similar, for once again your ownership is
conditional on your paying all the instalments. The main legal
difference is that you do not have room for that final change of

mind, at the end, if the goods you bought are worth more than £5,000. But, even now, few contracts are going to be for anything like so much.

*Credit sale* works differently. This time you get your loan, specifically to pay the balance of the cost of an item after you have produced the deposit. But the lender can only sue you for the money if you default and has no rights over the car or the refrigerator at all.

*Personal loans* provide you with money, but, at least in theory, do not force you to spend it in a particular way. In practice, personal loans are usually for something specific. If that is so, there is a good case for getting an agreement to make the fact that it is a personal loan clear. Lenders can sue you for debt if you default, but they cannot take back the goods.

*Second mortgages* provide an alternative way of getting a loan, though they have nothing whatever to do with building societies. Even so, they will only work if you own your house or at least are buying it on a mortgage which has been running for a while. You will not necessarily be able to use the money to borrow for whatever you want, for some finance companies restrict the loans to use for home improvements.

The idea behind them is simple enough. As you pay off the building society's loan, you gradually own an increasing proportion of the house. At the same time if prices rise, perhaps doubling in the course of five years from £10,000 to £20,000, you have a considerable stake in the place. Your 'equity' in the house – to use the financial jargon – is well over £10,000. Second mortgages allow you to borrow against that value, which becomes the finance company's security. But before doing so, you must ask the first lender, in practice the building society, if you are still paying off their loan.

If you default, the lenders will not find it easy to get their money back – and you may be charged little less than someone who can offer no security at all. So rates are high. At the same time, people in Britain move house, on average, about once every six years. If you want to migrate elsewhere and have borrowed on a second mortgage in the meantime, it could mean that half the money you need to buy your next house is locked up elsewhere.

*Instant loans* from moneylenders, which allow you to borrow up to £100 or £200 with no security, imply that the lender is taking considerable risks and he will make a point of charging, and perhaps overcharging, for the extra risks he takes.

## Revolving Credit

Credit cards, budget accounts and trading checks all depend on a different idea. This time, you have a permanent right to borrow, provided that you do not go over a fixed limit. As you pay off one debt, you can take on another – though you cannot choose to skip a repayment each month. The system will always insist on it. Assume that you have an overall borrowing limit of £500 and now have £250 outstanding. Inevitably you cannot borrow more than the other £250. But in the next month you return £125 and so you are free to borrow up to £375. As your debt goes down, your borrowing limit goes up – almost like a see-saw.

The standard *credit cards* usually work on these lines. Access and Barclaycard usually have a limit of £500 or £600 on them and the law insists that you should return 5 per cent of what you owe each month with a minimum payment of £5. There will be a regular bill for what you have bought in the preceding month, but what happens then depends on you. If you settle the whole of your Access or Barclaycard bill within twenty-five days of its being sent to you, there will be no interest charge on what you have borrowed.

Assuming your particular account goes out regularly on the fourth of the month, you can make a point of using your card on the fifth for some big item. It will not appear on your credit-card bill until the following month, so that you can borrow money for nothing for up to seven weeks, assuming you then repay the lot.

The rules differ, though, if you only settle part of your bill. Access will charge you interest from then on, only on what you still owe. But Barclaycard will want interest both on what you have paid and on the debt you have left outstanding back to the date when the bill went out. The problems with an Access card come at the end, for you have to pay interest on what you owe even in the month after you have cleared your bill. Overall, Barclaycard is slightly more expensive.

What do you have to pay when the companies start charging you? Both cards charged $2\frac{1}{4}$ per cent a month late in 1980, which works out at 30·6 per cent according to the official government formula. But in fact it is not quite so bad in practice because there is between four and seven weeks' delay built into the system. The one exception comes when you use the cards to take money from your current account. If you have an Access card, interest starts clocking up immediately. The rules on Barclaycard are more complex; it doubles up as a cheque card and normally when you withdraw money from the bank, using Barclaycard to back your cheque, the funds will come from your current account. But you can make a point of asking that money you withdraw from your bank – or indeed any other bank for that matter – should be taken from your Barclaycard limit and not your current account. If you do that, the group will impose a $1\frac{1}{2}$ per cent levy on what you take out. But you are given the same free credit period which normally applies.

Both cards work abroad. Access belongs to the Interbank group in Europe and comes under the Mastercharge card chain in America. Barclaycard, meanwhile, belongs to Visa. But coverage, at least in Europe, varies from country to country and it is probably at its worst in Belgium, Holland and Germany. Neither card is widely accepted there, but Access fares slightly better than Barclaycard. There is one new, general point to watch, wherever you use the cards. The government has given its backing to an official report, published late in 1980, recommending that shops which take credit cards should be free to charge their users more than they charge cash customers. So it makes sense to check prices.

*Shop credit cards* have been one of the big developments of the last few years. Woolworths, for instance, set up its own card whereby you pay a regular sum each month of at least £5. You then have the right to borrow up to twenty-four times your regular contributions via the card.

Marks & Spencer, too, went into the card business – though you have to go through the American group Citibank to get the card, and the cheques with which you must use it. Tesco, Boots, Asda and a whole series of other retailers have established their own cards recently, though you cannot use them outside their particular chain of shops.

Rates of interest vary. Often they are below the rates Access or Barclaycard charge, at least in terms of the charge per month. But there is no twenty-five-day free-credit period for people paying their bills in full. One other point is worth checking. Some groups impose their charges from the moment that you buy something over the counter, while others wait until your monthly statement goes out. Clearly, the first method will produce higher charges than the second, assuming that you start with the same interest rate.

*Travel and entertainment* (*T & E* ) *cards* are very different. The two best known in Britain are American Express and Diners Club and they depend not on charges, but on regular fees. You have to pay a £15 fee to join American Express and £12·50 for Diners Club. After that comes a regular membership fee which is £10 with Diners Club or £15·50 a year with American Express, which again proves the more expensive of the two.

This time there is no overall limit to what you spend, but a regular bill will come once a month and you are then bound to pay off your debts in full – without delays. Diners Club will impose a default charge – demanding 1½ per cent interest a month on what is due or rather overdue. The group stresses that it is a penalty clause and not a borrowing charge. At the same time, if you fail to pay back your funds on time more than once with either group, they are likely to take away the card.

Like Access and Barclaycard, the two companies will charge shops for the right to take their cards, but in this case the fees make up a considerably higher proportion of their income. But on one point all the card companies are united. They want people who use the cards to settle their debts to pay exactly the same as anyone else and be entitled to any rebates or special offers which apply to what they are buying. But they cannot insist

*Budget accounts* work on the standard credit-card lines even if you do not actually carry around the magic piece of plastic. Most of the big retailing groups, like Selfridges, Debenhams and John Lewis will offer them. The John Lewis variety, for instance, allows you to choose to pay a regular sum of somewhere between £6 and £15 a month, though once you have done so, you remain committed to it. You then have the right to borrow up to twenty times your standing order, taking on new debt only as you pay off old.

*Check trading* and *mail order* are two other forms of revolving credit, though they pre-date Access and Barclaycard by a century or more. Check trading used to be strong among working-class people in the north of England. The issuing company provides you with a check, or credit, and you can then use it at a series of shops. If you do not spend the full sum, the trader will mark the check so that you can use the outstanding balance elsewhere. Collectors deliver the checks, and you repay the money over twenty weeks, though as you settle one check you can always take on another. Shops may give you a discount on what you buy, but the interest rate on an annual basis is not cheap.

Mail order works on the same idea. The companies often claim that borrowing is free, but all that means is that you will not get a discount for settling bills in cash. Even so mail order can work out cheap – for the companies use bulk buying and large warehouses and employ relatively few staff. So you can sometimes make savings there.

## Early Repayment

If you settle a credit-card bill early, you may save yourself interest – and the move may make sense. But it is much more problematical if you want to repay a fixed loan before it is due. It always looks like good housekeeping, but it is probably bad economics. If you pay the rest of what you owe on a two-year loan after twelve months, it is easy to assume that you only have to return half of what you borrowed originally to be square.

Alas, it does not work like that. When interest rates are high, for instance, you have actually provided only one-third of the original capital, even when you are half-way through paying off the debt on many bank and hire-purchase loans.

The reason lies in the way that the loans are arranged. Each instalment may be the same size, but the balance between the interest you are paying and the capital you are returning shifts as the loan goes on. At the beginning the instalments are almost all interest and you pay off a quarter of the charge which the company levies in the first three months of a two-year loan. So there is a considerable part of the original loan outstanding for some time.

Banks insist that they do not levy penalties on people who pay off their debts before they are due. But the way the loans are organized ensures that you will owe more than you think. So check your figures before rushing off to clear a debt. You can always put the money you have earmarked for debt settlement into savings, and earn a reasonable return on them in the meanwhile.

## The Legal Framework

The Consumer Credit Act is changing the whole legal framework within which lending money takes place. The main aims are to ensure that only respectable people are involved in the lending business and that if you are going to borrow from them you should be able to compare what they charge on the same basis. Anyone who offers credit, from a bank to a back-street pawnbroker, has to register with the Director-General of Fair Trading. He has the right to turn them down or indeed withdraw any licence he has already given them if he has good reasons to believe that they are not 'fit and proper persons' to be in the business.

People who arrange loans, like estate agents, motor dealers and so on, also have to register and can also have their licences to arrange loans withdrawn. One other point comes up, though it is not part of the Consumer Credit Act. One or two motor dealers used to make a point of advertising as though they were just private motorists who happened to be selling their old cars.

The point was to avoid their legal responsibilities. Anyone who buys from a private individual is on his or her own, legally, and has no comeback if the car later proves to be defective. But a dealer is responsible, like any other trader, for the quality of what he sells. But the law now ensures that a dealer who goes through the charade of pretending to be something he is not is committing a criminal offence.

High-pressure salesmanship designed to badger you into taking money should disappear. No one has the right to call at your home unasked to offer you a loan. Meanwhile you also have time to reflect on what you have done and think better of it – at least if you have signed the loan agreement off 'trade premises' like a bank, a shop, or a motor-car showroom. If you did it elsewhere, there is a seven-day cooling-off period, and there is still time for more second thoughts if the transaction involves using your house as security for the money, as a second mortgage does.

The credit middleman – or credit broker in the jargon – can always introduce you to some potential lender in the hope of getting commission if the deal goes through. Occasionally, he may ask you for an introduction fee, though, as he is getting commission from the other side, it seems greedy. If you agree, and he manages to find you a lender within six months, you are committed to paying it. But if you have not borrowed money within that time limit, all he can demand for his troubles is the sum of £1.

The Truth in Lending provisions, which were to become effective late in 1980, will ensure that every lender has to show the rate of interest you will be paying on his loan on the same basis. As we said earlier, it will have to include all his charges without any extra remaining outside.

Shops will have to show the 'true rate of interest'. As you pay off a loan, the original debt as well as the interest will go down. There will be a declining balance – to use bank jargon – though it will not fall as fast as you think, because of the way it is skewed. However, it will decline all the same. The 'true' interest rate is based on the actual debt you owe at any time. If you borrow £500 for two years at 18 per cent, for instance, the interest will start off based on £500. But by the time you have repaid half the loan, the interest will be 18 per cent of £250. When you have repaid all but the last £50, the 18 per cent interest will be calculated on the basis of the £50 you still owe ... and so on.

The old alternative 'flat' way of doing the sum worked out the interest on what you had borrowed originally even when you had only one more repayment to make. So flat rates look deceptively cheap. Indeed, the standard way of converting a flat rate to a true rate is to double it, and then take away one, which shows just what a difference the favourable calculation can make.

You may still encounter flat rates, by the way, but unless the shop or lender is breaking the law, the true rate should also appear. If you have any doubts, ask about it.

*Lender's liabilities* often cover the goods for which they have provided the loan. If the money you have borrowed has been specifically tied to buying some particular object, whatever it may be, then the lender is jointly liable for its quality with the shop or dealer who sold it to you. The seller is your first target in practice, but if he proves awkward or perhaps goes bankrupt, you have a second string to your bow.

Access and Barclaycard are also liable, if the goods which you have bought through your card are worth more than £30, though there is also a legal wrangle on whether they would have to pay for 'consequential damage' caused by the defect. If your car's defective brakes meant that you ploughed into a bus queue, the card companies claim that they would not be legally responsible for damages unless you had been given your first card after July 1977. The government says that they would, but it is a matter of academic interest for most people.

*Legal help.* If you take out a loan, and feel on reflection that you are being squeezed, you can always take the issue to court. The courts have the power to set aside rates if they are too high, though there is little guidance as to what the phrase means. Even so, the rules are very unlikely to cover you unless you are dealing with the seamier edges of the credit fringe. The moral, of course, is to look at how much interest you are paying in the first place.

There are plenty of people who can advise you if you do find yourself in difficulties – and they include the company from which you are borrowing money. Other sources of help include the Citizens' Advice Bureaux (CAB) and the local Legal Aid Centre, if there is one. Finally, the Law Society, which represents Britain's solicitors, runs what is known as 'the green form scheme' which allows you to get half an hour's legal advice. Charges vary with the size of your income. The service is free if you have a low income, but moves up on a fixed scale in line with your earnings. Most firms of solicitors take part, and you will find at least some of the names listed in the local Yellow Pages – along with the CAB and Legal Aid Centre.

# 5. Buying or Selling a House

Buying a house can be the best investment of your life – but there are many pitfalls to watch for. You have to choose the right type of mortgage, for instance. The choice includes not only the ordinary building-society repayment method, but also the 'option'-mortgage method and at least three varieties of endowment mortgage. Endowment and option loans may have drawbacks which are often not appreciated until it is too late. But even plumping for an ordinary building-society loan is not without problems, because individual societies vary considerably and unexpectedly in their lending rules.

Professional fees and other expenses of buying or selling a house can easily come to £1,000 or more. It is tempting to look for ways to reduce the cost: some of the ideas occasionally mentioned are useful, others may prove false economies. Above all, the choice of home needs care. Many first-time buyers, in particular, make bad buys which they would have avoided if they had had a little foresight or taken advice.

Given the right decisions, you will probably make a handsome profit on your home. Why? House prices tend to rise over the long term roughly in line with inflation but for many years the net cost of a mortgage after tax relief has been well below the rate of inflation.

In a period when inflation averages, say, 10 per cent, a £15,000 home will rise by about £1,500 in a year. With a mortgage interest rate of, for instance, 12 per cent and basic-rate tax at 30 per cent, the net interest cost of a 100 per cent mortgage will be about £1,260 a year. So the home buyer is making a profit of about £240 in a year.

The bigger your mortgage the better if you want to make the most of tax subsidies – the only constraint is the government's limit of £25,000 on the amount of borrowing that qualifies for tax relief. It makes sense to make extra sacrifices to cope with a large mortgage in the difficult first years. Later, with inflation and pay rises, your borrowing will seem less of a burden. It usually makes sense also to borrow for as long as possible.

## Choosing a Building Society

Ideally a would-be borrower should aim to be a saver for at least two years before asking his building society for a loan. Otherwise he may be forced to resort to getting a loan by the back door and may have to accept terms that do not suit him.

Before you start saving with a building society, you should check on its lending practices and rules. Even the major societies differ widely in their attitudes to certain types of home and charge varying interest rates for different types of loan. In a recent survey, for instance, both the Leeds and Bradford & Bingley societies indicated that they are often chary about lending on flats made by converting Victorian mansions. At many other societies there is strong resistance at branch-manager level to converted flats, even if there are no head-office rules against them. The Nationwide, Abbey National and Halifax are among the few major societies which over the years have lent freely on conversions.

The same survey also confirmed would-be borrowers' complaints about the difficulty in raising a mortgage on a house in a run-down area. Few societies admit to having a ban on what estate agents call red-lined areas but many said they cut down the term of the loan. Often the maximum loan a society will offer in such an area will be lower than its usual maximum percentage – so you will need a much bigger deposit than for a standard semi at the same price. One society which has publicized its concern to help run-down areas, in recent years, is the Abbey National.

Most societies charge higher interest for larger loans. Usually the scale is $\frac{1}{2}$ per cent extra for loans between £15,000 and £20,000, 1 per cent extra between £20,000 and £25,000 and $1\frac{1}{2}$ per cent above £25,000. The extra is charged on the full amount of the loan, not just the excess above the trigger point: so if you find you want to go just above a trigger point it may well be worth while to have a rethink and keep below the threshold, borrowing the rest from a bank or a relative.

Nationwide is one of the few major societies which is out of line on charges for larger loans. Its scale starts at £13,000 and rises by ¼ per cent for each £2,000 band between £13,000 and £21,000. Between £21,000 and £25,000 the extra is 1¼ per cent and above £25,000 1½ per cent. The Bradford & Bingley's scale starts at £15,000 but rises in steps of ¼ per cent for each £2,500 band up to £30,000. Above £30,000 the extra is 1½ per cent.

One well-known society, the Burnley, actually charges less than the usual building-society interest rate. The discount depends on the general level of interest rates but, for instance, when the standard building-society mortgage rate was 15 per cent, the Burnley's equivalent rate (calculated on the same basis) was only 14·9 per cent. The difference meant that a £10,000 twenty-five-year loan that cost £128·92 a month at other societies cost only £128·10 at the Burnley. The Burnley actually uses the same stated interest rate as the others – but does its sums in a different way. For it gives the borrower immediate credit for each monthly reduction in his debt whereas other societies wait until the end of the financial year. The interest bill at the Burnley is therefore lower because it is calculated on a smaller principal.

Most societies charge ¼ per cent extra on endowment loans, but some societies, including the Leicester and Burnley among the majors, charge an extra ½ per cent.

If your pay is low in relation to the amount you expect to borrow, a society like the Nationwide or the Alliance may be a good bet. They are often happy to lend up to three times a borrower's yearly pay whereas many societies may not go above two and a half times. The maximum multiple is not fixed but varies with the level of interest rates: most societies apply lower multiples when interest rates – and repayment rates – are high. When the mortgage rate rose to 15 per cent in 1980 many societies reduced the maximum multiple to twice a borrower's annual earnings. But at the Nationwide and Abbey National, for instance, the multiple remained as high as two and a half times for first-time buyers.

Where a wife goes out to work, most societies are prepared to add something to what they would lend on the husband's income alone, particularly if she can show that she is planning to remain at work for some time. Often the formula for the maximum mortgage is the total of the lower salary plus whatever the society would lend on the higher salary alone. But some societies will take account of only half the lower salary.

Loans of up to 95 per cent of the official valuation of a home are now freely available from many societies where the borrower is a first-time buyer. Some societies even lend up to 100 per cent of valuation to young borrowers who have just graduated or finished apprenticeships. Other societies regard 80 per cent as their absolute maximum.

Many would-be borrowers are tempted to save with local societies in the hope that they will get more personal and sympathetic attention for their loan application than they would from a national society. A major attraction of some small societies, for instance, is that they may be more willing to lend on homes in local problem areas. But the drawback of a small society is that if you later move to another part of the country it may well turn you down for a loan on your new home. Then when you apply to another society you will find yourself at the back of its mortgage queue.

Some small societies offer temptingly high interest rates to savers – but this usually means that their mortgage rates are also higher than the norm.

The majority of societies these days are happy to lend to single people – and single women particularly are regarded as very reliable borrowers. Many societies are prepared to lend to unmarried couples, including homosexual couples, on the same basis as they would to a married couple. The Nationwide's view, for instance, is that the criterion that matters in judging an application for a joint mortgage is the stability of the relationship between the borrowers.

Most societies prefer not to grant loans for more than twenty-five years. And for older houses the maximum is often twenty years, particularly if they are unmodernized. But societies like the Woolwich, Alliance and Nationwide are happy to lend for thirty years and in some cases thirty-five. The Alliance and Nationwide say they are prepared to allow mortgage terms that will run until the borrower is seventy-five. The Nationwide is sometimes prepared to advance 'interest-only' mortgages, that is, the borrower has to make no regular repayments of capital, which will be paid off in one go from the proceeds of his estate when he dies.

Whatever a society's rules about the term of loan for first-time buyers it will probably relax them for existing borrowers who want to extend the term of their loan when interest rates go up. Then terms of thirty years or more are often allowed as a means of cushioning a borrower from the full impact of the rise.

The Alliance runs a special scheme to ease the repayments burden for first-time buyers in the difficult early years of a loan. In the Alliance Easi-Start plan, your repayments in the first three years are about one-seventh less than with an ordinary twenty-five-year loan. Your repayments are in fact so low that they do not even cover your full interest costs let alone clear any capital. In the fourth year the repayments start rising and in the seventh they level out at a little more than you would have been paying all along with an ordinary twenty-five-year loan. The snag is that to pay for the benefit you get in the first years, the Easi-Start scheme requires you to continue repayments for ten years after an ordinary loan would have finished.

Some smaller societies penalize borrowers who need to wind up a mortgage in the early years. A typical rule is that you have to pay an extra three months' interest on repayment of a loan inside the first five years of the term. The rule is not applied where a borrower wants to borrow for his new home from the same society. But it is often applied rigidly where the society refuses to provide the new loan and the borrower has to go to another society.

One of the few societies which is prepared to lend on homes where a sitting tenant occupies part of the building is the City of London. It will sometimes lend up to 70 per cent of the valuation in such cases.

## How Long Do You Need to Save?

Few societies will consider lending to someone who has been a saver for less than six months and often the minimum period is a year. The rules vary depending on how much money the societies have to lend and can even vary between different branches of the same society. Ideally a borrower should aim to save the whole of his deposit with a society, which means at least 5 per cent of the purchase price of his home and probably more than 10 per cent.

Many societies have 'subscription share accounts' which are tailor-made for anyone saving for his or her first home. You are committed to saving a set amount each month and you usually earn a handsome 1¼ per cent more than the standard rate for ordinary building-society investors.

To hedge your bets it may be worth putting a small sum in another building society. The fact of having had even a token deposit with a society for, say, a year will give you a useful edge over anyone applying completely cold.

If you want to buy in a hurry and have not established a savings record, you may still have a chance of a loan. Societies sometimes lend to people who come in off the street at times when money is flowing freely. At other times, a borrower can try getting professional advisers to intercede on his behalf. Solicitors, estate agents, accountants and insurance brokers place a lot of clients' money with building societies, so if they back your application you will probably have a better chance. Such queue-jumping, however, has its drawbacks. For one thing you are in a poor bargaining position to get the loan best suited to your needs. You will probably have to accept an endowment loan, which in most cases will provide your adviser with hefty commission, but you may feel that on examination of the figures you would be better off with an ordinary repayment loan.

### The Government's 'Homeloan' Scheme

First-time buyers now receive a special subsidy through the government's 'Homeloan' scheme when they take out a mortgage. To get a cash bonus of £110, you have to save for two years in a qualifying savings account and build up at least £600. You have to be at least eighteen and have to take out a mortgage of not less than £1,600 and at least one-quarter of the home's price. The home has to be below a certain price, which varies according to region.

You have to have had at least £300 on deposit throughout the twelve months before your application. Institutions which run savings accounts that qualify include building societies, high-street banks and the National Savings Department. When you open your account, stake your claim to the bonus by filling in a special form.

## Endowment versus Repayment Loans

There are two main ways of clearing a mortgage loan: the 'endowment' method and the 'repayment' method. With the endowment method you pay the whole loan off in one go at the end of the term. The cash to do this comes from an endowment policy which is timed to mature on the date the mortgage is due to be repaid. The monthly payments you make on an endowment mortgage are made up of interest on the loan and premiums on the policy – there are no capital repayments as such.

With the repayment method the debt to the building society is reduced each month. In the early years most of each monthly payment goes to meet interest but as the debt reduces more of the payment each month goes to clearing the capital.

Insurance brokers' comparison sheets often obscure the way that inflation undermines the advantages of the endowment method. A fair comparison of endowment and repayment mortgages is much harder to make than many brokers suggest. But on analysis of the detailed figures many independent experts have concluded that endowments have little to offer anyone except high-rate taxpayers. And for first-time buyers, endowments often prove financial millstones at a time in life when it is usually hardest to make ends meet. You get full tax relief on the interest and relief at half the basic tax rate on the endowment premiums. Because you make no reductions in the debt during the term of the loan your total interest bills come to much more than with the repayment method. Hence the somewhat misleading point often made in favour of endowments that they earn you much more tax relief.

On analysis it emerges that the main reason for higher tax relief with the endowment method is that your total costs are higher. The question for home buyers is whether it is in their interest to incur higher costs simply to claim tax relief. What matters in the end is not the total amount of tax relief but the net costs to the borrower after tax relief; and here the balance of advantage between the two methods is far from clear.

The cheapest form of endowment is the 'low-cost' variety, where the initial sum insured is only a fraction of the loan. The policy is with-profits and the hope is that with bonuses rolling up over the years there will be a big-enough pay-out at maturity not only to repay the loan but to provide a little extra for the policy-holder. The amount of this windfall can never be predicted accurately because of uncertainty about insurance companies' future bonus rates. Predictions based on policies maturing now can be misleading – and many top insurance companies have recently warned that 'terminal' bonuses in particular may well fall from the high levels of the last few years.

In the early years the main policy in a low-cost package will not be enough to cover the debt should the borrower die. Most endowment packages, therefore, include a small extra policy providing pure life cover to meet this shortfall.

The traditional endowment mortgage sold to well-off borrowers – the 'full endowment' – is based on a with-profits policy with a sum insured equal to the full amount of the loan. This works out by far the most expensive of all mortgage varieties on monthly cost; but the bonuses added to the initial large sum insured mean that at the end the maturity value is often three times the amount of the loan. It is thus primarily a savings vehicle. With the introduction of the low-cost method in the early 1970s, brokers rarely promote it these days.

Some insurance brokers still sell non-profit endowment mortgages, although these are considered by experts to have nothing to offer any category of borrower. The policy is for the full amount of the loan but, because there are no with-profits bonuses, there is no windfall element at the end.

The basic life cover included automatically in endowment packages is a vitally important feature for most borrowers. It is not included automatically with repayment mortgages but a simple 'mortgage protection policy' can be bought separately which for a very small premium will repay the balance of the debt outstanding if the borrower dies during the term.

The net cost of an endowment mortgage after tax relief remains fixed throughout the term (assuming unchanged tax and interest rates). The net cost of the repayment method rises over the term, reflecting the lower rax relief you get in later years as progressively more of each repayment is capital.

The net cost of the repayment method starts out lower than all the endowment varieties. But eventually with the reducing tax relief the net cost will rise above that for most endowment loans.

Tables 3, 4 and 5 compare how the different methods work for a thirty-year-old man paying income tax at 30 per cent. The standard mortgage rate is assumed to be 12 per cent, close to the average for the last five years. And, in line with building-society practice, there is a ¼ per cent interest to pay on the endowment loans. Insurance premiums are stated net of a tax subsidy of 15 per cent, the rate that applies from April 1981. The repayment method's costs include premiums on a mortgage protection policy, which will ensure that the debt outstanding is immediately repaid in full if the borrower dies early.

Table 3 shows that in the low-cost version of the endowment method the monthly cost of a £10,000 twenty-five-year loan after tax relief is £84·89 – £2·72 a month cheaper than the without-profits method shown in Table 4. But, as Table 5 shows, the repayment method is cheaper again. In the first year the net monthly cost works out at only £77·80 a month – £7·09 cheaper than the low-cost endowment. The repayment method's cost will gradually rise over the years; but even after ten years the net cost at £81·75 a month has risen by only £3·95. And, as Table 5 shows, even in the fourteenth year, when the debt outstanding has been cut to £7,898 and the tax relief has been cut by £6·31 a month, the net cost of £84·11 is still a little less than the low-cost endowment.

The low-cost endowment will show a surplus, on current projections, of £3,750 when the debt is repaid out of the policy's proceeds at the end. About £2,750 of the surplus is formed by a terminal bonus – and there is no obligation on an insurance company to maintain its terminal bonuses. In any case inflation will slash the surplus's real value. If, for instance, inflation averages a modest 10 per cent a year over the next twenty-five years £1 at the end will be worth less than 10p of today's money. And £3,750 will have the purchasing power of about £350 today.

Of course, from the fifteenth year onwards the repayment

method will cost more than the low-cost endowment. But its average cost over the whole period works out at only £85·93 a month, just £1·04 more than the low-cost. And all of the saving with the endowment comes more than half-way through when money has lost much of its value.

The endowment method cannot usually match the flexibility of the repayment method in coping with interest-rate rises. Usually, with an endowment, a borrower has to bear the full brunt of a rise immediately because there is no provision for him to extend the term of the loan.

**Table 3 Mortgage Payment: Low-Cost Endowment Method**
£10,000 low-cost endowment loan repaid over twenty-five years at 12¼ per cent

| | | | |
|---|---|---|---|
| Net monthly premium | £13·43 | Projected maturity value | |
| Monthly interest bill | £102·08 | of policy after | |
| | ——— | twenty-five years | £13,752 |
| Total cost before tax | | | |
| relief | £115·51 | Deduct mortgage debt | £10,000 |
| Deduct tax relief | £30·62 | | ——— |
| | ——— | *Surplus cash for borrower* | *£3,752* |
| *Total net cost* | £84·89 | | |

**Table 4 Mortgage Payment: Without-Profits Endowment Method**
£10,000 without-profits endowment loan repaid over twenty-five years at 12¼ per cent

| | | | |
|---|---|---|---|
| Net monthly premium | £16·15 | Maturity value after | |
| Monthly interest cost | £102·08 | twenty-five years | £10,000 |
| | ——— | Deduct mortgage debt | £10,000 |
| Total cost | £118·23 | | ——— |
| Deduct tax relief | £30·62 | *Surplus* | *Nil* |
| *Total net cost* | £87.61 | | |

**Table 5 Mortgage Payment: Repayment Method**
£10,000 repayment loan repaid over twenty-five years at 12 per cent

| | | | |
|---|---|---|---|
| Monthly repayments | £106·25 | *Position in Year 14:* | |
| Monthly life-insurance | | Debt outstanding | £7,897·83 |
| premium* | £1·55 | Total monthly cost | £107·80 |
| | —— | Deduct tax relief on | |
| *Total cost* | *£107·80* | interest | £23·69 |
| | | | —— |
| | | *Net monthly cost* | *£84·11* |
| *Position in Year 1:* | | *Average position over* | |
| Debt outstanding | £10,000·00 | *twenty-five years:* | |
| Total monthly cost | £107·80 | Total monthly cost | £107·80 |
| Deduct tax relief on | | Deduct average tax | |
| interest | £30·00 | relief | £21·87 |
| | —— | | —— |
| *Net monthly cost* | *£77·80* | *Net monthly cost* | *£85·93* |

\* Net cost of mortgage protection policy.

The repayment method is also more flexible if you want to move. You can usually choose either to repay the new loan within the time span agreed for your original mortgage or repay it on a new twenty-five-year term. With the endowment, you will have to repay most if not all of the new loan by the maturity date agreed for your first loan.

The relative merits of endowments and repayments vary with different levels of interest rates. With the mortgage rate at $8\frac{1}{2}$ per cent – its level a few years ago – the repayment method's net costs exceeded the low-cost endowment's after eleven years. With the mortgage rate at 15 per cent (its level in 1980), the repayment method remains cheaper for fifteen years. High interest rates help the repayment method because the interest content of the repayments remains higher for longer – and so the tax relief remains high.

High tax rates, however, tend to favour the endowment method because the large continuing interest bills attract that much more tax relief. Academic studies indicate that the low-cost endowment method is the better bet for people paying tax at more than about

50 per cent (provided, of course, they can set off their interest payments in full against tax). On that showing, a low-cost endowment is worth considering for someone earning more than about £16,000 at present.

Table 6 shows how the cost of the repayment method varies at different rates of interest.

Table 6 **Mortgage Repayment Rates**
The cost of a £10,000 twenty-five-year loan repaid by the standard building-society repayment method

| Interest rate (%) | Repayments* (£) | Interest rate (%) | Repayments* (£) |
|---|---|---|---|
| 8 | 78·06 | 13½ | 117·45 |
| 8½ | 81·43 | 14 | 121·25 |
| 9 | 84·84 | 14½ | 125·06 |
| 9½ | 88·30 | 15 | 128·92 |
| 10 | 91·81 | 15½ | 132·79 |
| 10½ | 95·36 | 16 | 136·68 |
| 11 | 98·95 | 16½ | 140·59 |
| 11½ | 102·58 | 17 | 144·52 |
| 12 | 106·25 | 17½ | 148·47 |
| 12½ | 109·95 | 18 | 152·43 |
| 13 | 113·69 | | |

* Monthly cost before tax relief.

## Option Mortgages

'Option mortgages' are home loans with specially subsidized interest rates. Interest payments, however, do not qualify for tax relief. The interest rate usually works out about the same as the standard mortgage rate after tax relief and the point of the scheme is to give borrowers paying little or no income tax the same help as better-off borrowers. The government pays the subsidy direct to building societies and other lenders to meet the difference between the option rate and the ordinary rate.

Despite the government's efforts to match the tax relief of an ordinary mortgage, option mortgages are more expensive in early years. This is because the borrower has to pay off the debt faster: he gets the benefit of this if he moves house, when the debt outstanding will be smaller than with an ordinary mortgage.

For a £10,000 loan, the extra repayment burden may be about £5 a month, the exact figure depending on rates of interest and tax.

Option mortgages are a bad bet for people who pay higher rates of tax or may do so in the foreseeable future. Such borrowers have to switch to an ordinary mortgage if they are to get tax aid at rates higher than the basic rate. Option borrowers are allowed to switch – but there may be a delay before the switch takes effect.

## Local-Authority Mortgages

Local authorities can be a useful source of mortgage funds, particularly if you are buying a house whose condition is unacceptable to a building society. Local authorities are generally less demanding in their standards and often have specific policies to revive run-down areas shunned by many building societies.

The flow of local authority mortgage money, however, fluctuates greatly depending on national economic conditions. Local authorities are required by law to give priority to council tenants and families on the housing waiting list.

To be considered for a local authority loan you usually have to show that you have been turned down by at least one building society.

## Other Lenders

Home loans are offered by many life-insurance companies but invariably as a condition of the deal the borrower has to take out an endowment policy. Life-insurance companies are particularly useful for larger loans – in many cases they lend up to £75,000 to well-off borrowers. Often, however, life companies prefer to provide 'top-up' loans – that is they leave it to the building society to provide the bulk of the money and they just add a small second mortgage on top.

Companies which in the recent past have been willing to provide the whole mortgage package include Eagle Star, Equitable Life, London & Manchester and Royal Insurance.

Most of these companies also provide top-up finance. Other companies in the top-up field include Guardian Royal Exchange, Legal & General, Sun Life, National Mutual and the insurance arm of the Save & Prosper unit-trust group.

Insurance companies' interest rates are usually higher than the building-society mortgage rate. A recent survey showed that most insurance companies were charging at least 14 per cent at a time when the building society mortgage rate was $11\frac{3}{4}$ per cent. A further snag is that even where the insurance company is providing only a top-up loan it usually insists not only that the whole of the borrowing should be backed by an endowment policy but that the policy should be non-profit. Where a borrower has no option but to accept a non-profit endowment loan, he should at least shop around for the cheapest non-profit policy. Non-profit-policy premiums are directly comparable, and unless there are worries about the financial stability of the company concerned the policy with the cheapest premium is generally the one to choose.

Some companies confuse the issue by charging a relatively low interest rate on the loan combined with a higher-than-usual premium for the endowment policy. The package needs careful examination. It may not be the best value, particularly where the insurance company is providing only part of the finance but insists on a policy covering the total amount.

If you want to pay off an insurance loan early you may face a hefty penalty. Often this is six months' interest but the norm is three months'. Companies which, in a recent survey, said they make no charge on winding up a loan include Cornhill, Guardian Royal Exchange, MGM, National Provident, Norwich Union, Provident Life, Scottish Amicable, Scottish Equitable, Scottish Mutual and Wesleyan & General.

Insurance companies usually do not like the total borrowing package to come to more than twice your annual income. And they rarely like the borrowing to exceed 75 per cent of the price of the house.

The Trustee Savings Banks have recently become a sizeable force in the mortgage field. When their home-loan scheme was introduced in 1979 their interest rates ranged up to 16 per cent, compared to the standard building-society mortgage rate of $11\frac{3}{4}$

per cent at the time. The TSBs lend up to about twice a borrower's annual income; their rule is that mortgage payments should not exceed one-quarter of the borrower's income. Other banks which have started to provide mortgages include Lloyds, Midland, Williams & Glyn's and Citibank. They specialize in larger loans, sometimes as much as £150,000. But Lloyds Bank will consider applications for loans of as little as £10,000.

## Buying a Council Home

Under the 1980 Housing Act, most people who have been tenants of a council for at least three years have the right to buy their home at a discount to its market value. The discount depends on how long you or your family have lived in council property. It starts at 33 per cent for three years and reaches a maximum of 50 per cent for twenty years or more. There is an overriding rule for homes built within the last six years that they cannot be sold for less than what they cost to build. Buyers have to refund a proportion of the discount if they sell within five years. The proportion is on a sliding scale depending on how long after the purchase the sale takes place.

The first step for a would-be purchaser is to complete a 'Right to Buy' form (R T B 1) which should be available from the council (if it is not, appeal to the Department of the Environment). If your council will not help you fill in the form, go to a Citizens' Advice Bureau or a solicitor. Mistakes in giving information can cost you thousands later. If, within four weeks, the council has not acknowledged your right to buy, write to the Department of the Environment, which will invoke special procedures. In most cases, a council which is not in favour of selling will, because of the law, pay lip-service to your rights – but try to wear you down by dragging its feet in, for instance, delaying telling you the home's 'assessed market value' and the discount you are entitled to.

If you act within three months of receiving an offer price, you can secure a council mortgage. You can claim up to 100 per cent of the price provided the loan would not exceed two and a half times your income or, in the case of joint applicants, provided it would not exceed the lower income plus two and a half times the higher. If the council's mortgage offer is less than you need, you can, by depositing £100 within five years, ensure that the home's price is frozen for two years.

If you live in a house, you get the freehold. If you live in a flat, you get a 125-year lease – and you will be liable for maintenance and service charges which may come to more than your rent. In the case of both a house and a flat, you have to budget to pay rates (which were previously included in your rent).

## House-buying Procedures

Before you go house-hunting be clear about how much you can afford to pay. A preliminary visit to your building-society manager should establish how much you can borrow, particularly if you can give him a clear idea of the sort of place you are looking for.

Remember that you will face a hefty bill for solicitors' and survey fees, probably stamp duty and other costs (see Table 7). A

Table 7 **House-Purchase Costs (£)**

| Purchase price | Building-society survey* | Land registry fee | Solicitor's charge for conveyance* | Solicitor's mortgage charge*† | Indemnity premium† |
|---|---|---|---|---|---|
| 8,000 | 17·00 | 20·00 | 80·00 | 40·00 | 28·00 |
| 10,000 | 21·00 | 25·00 | 100·00 | 42·50 | 35·00 |
| 12,000 | 25·00 | 30·00 | 120·00 | 46·00 | 42·00 |
| 14,000 | 29·00 | 35·00 | 140·00 | 48·00 | 49·00 |
| 16,000 | 32·00 | 40·00 | 160·00 | 50·00 | 56·00 |
| 18,000 | 34·00 | 45·00 | 180·00 | 51·60 | 63·00 |
| 20,000 | 36·00 | 50·00 | 200·00 | 52·40 | 70·00 |
| 25,000 | 41·00 | 62·00 | 250·00 | 55·80 | 87·50 |
| 30,000 | 46·00 | 74·00 | 300·00 | 58·20 | 105·00 |
| 35,000 | 49·00 | 86·00 | 350·00 | 61·20 | 122·50 |
| 40,000 | 51·00 | 98·00 | 400·00 | 63·60 | 140·00 |

* VAT, currently at 15 per cent, is extra.
† Assuming a 90 per cent mortgage.
*Source:* Building Societies Association.

recent analysis by *Money Which?* magazine showed that, for a typical buyer paying £28,000, solicitors' fees, stamp duty and other legal costs totalled £893. If the buyer was at the same time selling a £25,000 home his solicitors' and estate agents' bills for the sale would total a further £690. Then there is the bill for removals, probably at least £100.

*Money Which?* established that the total bill for all direct expenses of the move would come to about $7\frac{1}{2}$ per cent of the value of the house being sold. On top of this there might be bills for new carpets and curtains.

Most home-hunters find the place they buy through estate agents, and the first step is usually to get yourself on the mailing list of the estate agents covering the area you are looking in. But it may be worth looking for private sellers advertising in the local newspapers and in tobacconists' windows. By buying from a private seller you may save hundreds of pounds: he can afford to undercut prices in estate agents' lists because he is saving the estate agents' bill, which often works out at as much as 3 per cent of the house price.

Usually sellers price their homes a little higher than they expect to get. It may, therefore, be worth trying an offer well below the asking price, particularly where the house has unique features which make it hard to value. If you are dealing through an estate agent, he has a legal duty to put all offers to the seller.

Once the seller has accepted your offer, you usually have to put down a small deposit – £100 in most cases – to show good faith. Offers do not become legally binding at this stage under the law in England and Wales, provided you state in writing that the arrangement is 'subject to contract and survey'. You can withdraw later from the deal without giving a reason and get your preliminary deposit back.

If an estate agent is involved he will normally hold the deposit on behalf of the seller, and the receipt he gives you should state that he is holding it 'as stakeholder'. You ought to be sure of his credentials and that he has insurance so that if he goes bankrupt you will be able to get your money back. Generally it is better to leave the deposit with the estate agent than with the seller because if you withdraw later you should have less trouble getting your money back.

The next stage is to apply to the building society for a loan on the house. Usually you will have to fill out a special form and provide proof of your income. You will probably need to get a surveyor to check on the house's condition. The building society will also want a surveyor's report. You may save money if you use the same surveyor as the building society. The survey report for the building society is not normally available to buyers, partly because it is usually based on a less exacting examination of the property than a buyer would want. The Abbey National, however, makes its surveyors' valuation reports available to buyers.

The surveyor should be a member of one of the recognized organizations of the profession. Members of the Royal Institution of Chartered Surveyors, the best-established body for estate agents, have the letters FRICS or ARICS after their name. The other major body is the Incorporated Society of Valuers and Auctioneers, whose members use the letters FSVA or ASVA. A good survey should include an examination of the roof, ceilings, walls, floors, doors, windows and any outbuildings. The surveyor should comment briefly on the electrical system, plumbing and heating, but if you want a full examination you will have to ask specifically and probably pay extra. You can save money by having a verbal report rather than a written one, but this could be a false economy. You will have little evidence of negligence to back your case if, later, you want to sue the surveyor for failing to spot something vital.

A full survey for a three-bedroomed semi costs at least £100 in most cases and often more than £150. There is a standard scale of fees for building-society surveys, ranging from £21 for a £10,000 house to £51 for a £40,000 one; in each case value-added tax is extra. A survey report usually includes an estimate of the value of the house, but if this is not included you can usually get it on request. The next stage is to 'exchange contracts'. This is when the deal becomes binding on both sides and the buyer has to increase his deposit to 10 per cent of the house's price.

Most of the legal work which buying a house entails has to be done in the weeks leading up to exchange of contracts. Usually you need a solicitor to handle it: you are legally entitled to do the work yourself but this is time-consuming and demands patience and care if you are not to make a potentially disastrous mistake.

Most solicitors will give you an estimate of their bill if you ask, so you can save money by shopping around for the cheapest quotation.

The building society needs a solicitor to check that the legal procedures have been executed correctly. Usually the same solicitor can act for both the society and the buyer, and this should save the buyer money. Before engaging a solicitor it is worth checking that the building society will be prepared to accept him to act for it. Until 1973 solicitors' fees for conveyancing work were laid down in a set scale linked to the value of the house. Solicitors are now free to charge whatever they think is 'fair and reasonable' but in practice there is still a correlation between the size of the bill and the value of the house.

If you are buying a £15,000 house, you will usually have to pay about £200, including value-added tax and the solicitor's fee for acting for the building society. For a £30,000 house, a typical bill is about £300. These figures do not include Land Registry fees or stamp duty.

Before exchanging contracts you or your solicitor have to check whether the local authority has any plans which might reduce the value of the house – proposals for a motorway, for instance. You need to be sure the seller's ownership of the house is undisputed – and that no one else has an interest. You also need to check on any 'restrictive covenants'. These are restrictions on how you can use the property. You may, for instance, be required to get someone else's consent for any alterations.

Both buyer and seller have to sign a separate contract and send it to the other side. The most important element in the contract is the price, which your solicitor will normally write in. It is worth checking that he has got it right, particularly if you have negotiated a reduction since he first became involved.

The final stage is 'completion', when the buyer hands over the balance of the money and the house is fully his. Completion usually takes place about a month after exchange of contracts, and probably as much as three months after the seller accepted the provisional offer. Once contracts have been exchanged the property is at the buyer's risk. If it burns down between exchange and completion, he will be forced to pay the full purchase price. The buyer should therefore make sure his solicitor arranges temporary house insurance.

Usually where the loan exceeds 80 per cent of the building society's valuation of the house, the borrower has to provide additional security in the form of a special insurance policy. Under this, the insurance company indemnifies the building society against loss if the borrower defaults. The insurance guarantee usually covers the amount by which the loan exceeds 80 per cent of the valuation. The borrower has to pay a single premium of about $3\frac{1}{2}$ per cent of the amount covered.

The buyer has to pay stamp duty if the price is more than £20,000. For homes between £20,001 and £25,000 the rate is $\frac{1}{2}$ per cent; for homes between £25,001 and £30,000 it is 1 per cent and between £30,001 and £35,000 it is $1\frac{1}{2}$ per cent. Above £35,000 it is 2 per cent. In each case the rate is applied on the whole of the price. There can be a big saving, therefore, if you can reduce the price below one of the thresholds which trigger a higher rate. Often this can be done by paying for carpets, curtains and other fixtures and fittings separately. Take, for instance, a house costing £26,000. The stamp-duty bill would normally be £260. But if the price includes £1,000 worth or more of fixtures and fittings, these can be paid for separately to bring the house price below £25,001, whereby the stamp duty will be cut to less than £125.

The Land Registry is a government organization which keeps tabs on the ownership of most of the country's property. If the seller is listed as the owner at the registry, there is usually no need for further inquiries. The buyer has to pay the registry for recording the transfer of the property's ownership. For a house costing £15,000 the bill works out at £37·50; for a £30,000 house, £74. If the house is being registered for the first time, you pay slightly less.

If you want to do your own conveyancing, a good starting point is the Consumers' Association's book *The Legal Side of Buying a House* (England and Wales). This is available from booksellers but if you have difficulty finding it write direct to the association at Caxton Hill, Hertford SG13 7LZ. The association also publishes *Which? Way to Buy, Sell and Move House*, which is of slightly broader scope.

Several specialist conveyancing firms have recently been challenging the solicitors' monopoly. Usually they charge less than a solicitor – but you may not be as well protected if anything goes wrong. Solicitors must have professional indemnity insurance to cover you if they are negligent. And they must keep clients' money in a special account so it is safe if they go bankrupt. Clients are also protected against fraud by a solicitor or his staff.

If you use a conveyancing firm you may find the seller's solicitor is obstructive. Sometimes solicitors refuse to deal direct with conveyancing firms and instead route all communications through the buyers. You can get a list of conveyancing firms from the National Association of Conveyancers, 44 London Road, Kingston-on-Thames, Surrey (tel. 01 549 3636).

## How Running Costs Affect the Value of a House

In assessing the price of a home, many house-hunters do not take enough account of the costs that go with it – rates bills, season tickets, ground rent and, in the case of flats, service charges. Commuting costs, service charges and rates tend to rise at least as fast as inflation: so in a few years they may become a bigger burden than the mortgage.

How much credit should you give for low outgoings in comparing home prices? There are no easy answers but an example may help. Suppose you have a choice between two almost identical flats: one costing £25,000 with a service charge of £300 a year and the other £23,000 with a charge of £500. The estate agent's best guess is that both service-charge figures are likely to rise in line with inflation. If you have the money to buy the dearer flat but instead buy the cheaper and invest the difference – £2,000 – in a unit trust, you will face an extra outlay initially of £200 a year in management charges. Assuming the unit trust holds shares with prospects of dividend growth matching inflation it might offer a return of around 6 per cent before tax – that is about £120 a year. After tax at 30 per cent that works out at £84. Seen in this light the extra you pay for the flat with lower management charges is a good investment. Arguably, in fact, you could pay an extra amount of up to twenty times the difference in annual management charges for the flat with lower charges and still be on the winning side.

You can do similar sums to assess the value of a low rates bill –

but the problem here is complicated by the suggestions that the rates system may eventually be scrapped.

A saving in commuting costs can be at least as valuable as a saving in flat service charges. Savings in ground rent are not usually so valuable because even where ground rent is on a rising scale it rarely increases as fast as inflation.

## Selling a House

The biggest expense in selling a house is often the estate agent's commission.

Estate agents are free these days to charge what they like and a typical commission is 2 per cent of the price of the house. You usually have to pay value-added tax on top and may have to pay the agent's advertising bills. There are three main types of agreement you can come to with estate agents:

*Multiple agency*. This is where you put the house in the hands of several agents but you pay commission only to the one who comes up with the eventual purchaser. You thus cast your net widely, but with the drawback that none of the agents will have a strong incentive to work for you because they will fear that they will be beaten to a sale by one of their rivals.

*Sole agency*. This means you put the property in the hands of one agent, but you retain the right to pay him no commission if you find the buyer yourself. Often estate agents give you a discount off their normal commission rates if you give them a sole agency. Usually it is best to put a time limit on a sole agency – say, a month. That gives the agent a reasonable chance of finding a buyer, but puts some pressure on him to get a move on.

*Sole selling rights*. This is like a sole agency except that you have to pay the agent's commission even if you find the buyer yourself. It is by far the worst option and few good agents suggest it.

The estate agent's first task is to suggest the asking price. He may be tempted to suggest a high price in the hope of improving his chances of getting a sole agency; then, after the property has been languishing on his books for weeks, he will persuade you to drop the price. Sometimes an estate agent will suggest a price several hundred pounds below a house's true value. This will make for an easy sale – and less work for him.

It may be worth trying to find a buyer on your own, particularly if your home is similar to many others in the neighbourhood and is therefore relatively easy to value. Such properties also have the advantage that there is usually a constant flow of prospective buyers searching the area who can recognize a reasonable price when they see it. A For Sale sign is one of the cheapest and – often – one of the most effective ways of advertising your home. If you advertise in the press, choose a newspaper which carries estate agents' advertising for similar homes (estate agents know from long experience which papers are best for which types of property).

One pitfall is that you may underprice your home. You can guard against that by asking an estate agent to do a special valuation. Another worry is that you may not be as adept as an estate agent at spotting a frivolous offer from a buyer who has little intention of going through with the deal. You need to chase the buyer to make sure his building society surveys your home promptly and makes a mortgage offer. If he has a home to sell, check that he has a firm buyer.

Solicitors' fees for selling a house are usually lower than for buying – and there are no bills for stamp duty, Land Registry fees or surveys. A recent report by the Consumers' Association indicated that a typical solicitor's bill for selling a £15,000 home averaged about £160 – £10 less than for buying. For a £30,000 home the bill averaged about £210 – £70 less than for buying.

## Grants

Local authorities have considerable discretion to help you improve or repair your home. They can make 'improvement grants' for a wide range of improvements and repairs such as putting in a damp-proof course, installing power points, rewiring, repointing and converting a house into flats. 'Repair grants' may be available for basic repairs to pre-1919 homes and to homes in specially designated run-down areas. In England and Wales, houses shared by two or more families may qualify for 'special grants' for putting in basic amenities like a lavatory or bath.

Some councils are much more tight-fisted than others in their policy on these grants, which are discretionary. But they are required by law to provide 'intermediate grants' for installing basic amenities like lavatory and bath, where the applicant satisfies certain conditions. To qualify for a grant, you generally need to be living in the house concerned and to intend to continue living there for a certain number of years. The work must meet certain standards and must not be started before grant approval. You may be ruled out if your home's rateable value exceeds a certain amount.

In most cases, the maximum grant is 50 per cent of the estimate of the cost of the work involved – but up to 75 per cent or more may be available in certain, mainly hardship, cases. There are upper limits on the amount of the estimate that is counted: £2,000 in the case of an intermediate grant, £5,000 for an improvement grant and £2,000 for a repair grant.

Other grants are available for insulating your loft and lagging water pipes and tank; providing amenities for elderly or disabled members of the household; and for repairs to houses of cultural interest. A Department of the Environment leaflet, *Your Guide to House Renovation Grants*, is available from Citizens' Advice Bureaux and council offices.

# 6. Household, Car and Other Insurance

You can insure almost anything. Whisky-tasters insure their sense of smell, pianists their fingers and film stars their legs. If you want to cover yourself against the risk of having triplets that is possible too. One company even insured itself against the risk that someone would discover the Loch Ness monster, and so win a vast prize it was offering as a publicity stunt. For ordinary people, though, there are five kinds of insurance that matter. We have dealt with life insurance in Chapter 2, and this chapter is mainly about the four others which most people need in some form: domestic insurance (house and contents cover); motor insurance in all its varieties; travel insurance; and medical insurance.

## Domestic Insurance (House and Contents)

If you own a house, or indeed are buying one on a mortgage, you should certainly cover yourself against the risk that it will be damaged through fires, storms or anything else. The cost of repairs can come close to bankrupting you if you are on an average income. Insuring a house sounds simple enough, but it is easy to start on the wrong assumptions. You have to cover the cost of rebuilding the place from scratch if it is burned down or destroyed in any other way. The price you could get if you sold it has nothing to do with it.

Building costs are bad enough on their own. But you have to add to them the cost of clearing rubble, architects' and surveyors' fees for drawing up plans and so on. How much this package of expenses costs will vary with the kind of house and where you live. According to figures produced by the British Insurance Association in June 1980, the cost of coping with a nineteenth-century terraced house in London will come to £41·10 a square foot, whereas the same work would cost £33·00 a square foot in the North. But the figures come sharply down on modern properties. If you have a small house built since the war, the BIA believes that building costs will come to £33·00 and £26·63 if you take London and the North once again.

The industry has calculated its own figures on square footage. A large Edwardian terraced house will probably contain just under 3,500 square feet, whereas the average semi-detached bungalow at the other extreme is not going to run to more than 800 square feet. Assessing the figure yourself is quite easy. You take the external measurements of your house – length and breadth, which gives you the area of the ground floor – and multiply your answer by the number of floors. If the second floor is smaller than the first, you have to do the best you can by adding the two sets of internal measurements together. But you only have to allow for three-quarters of the area of any higher floors.

In a perfect world, your sum insured – the most that your company will pay out whatever the circumstances – should be the same as the cost of rebuilding the house from scratch. If the figures are close, no one is going to quibble. It may be simple to get the figures right when you start, but all too easy to let matters slide after that. In the past, companies regularly wrote to their customers suggesting they should increase their insurance to allow for higher building costs, and of course pay higher premiums for doing it. Lethargy ensured most people did not bother, and became steadily more under-insured.

The industry then changed its tactics, using lethargy as an ally. Companies wrote to their customers announcing that they were going to raise their insurance cover by a fixed percentage, whose size depended on when it had last been altered – unless they wrote back to object. The companies used the 'buy now, pay later' principle as a sweetener. Your total insurance went up by perhaps 50 per cent immediately, but you did not have to pay higher premiums to match it until twelve months later.

A few insurers left it at that. But most have switched their customers to a system where premiums and the potential pay-outs both rise steadily. The total for which the house is insured goes up month by month with an index of building costs, usually compiled by the Royal Institution of Chartered Surveyors. You then have to pay for the twelve months' inflation-proofing at the beginning of the following year.

What happens if you reject the offers? Being out of pocket on big repairs is not the only danger. Some companies will impose an 'average clause'. If you have insured your house for half its value, you receive from the company only half the cost of any repairs. Other companies are expected to introduce average clauses soon.

Although the number of insurance companies runs into hundreds, if you are starting with a mortgage your choice is very limited. Your building society will steer you in the direction of a particular firm and, if you have any objections to it, you have the right to choose among three or four others they may suggest. But they certainly do not have to accept an insurer who is not on their list.

*Cover*. Structural insurance will cover you against all the major risks like fire, storms, and the more surprising risks or acts of God, like thunderbolts, lightning and even earthquakes, which are not unknown in Britain. Damage from aircraft, falling trees, escaping oil or water from your pipes or central heating are all insured too. Malicious damage by someone who happens to have a grudge against you is also an 'insured peril'. If the house needs repairing after riots or civil commotion – a phrase which could only occur in the Prayer Book or an insurance contract – the company is there to pay the bills. Northern Ireland is the one exception. There it is the government's responsibility to make good losses of the kind. Policies will usually pay the bill, up to certain limits, for alternative accommodation if the damage is so bad that you cannot live in the house.

There is a lot more, too. The important point is to look through the contract the insurers send you, and see what it contains and more important still what it does not. Sometimes you are on your own. For instance, any damage to fencing or gates is usually your responsibility. [1]

'Excesses', as they are known, will appear where you and not the company are responsible for the first part of any loss. Subsidence, where a house begins to shift on its foundations, is the main

1. If it has been damaged by storm or flood. But when people, not nature, swing it off its hinges, the insurers will pick up the bill.

one. It hit many houses in south-east England after the drought of 1976, and the industry toughened up its rules. The insurers may make you responsible for the first 3 per cent of the rebuilding costs. That does not mean 3 per cent of the bill for repairing the damage subsidence has caused. The companies calculate what it would cost to rebuild the whole house, and charge 3 per cent of that. Many insurers still insist that you should meet the first £250 of damage anyway – though more recently some have softened the approach. Some firms have brought a ceiling of £500 to your contribution. Many old policies do not cover subsidence at all – and the same goes for flood damage. It is well worth including, particularly if the house is built on clay soil. The other 'excesses' are trifling. If the pipes burst, or a flood damages the structure of the house, you have to pay the first £15 of any bill – unless you agree to pay another £4 or so in premiums, when the company will pay the lot.

Many new contracts now insist that you should pay the first £50 of any other claim you make – except for fire damage and for 'liability' claims, which we come to later.

Insurers should know about any damage as soon as possible – but you should not wait for permission to do repairs which prevent matters from getting worse. If your house is one of many others damaged – as storms sweep across the West Country for instance – you do not have to wait for individual permission before starting. If the sums involved are not out of line with their estimates, the company will not baulk at repaying you what you've spent.

Inflation-proofed contracts of the kind we have described mostly work on a 'new for old' basis. Even if you have had your roof for years, you get a new one without deductions. Earlier and less expensive policies cut back what they paid, to allow for wear and tear. Inflation proofing is fine as long as there are no changes to the house and you have started with the right figure in the first place. But if you add a garage or build on an extra room, the area you want covered is higher than it was – and so you need to readjust your figures.

*Contents*. Insuring what is inside the house – 'contents' to the trade – works in the same way. But an amazingly large number of people don't bother. One house in four has no contents insurance at all, and that lethargy combined with rapid inflation has meant that many of those who are insured could not get back anything like enough to replace what they would lose if thieves stripped the house or there was some disastrous fire.

In the early days insurance was based on making up the loss you had made. If you had lost a five-year-old sofa in a fire, companies would give you the value of a second-hand five-year-old sofa. That has long since gone, giving way to the principle of cost of replacement.

The basic form of cover has, like any other insurance, a fixed total, beyond which the companies are not prepared to pay. Within that limit the insurance will give you the cost of replacing what has been burned or stolen provided it is less than two or three years old. If you have had it for longer they will make a deduction on big items, which includes not only furniture but televisions, hi-fi and the like. The deductions depend partly on the object and partly on the firm. As a very general rule, the companies may give you half the cost of replacing a five-year-old sofa. Under the terms of your contract you have to insure everything for the full value. If there is a vast discrepancy, companies are legally free to refuse the claim.

*New for old* is an alternative which the industry has developed since. In general it will give you replacement costs in full if they come to less than the total for which you are insured. The arrangement does not cover everything. Companies will not include clothes, sheets, towels and other 'household linen' if you have had them for more than two years.

*Inflation-proofed*, or *index-linked*, insurance is the final development, for the figures stay right, provided the original figures are right. The total insurance for the contents of the house goes up in line month by month, sometimes with the Retail-Price Index, but often with official price figures which apply specifically to such things as furniture. Your premiums then rise to pay for the extra protection you have had at the beginning of the following year.

How can you gauge the value of what is in the house? The answer is to go round the house with a pen and pad room by room, writing down not only the various gadgets – hi-fis, cameras and record-players – that you possess but also clothes, furniture and so on. You will need to pull out drawers and look through cupboards to make a proper job of it. The list is likely to be far longer than you think. Finally you try to work out the cost of replacing them all when you go down to the shops, by noting comparable prices. It may not be an entertaining exercise but its one great virtue is that you will almost certainly find that you are far richer than you thought.

If you do make such a list, and remember to add new possessions to it as you buy them, insurance levels should be about right. Whatever cover you have, one final point covers hired televisions. If you lease them, you and not the rental company are responsible for insuring them.

*Personal indemnity*. Most policies include indemnity insurance, to cover the risk that you cause some accident and then have to face a vast bill for damages as a result. There are plenty of ways in which it could happen. Perhaps you may open a door of a train coming into a station and injure someone who is then off work for many months, or alternatively your dog may rush into the road and cause a serious accident, so that you are found to be legally responsible. If that happens, personal indemnity cover will pay for the damages awarded against you up to £250,000 or so.

*Limitations*. Some companies limit what they will pay on certain items. Many will not provide more than 5 per cent of the total for which you have insured the contents on any one small item, however valuable that item – brooch, painting or whatever – may be.

Another standard limitation is that you will not get more than one-third of the insurance on 'valuables' like jewellery, fur coats, paintings or small antiques taken as a whole. Separate lists itemizing each object are the way to get full insurance, though inevitably it will cost you more. If you make the move, the police suggest you should have your valuables photographed at the same time, for it makes it infinitely easier to identify them if they turn up.

Companies restrict the terms on which they will insure property in flats or houses containing a group of students or three or four people who come together via an agency, but do not know each other beforehand. Insurers do not just demand that thefts should be reported to the police – a rule which applies to everyone – but also refuse to pay out on theft claims unless there has been forcible entry. Other conditions too can appear. Companies have been known to demand that flats should not be left empty all day.

Extensions widening the scope of the insurance are always possible; one standard extension covers freezers, guaranteeing that the company will pay for damage to the food inside them if storms or snow interrupt the supplies of electricity. But it may not do this if the electricity board cuts them off deliberately or strikes or go-slows are responsible.

*All-risks insurance* protects property against theft or damage if it is stolen elsewhere – perhaps if you are robbed of jewellery in the street. It also insures you against losing things covered under its terms, which no normal household policy will do. The cover does not come cheap. It will cost you at least twice as much as insuring it at home, though exact rates depend on your job and how much you travel. Its other great virtue is that it will pay for accidental damage to what you own wherever it happens – a risk that ordinary contents policies always exclude.

Many firms produce packages of insurance which can cover a series of unconnected areas, including health insurance, accident cover and protection for the house and its contents. Every company has a minimum premium which you have to pay, however little you may want to insure under your policy. But if all the contracts are rolled into one, you do not have that worry. Bulk buying also keeps rates cheaper overall.

## Car Insurance

Drivers are often concerned by just one aspect of their motor insurance: its cost. Many giants in the past, from Vehicle & General to Fire, Auto & Marine, have started and flourished by offering cut-price cover, only to collapse under the weight of claims as a result. Admittedly, there are tight legal controls to prevent anything of the kind from happening again. All the same, cut-price insurance can too often mean cut-price cover. In broad terms you do not get what you do not pay for. Companies which provide specially low terms for everyone may well quibble on claims that others would settle, or impose tighter conditions. So bargain premiums are not always the bargain they look.

The biggest factor in deciding how much you pay is the protection you buy, and the varieties are considerable.

*Road Traffic Act cover* is the legal minimum insurance you must have to drive at all. If you injure another motorist, a passenger or someone on a public road you are protected against the cost of any legal claims they may have against you. You are not covered on private roads, perhaps running through an estate. The cost of repairing the car itself, or indeed of any damage it may do to other vehicles or property, is your own responsibility. The other cost which Road Traffic Act insurance will settle is the various National Health Service charges for medical treatment, if you are damaged in a crash.

If you have a series of convictions for drunken driving it may be the only cover your insurer will give you as a last resort. Very few other people have it.

*Third-party only* is more common. It covers you against all the Road Traffic Act perils, and also insures you against the cost of damage you may do, either to other cars or to property. It is worth remembering that if you knock down a lamppost or bollard, for instance, the local authority will sue for the cost of another. Like all but the most basic legal minimum, it applies if you drive on private roads. Between 10 and 15 per cent of British drivers have this insurance, which gives you no help with your own car.

*Third-party, fire and theft* starts with that base, but also ensures that if your car is stolen or burnt out your company will settle the bills. But you are responsible for any damage to your own car done in an accident – assuming you cannot claim from the other driver. Contracts of this kind can make sense if you are young and run an old beaten-up second-hand car where major repairs would not be worth while and the cost of repairs will be disproportionately high.

*Comprehensive insurance* covers the widest range of risks. It will pay for the cost of repairing your car if it is damaged in an accident, as well as giving you the insurance cover the other contracts provide. You are usually covered for rugs, luggage and so on if stolen when they are inside the car, though portable radios are not always included. It is worth looking at the policy to see how you are placed on this point. About seven motorists out of ten are insured in this way. You may not get the cost of repairs in full. Young drivers, people who have just passed their driving test or those who have a bad record are normally loaded with an 'excess' – so that they are responsible for the first £50 or perhaps £100 of any claim. A young driver with a sports car in central London – statistically one of the worst risks a company can take on – or people with a bad driving record may well find themselves paying more.

Whatever type of cover you choose, the insurance contract is based on the principle of utmost good faith. So you have to fill in with absolute accuracy all the details on the 'proposal form' that the company wants to know about the car, your driving record and so on before assessing what premium to charge. If you have had a conviction for anything in the past, it is as well to state it, for occasionally insurance companies will claim that it makes a material difference – even if it has nothing to do with motoring. You should always check what any broker writes on your behalf. If you do not do so, and then make a claim in which inaccuracies come to light, your insurer can refuse to pay out money.

The contract also lays down that, when you drive, your car must be in a 'roadworthy condition'. If the tyres are so bald that they contribute towards an accident, companies can again refuse payment on the grounds that you have not fulfilled your side of the bargain.

Usually policies will cover you for domestic use of the car, taking the children to school, driving to and from work and shopping and so on. You can give people lifts in the car without any problems, provided that you do not charge more than you need to cover the costs. You must not make a profit. Usually you, but only you, can use the car for your business. If you use the car professionally, perhaps as a sales rep, and so are driving much of the time, you also have to tell the company because the standard policies will not cover you. The same applies if the car is taken on big rallies and competitions.

Most companies offer you discounts if you are prepared to limit the policy. You may get a discount for restricting its use by agreeing not to use it for commuting. The same principle applies to drivers. Most contracts do not insist that you should name all the drivers beforehand. But you can do it voluntarily, and get a discount. If you restrict driving to yourself, you will get a saving of around 15 per cent. There is a similar cut of 10 per cent in what you would otherwise pay if you limit driving just to yourself and your wife or husband.

Restrictions of this kind have their disadvantages. If someone who is not insured to do so has to drive your car in some emergency, both you and he are breaking the law. Even if he is insured for his own car on a comprehensive policy, he will be restricted to insurance for the damage he does, and not the damage done to him if he drives other vehicles. So you would be responsible for damage inflicted on the car and by the car.

Once you have decided which model to buy and whether you are going to limit your insurance there is nothing you can do about the other factors which go into deciding your first premium. They will include your age, previous driving experience and where you live. Later on, of course, come the no-claims discounts.

Accidents are far more common in busy streets than deserted ones. The premiums you pay will partly reflect where you live, and the country is usually divided along the following lines (the cheapest areas come first):

*Area One*     Rural counties, like Shropshire and Lincolnshire; the West Country; the Scottish islands.

*Area Two*     Much of Scotland; most of Wales; semi-rural areas like Hampshire, Avon, North Yorkshire.

*Area Three*   Surrey and Kent, and counties with average populations like them. Oxford, Luton and other medium-sized towns.

*Area Four*    Greater Manchester, Merseyside, Birmingham, Edinburgh, Cardiff, Greater London outside the postal areas.

*Area Five*    Liverpool, inner Manchester; outer Glasgow.

*Area Six*     Central Glasgow; outer London.

*Area Seven*   Inner London; Northern Ireland.

As the list shows, London is the most expensive place in which to drive. A motorist there will have to pay as much again as he would if he lived in Devon or Cornwall. Younger drivers always have more accidents than older ones, so the odds are always against them. Insurers divide cars into at least seven categories, based on the car's performance, speed, acceleration and so on, as well as the cost of repairs; the availability of spares will also come into it. The list for one typical company is as follows:

| | |
|---|---|
| *Group One* | Citroën 2cv/Dyane; Fiat 126; Fiesta 950; Mini 850; Mini 1000; Renault 4; Sunbeam 1·0. |
| *Group Two* | Allegro 1300; Chevette; Cortina 1300; Escort 1300; Fiat 127; Sunbeam 1·3; Viva 1300. |
| *Group Three* | Avenger 1600; Cavalier 1300; Cortina 1600; Dolomite 1500; Fiat Strada; Fiesta 1300; Marina 1700; Renault 5 TL; VW Golf 900. |
| *Group Four* | Citroën GS; Datsun Sunny; Honda Civic; Peugeot 305/504; Princess; Renault 14/18TL; Toyota Corolla; VW Golf 1100. |
| *Group Five* | Alfasud; Alpine 1442; Audi 80; Granada 2300; Honda Accord; Vauxhall Carlton; Volvo 244DL/343. |
| *Group Six* | Citroën CX; Fiat 132; Jaguar XJ6; MGB; Renault 20/30; Rover; VW Sirocco. |
| *Group Seven* | Audi 100; BMW 320; Porsche; Saab Turbo. |

There are advantages if you work in certain professions. Civil servants are one favoured group. They get particularly good rates if they insure themselves through the Civil Service Motoring Association, for there they also get the advantages of bulk buying. Bankers, teachers and nurses are also all better-than-average risks in the industry's eyes and so get better-than-average terms. Journalists, pub-keepers and students come at the other end of the scale, and may well find premiums loaded against them. So, too, will entertainers and professional sportsmen. If you work in some perfectly anodyne office during the day, but belong to a touring pop group at weekends or do a job in a pub in the evening, insurers will want to know about it. Whatever figures you are quoted, there is always a case for shopping around, for different firms dislike these different categories in different degrees.

*No-claims discounts* make an enormous difference to your costs. The only way you have of avoiding the full rate, when you begin, is to show that you have had some previous driving experience, perhaps on your husband's or wife's policy. In that way you may get a 10 or 20 per cent reduction. It could be higher still if you have done a lot of driving, but terms vary from one company to another, so you have to pick and choose. Everyone else starts at the full rate, and works – or does not work – their way up to the top rate of discount in four or five stages. Discount and bonus are the same thing, by the way, at least as far as motor insurance goes. Different firms use different terms.

The discount scales will vary. After one, or occasionally two, years of claim-free driving, there is a 30 per cent discount on whatever the starting rate happens to be at the time. That widens to 40 per cent after you have completed another twelve months without a claim. In the third or fourth years, you provide only half the starters' rate. Finally as you enter your fourth or fifth year without a claim you get a 60 per cent discount, the top bonus rate. Even when you get the extra bonus, inflation over the last few years has often ensured that you merely stay where you were. Higher charges have cancelled out the extra discount.

Drivers make a claim about once every six years, on average; when they do they do not have to go back to the beginning again. They will usually drop two stages in the bonus ladder. Falling two stages can mean losing a lot of money – so that if you are comprehensively insured there may be a case for doing small repairs yourself. Indeed you can always save about 15 per cent on your insurance bill if you agree to pay the first £50 of any claim you make. But, of course, you will lose your bonus when damage after some accident is considerable and you have to make a claim anyway. But if you are a young driver with an obligation to pay the first £50 of any claim you let yourself in for the first £100 and so on by taking this option.

*Choosing a policy.* The choice of insurers and special offers is bewildering. Companies are always trying to find particular groups of people with good driving records to whom they can give small concessions and so attract them away from the opposition. One firm, for instance, gives better rates to girls under twenty-five than to men under the same age. Others try to isolate experienced middle-aged drivers, offering them special terms, but only on condition that they will exclude their teenage children from using the car. The companies have their own little come-ons. Some give you the right to claim for a shattered windscreen (within certain limits) without endangering your no-claims discount. One firm will allow you to hire a car for up to a fortnight on your insurance, while your own is off the road.

How do you choose between them? The answer is probably to

go to an insurance broker. He is supposed to have the details of most policies and so can fit you with the exact insurance policy to suit your particular circumstances. What is more, he does so for nothing, because his fees come not from his clients but from the companies to which he 'introduces' them. That is how it should work. But a survey in the consumer magazine *Which?* late in 1979 suggested that some of the brokers they tried had only shown the premiums offered by one or two companies and had missed the most suitable offer.

There is no way of guaranteeing that will not happen to you. Matters may improve when only people who have been in the insurance business for five years (without qualifications) or three (with them) can set up as brokers. The law already gives the government power to enforce the principle, but at the beginning of 1980 there was no news of when the law would become effective. The odds are that it will be some time in 1981. Until that happens anyone can set up as a broker just by declaring that he is one. Your safest bet is to go to someone who belongs to the trade's professional body – the British Insurance Brokers' Association.

There are several computer systems to which brokers can subscribe. They show the best figures of those offered by up to forty or fifty companies for people of a particular age, driving experience and so on. The two main systems are Quotel, based in London and Quickquote in Brighton. They should be able to tell you the nearest broker who uses their services. There is one caveat. The figures indicate the cheapest rates available but they will not show the conditions – which may be tougher than those elsewhere.

Finally, you can always do your own telephoning to find terms. When insurers change their rates as often as twice a year – as they did in 1979, for instance – getting in just before an increase can make a considerable difference. But insurers who always charge less than anyone else have to find money to pay for the concessions somehow. They may apply a tougher line on claims than companies elsewhere, or impose extra restrictions. Sometimes they may disclaim responsibility for a car at night, for instance, unless it is kept in a garage. It is always worth fighting your way through the small print to see the conditions whatever your policy.

*Knock-for-knock* agreements ensure that after an accident your insurer pays for the damage to your car while the other driver's insurer will do the same for him. Despite the mythology, you do not automatically lose your no-claims discount under a knock-for-knock agreement. You will keep it if your company believes that it could have got back the cost of the claim from some other insurer, if the knock-for-knock arrangement had not existed in the first place. The industry uses it to cut back costs claiming – and rightly – that without it, the cost of motor insurance would be considerably higher. For every six drivers who lose their bonuses under knock-for-knock agreements, four will keep them.

What happens if you face a lost discount after an accident? The one way to get it back is to try to get damages from the other driver – first through a broker or solicitor, and ultimately through the courts. If you win, the company will restore it, though there will be nothing for the time and money you have spent in pursuing the case. The insurers always stress that 'claim not blame' is the principle behind the arrangements. If the facts are clear, and there is another company on which to claim, all is well. But once shades of grey appear on responsibility the bonus will go. The same applies if there is no other company, which may happen quite easily.

Occasionally motorists refuse to report accidents to their insurers, and if that happens the company will not pay out money to outsiders. Admittedly, under the terms of an insurance contract the insurer should be informed about accidents even if a claim is not made. But if the other motorist does not report the accident to his insurers, there is little you can do, short of sueing him for damages.

Standard ways of losing a no-claims discount occur when you return to find your parked car has been damaged by someone who has driven on, or when it is hit by people who have stolen a vehicle for a joy ride. If you are a passenger or pedestrian injured by a driver who is not insured, there is one last port of call. The Motor Insurers' Bureau, at Aldermary House in Queen Street, London EC4 will pay for the damages you may be awarded against the driver. But the scheme does not cover damage to a car, or property.

It is all too easy to assume that you are insured and then to find yourself without cover, because you have put off the evil day when you actually have to pay the premiums. Usually the company will issue a 'renewal notice', containing a cover note which extends the previous year's policy by fifteen days. You need to regard it with caution. In theory it only covers you for the very basic Road Traffic Act insurance, though in practice companies may be more generous. The police and magistrates' courts sometimes do not consider this cover note as evidence of proper insurance anyway. You do not gain time. The company, if you stay with it, will backdate the new year's insurance to start at the point when the old one ran out. Finally, if you have made arrangements to change companies and have an accident during the cover-note period, you may well be completely uninsured. The note is only issued as a favour on the assumption that you stay with the same company.

Finding a full year's premiums all at once may be difficult, but it is not always necessary. Some insurers have special instalment schemes, though they cost slightly more than usual. Alternatively, you can sometimes use an Access or Barclaycard to spread your payments, though the interest they charge is not cheap and will push up your cost if you take some time to pay the money.

*Claims*. The odds are that any stolen car will turn up, particularly in big cities, so insurers do not settle claims immediately. You have to report the loss at once, but will only receive your money if the vehicle has not reappeared within four to six weeks.

You certainly do not get the price of a new car. Insurers work on the traditional indemnity principle, giving you back the value of what you have lost – and not the cost of replacing it with something new. If your five-year-old Volvo disappears, you will get the value of a five-year-old Volvo. Companies can send in assessors to work out what that value should be assuming that you had sold the car on the day it disappeared or was written off. The handbook *Glasse's Guide* is what the industry generally uses.

Some companies will make an exception if the vehicle is under one year old – for they will then replace your car with an identical model – assuming one is available. Fixing an agreed value on the car so that you know what you will get is sometimes possible, and may make sense if you happen to run a vintage model. But that option is not part of the standard contract and you will have to find a group which will accept the idea. The obvious underwriters are in the Lloyd's insurance market.

*Drunken driving*. A conviction for drunken driving will ensure that you lose your licence for one year, except in extremely special circumstances. When you get it back, insurers will be wary of you. They will certainly increase your premium, though how much depends on the circumstances of the case. It could be anything from 25 per cent to 100 per cent on top of the rate you would otherwise pay.

Some companies may move you down to third-party, fire and theft insurance so that you are protected against the damage you may do to other people's cars, but not against what you or they may do to your own vehicle. And, of course, you will have to pay well over the usual rates for getting the insurance anyway. The 'loading' of the premium falls gradually and it may take you four years to get back to full comprehensive insurance. Even then, you may have to take responsibility for the first £50 or £100 of any damage. A second conviction will almost certainly push you back to third-party, fire and theft.

Other companies will be very reluctant to take you on, but you may get help from groups like Cloverleaf, which specialize in people who present bad risks. But they will often insure them on a month-to-month or three-months-to-three-months basis, so that they can cancel if things go wrong.

*Holidays*. You will need extra insurance if you take the car abroad. Admittedly, a reciprocal insurance scheme exists inside the Common Market but it merely gives the minimum legal cover that the locals must have, to outsiders from other member-states. Details vary from state to state, but if there is any third-party insurance to cover you against damage you may do to property or other cars, it may be very limited.

Continental extensions which you can get from your own insurer ensure that whatever policy you have in Britain carries over to the country you are visiting. The arrangements cover most of Europe and also extend to one or two countries on the other side of the Mediterranean like Tunisia. There are other extras which are well worth having, and if your insurer does not provide them, it is worth looking elsewhere. They include the cost of hiring a car to continue your journey if you have an accident. One specialist group – Europ-Assistance – has a twenty-four-hour answering service which you can call for advice if need be.

Companies often provide you with a form called the European Accident statement. If you have a crash, you and the driver involved write down the details as you agree them at the time, sign each other's forms and off they go to the pair of your insurers. The form is not an admission of guilt or legally binding. But it is useful in showing the facts at the time that you are most likely to agree them. Usually your company will present you with a Green Card, which is evidence that you have the proper insurance you need to comply with the law of the country which you are entering. The card itself is not necessary in the Common Market countries, in Austria, Switzerland, Scandinavia or indeed in many East European states. But insurers suggest that it may still be worth having.

Bail bonds are useful in Spain. Under Spanish law you can be detained after an accident until the authorities discover whether you have enough money to pay any civil damages which the courts may award against you. The bail bond demonstrates that there is an insurer in the background who can settle any bills, and saves a lot of complications.

## Travel Insurance

Travel insurance is probably wise wherever you go on holiday abroad. If you are travelling with one of the big tour companies, you may actually have to opt out of the cover they provide if you do not want it. Otherwise the firm will assume that you do.

The insurance comes as a package. It will protect you first against the cost of losing your baggage or having it stolen, but it will also cover you against having to pay a proportion of the holiday bill if you are forced into cancellation in the last weeks before departure because there has been serious illness or death inside the family or you have been summoned to jury service. It will cope with the loss of any money you may have, and provides compensation if you are seriously injured or killed while you are away. But medical insurance is the most important point of the package. In some countries, admittedly, you will not need it. In Scandinavia, Ireland and most of Eastern Europe, treatment is free.

In the Common Market (apart from Ireland) problems can arise if you plan to rely on the state. Almost everyone in Britain has the same right to treatment as people living locally (the only exception is the self-employed and even for them it will vary from case to case). But the Common Market scheme is cumbersome. You fill in one document – CM 1 – from your local social-security office – and return it to them. In due course, they send you the form E111, which you have to carry round with you, like some talisman. In some countries you will have to go to the social-security office to be allocated a doctor, rather than going to him direct – except of course in emergencies. In others, like France and Belgium, you pay the doctor's fees and any prescription fees in full, keep the various dockets with which you will be provided and claim back a proportion of your costs later on.

So medical insurance is generally wise, albeit, as with all the other sections of the insurance, the companies set a top limit to what they will pay out.

Certainly, you will need it in Spain, where there are no special arrangements. In both Canada and America, medical costs are very high and you may well need four or five times as much cover as the standard packages may provide. Rules vary. There is an official leaflet – SA 28/30 – which sets out the details of health schemes all over the world.

If you do take out medical insurance, it is worth looking for a policy which allows you to vary your limits on it while leaving your other cover at the normal levels. A new policy issued by the Association of British Travel Agents, which you should be able to get through any travel agent, allows you to do so.

There are two points on which to be wary. Some contracts will not cover you for the cost of 'pre-existing conditions'. If you have had a heart attack in the previous three or four years the insurance will cover you for every medical risk except another attack – though that is just what you need protection for. Other policies will not insure very young children or people over a certain age – perhaps seventy-five or eighty. Big operators do not usually have these restrictions, but it is worth checking. If the clauses are there and you are affected, the answer is to take out another contract. Specialist travel insurers will almost always offer better terms than the rest of the industry provides.

Those who design the contracts are always cautious people who like to limit their risks, and their insurance will not give you blanket protection whatever you do. Details vary from contract to contract, but many firms will exclude accidents which happen when you are flying in a private plane, mountaineering, pot-holing or deep-sea diving. So again check the small print.

## Medical Insurance

Medical insurance divides into two. First come the policies which give you an income while you are ill. Others are designed to pay for the cost of any treatment you need.

*Sickness and accident* insurance is just designed to replace your income in the short term. If you have a serious illness or accident, the company has to provide you with a regular income until you are fit to work again – or for the first twelve months. At that point it stops. If both sides then want to go on with the policy, all is well. But if you have been off sick for most of the year, the insurers can wash their hands of you when the contracts run out.

*Permanent health insurance* is far more long-term, for the con-tract, despite its name, is really concerned with permanent illness. Once a firm has taken you on, it cannot break the contract as long as you pay your premiums. If you get some long-term illness or suffer an accident which prevents you from doing your job, or any other like it, the insurers will have to continue to pay you your money until you recover or you reach retirement age.

There are any number of factors which go into deciding how much you pay. First comes your sex. If you are a woman, you will usually have to pay between one and a half to twice as much as a man in the same position, because the industry believes that women are more likely to suffer illness than men. But one or two firms, including Langham Life, dispute the idea and charge the same rates all round, and will also take on housewives. The giants of the industry have been sniffy about the idea because they say housewives have no income to replace, though the impact of an illness on the family budget can be drastic enough.

The industry also divides people up into job categories. Office workers get the cheapest rates, and people who handle heavy machinery, like farmers for instance, will have to pay four or five times as much. Whoever you are, the money on a permanent-health-insurance contract does not appear immediately you stop work. You have to choose the time gap between the onset of your illness, or accident, and the moment that the first payment arrives. It can be anything from one month to two years.

Finally comes inflation. Insuring yourself for a weekly pension is not easy, when what seems adequate now may appear derisory after four or five years of rising prices. Many companies have schemes where the benefits rise at the rate of 3 per cent or 5 per cent a year, and indeed one group will even go to 10 per cent. But there is no way of guaranteeing yourself against the double-figure inflation from which Britain has suffered recently. The best hope lies in regularly updating the starting limit and going for a long deferment – like six months. Many companies allow you to increase the rate every so often, without asking for more evidence of what has happened to your health. But they can often be suspicious. In many cases they will not pay you more than two-thirds or three-quarters of your last salary.

If you are self-employed, PHI, as it is known in the trade, is almost essential.

The tax rules depend on whether you take the insurance out privately or as part of a group. If you insure on your own, benefits are tax-free for the year in which they appear and for one full tax year on top. The tax year runs from April to April, so that if the payments first appear in May, you get tax-free treatment for almost two years. On the other hand if they start in March, the concessions apply for no more than thirteen months. After that they will be taxed as income and, if your income is large enough, you could have to pay investment-income surcharge. You will probably do better if you or your trade union (if you have one) can badger your firm into providing PHI as part of your pension scheme. Bulk buying, as usual, produces cheaper rates. The tax rules will also be different this time; the benefits you receive will be taxed as earned income from the day you receive them.

*Hospital cash plans*, which started advertising heavily in the seventies, work differently. They exist to provide you with an income for each day that you are in hospital, though it is to replace your spending money and not to pay for the cost of private treatment. The contract is not permanent, so that the companies have the right not to continue to insure large claimants, and in one or two cases insurers will not pay more than a fixed total in any twelve-month period. If you have a serious long-term illness, you are likely to spend most of the time out of hospital, but this time no money will arrive. It makes sense to approach these plans sceptically.

Medical insurance designed to pay for the cost of hospital bills and private treatment is very different. The two giants in the business are the British United Provident Association (BUPA) and the Private Patients Plan, which are both based in London.

The schemes should give you a private room either in a National Health Service hospital or indeed in a private hospital, though they do not absolutely guarantee it. They can cope with sudden medical emergencies like a heart attack or a stroke, but then the National Health Service can handle emergencies probably just as well. Where the private schemes come into their own is when you have some complaint with which you can live perfectly well but which is painful all the same – like piles, hernia or a hip joint that needs replacing. They ensure that you can be treated quickly for them, whereas the National Health Service guarantees nothing of the kind. They will also give you advance warning of when you are to go into hospital, which you will not find elsewhere.

There is no one price. The companies offer a scale of benefits related to the cost of hospitals in various parts of the country, and the premiums vary accordingly. They will cover not only the bed, but the cost of surgeons' and anaesthetists' fees – and the price of drugs. The point is that if you occupy a private bed you have to buy drugs at their full cost to the National Health Service.

The variations in costs between one part of the country and another are enormous. Health-service charges for a room in a small hospital in Wales are between one-third and one-quarter of the comparable rates for a London teaching hospital. If you want medical insurance in a high-cost area, it is no use going for the cheaper rates. If you cannot cope with the higher premiums, you will not be able to make up the difference between what the schemes will pay and the full charge which the hospital demands.

Both the giant companies offer a variety of contracts. Some will provide you with a certain sum week by week under each heading for the bed, surgeon's fees and so on, which is the usual pattern if you take out the plan privately, or as one of a small group. Other schemes run for big companies will pay up to a global total for the whole year's insurance, and then give rebates if it has not been heavily used.

Hospitals may be the most important part of treatment, but both groups will pay for at least some nursing at home, while you are ill. There are some items which they will not touch. They will not pay for the cost of having a child – unless there are complications which need specialist treatment – and they will not cope with the cost of geriatric nursing, where age and not any particular illness causes the problem. Both are wary of mental illness. No private insurer will pay the cost of a private visit to your doctor, and though you can get insurance to cover the cost of seeing a dentist privately, it is not part of these contracts.

What you pay in premiums will depend on the number of people you want insured and where you live, and there is probably nothing you can do about either. But you can probably take out a plan not on your own but as part of a wider group, and so reduce your costs. At the lowest level of discount you can get a 10 per cent reduction in BUPA's charges if you join through the RAC and there are other discounts if you use your Access card to pay your subscription. Bigger discounts depend on joining a group scheme and the larger they are, the better the terms will be. Discounts of up to 25 per cent are possible if you organize the scheme through a company. If your employer will pay for the premiums, the discounts are bigger still, which makes it a comparatively cheap fringe benefit to offer.

## Legal Expenses Insurance

One old joke has it that the law, like the Ritz, is open to everyone. The legal-aid system was meant to remedy that, but it will not provide much help if you earn anything more than the average income. Courts can settle civil claims where you may sue your neighbour or one of the local shops, for instance, informally round a table if the dispute involves less than £200. It is known as the small-claims procedure, and if you lose your case you do not have to pay the other side's costs. Lawyers are discouraged. Otherwise you go to the county courts if disputes involve less than £2,000, but above that you could find it extremely expensive. If you lose your case, you are usually committed to paying your opponent's costs.

There are schemes to cover legal expenses. The best-known one is run by a Bristol-based group called DAS, half-owned by a German group which specializes in legal insurance on the Continent, where it is far better known than in Britain. There are two separate contracts, one for motor claims and the other for anything else.

Guarantees exist to protect people against the collapse of any insurance firm. A group called the Policyholders' Protection Board, run partly by the government and partly by the industry, can order a levy on all the companies to make up 90 per cent of any loss which their customers have suffered, and at worst would do so. In practice, though, it is far more likely that other companies would take over the failed firm's policies and run them as their own.

People sometimes have complaints about their insurers. If you cannot get them sorted out at a local level, it is worth writing to the chief public relations officer at the firm's headquarters, or indeed the managing director. If you think the firm is still unreasonable after that you can take it to the industry's trade association – the British Insurance Association – at Aldermary House, in the City of London. Do not forget, too, that in cases where some giant firm looks as though it is pushing people around, just because it is big enough to do so, the media are usually interested to hear of it.

# 7. Saving

Most savers want to put at least some of their spare cash in a place where it is absolutely safe, is easy to get at and earns a reasonable return. The traditional havens for this kind of saving are the building societies, the big banks and the National Savings Department, which all still have a role to play. But there are alternatives which can sometimes be better – local authorities and finance companies, for instance, regularly advertise high-income short- and medium-term investments in the weekend financial press. This uncomplicated type of saving will probably play a bigger role for a young saver than for one in middle age investing for retirement. If you are saving for the first time, perhaps for the deposit on a house, safety and ease of access are probably more important than the chance of long-term growth. But even a family man with a mortgage, insurance policies and stock-market investments should have some of his money in a readily accessible place.

There are big differences between the various options open to short-term savers – the tax position particularly varies widely. It is, therefore, worth shopping around for the investment that best suits your needs.

Many of the best-known ways of investing a lump sum allow you to withdraw at short notice – but if you can tie your money up for a year or two you can sometimes get a much higher interest rate. Equally, if you are planning to save regularly, you can get a better return by promising to invest a specified sum each month.

Interest rates change so often these days that it is difficult to find any general rules about short-term saving – but usually building societies are among the best bets for people paying basic-rate tax. Banks may be better for non-taxpayers. People paying higher rates of tax may be better off with National Savings investments, some types of government securities or insurance-linked arrangements. The National Savings Bank's Investment

Account is good for non-taxpayers. If you are uncertain about your tax position, see Chapter 8. And remember that your tax position may change drastically if, for instance, you intend to retire shortly.

## Building Societies

Building societies enjoy a special tax position which helps them offer a better deal to most investors than their main competitors. The societies pay income tax direct to the Inland Revenue on behalf of savers – so building-society interest is not subject to tax in the hands of basic-rate taxpayers. The rate at which societies pay tax on savers' interest is lower than the basic rate of tax, hence the societies' advantage compared to other savings institutions in competing for funds from taxpayers.

The tax-paid arrangements do not absolve investors from the need to declare building-society interest on their tax returns. But the saver will face a tax demand only if he is subject to higher rates of tax. And in that case, of course, he will get credit for having already paid basic-rate tax. Take, for instance, a saver who has invested £10,000 with a building society earning 7 per cent tax-paid. Suppose the basic rate of tax is 30 per cent and his tax rate on his investment income is 45 per cent. He will actually receive £700 from the society in each tax year but the Inland Revenue will treat the income as a gross payment of £1,000 on which £300 tax was deducted at source. His full tax liability will be assessed at £450 (45 per cent of £1,000). He will, therefore, be billed for extra tax of £150 – £450 less £300 already paid.

The snag about the building societies' tax arrangements is that if you are a non-taxpayer you cannot reclaim tax paid on your behalf. Building societies are not usually, therefore, a good bet for non-taxpayers.

Among the advantages of saving with a building society are that:

*Your money is safe.* No one has lost money through a building-society collapse in recent decades. Investors seeking absolute security should make sure a building society has 'trustee status'. This means it has the government's seal of approval as an institution suitable for trustees to invest trust-fund money. To merit trustee status, a society must have a certain level of reserves and liquid assets. Most sizeable societies have trustee status. You should also make sure your society is a member of the Building Societies Association. The association vets members and whenever one of them hits trouble other members normally mount a rescue bid. The last member to hit trouble, the Grays Building Society, was propped up to the tune of £7 million by the association. No Grays saver lost money; the society's branches, however, were shut for several months and no one could make withdrawals until the rescue operation was completed by a merger with the Woolwich.

*Building societies are convenient.* Investing is easy and can usually be done by post or across the counter of one of 4,000 building-society branches around the country. You normally get a passbook in which deposits and withdrawals are recorded. Interest is usually paid every six months (many major societies including the Woolwich and the Alliance pay interest monthly if you wish).

*A savings record with a building society helps you get a mortgage.* It is not essential to be an investor to become a borrower but, when demand for mortgages is strong, societies give preference to investors with a good savings record. When mortgage funds are tight, many societies expect would-be borrowers to have been savers for at least six months and often a year and to have accumulated 5 per cent of the price of the house they are planning to buy.

The most an individual can invest in any one building society is £20,000 – but he or she can invest up to that limit in as many building societies as he or she wishes. The limit for a married couple investing jointly is £40,000 in any one society.

These are the main types of building-society account for lump-sum investments:

*Ordinary-share accounts.* This is the standard type of account and about 80 per cent of all building-society money is in ordinary-share accounts. In practice building-society share accounts are similar to bank deposits. In law, however, holders of ordinary-share accounts are shareholders and can vote at the societies' annual general meetings. The main advantage of these accounts is ease of access: most societies will allow withdrawals of up to £200 on demand and you can take out anything above that at a few days' notice. The practice of paying interest each half-year means that the true interest rate is slightly more than the quoted rate (that is, if the stated rate is 8 per cent, for instance, you actually get 4 per cent compound each half-year, which is equal to a true rate of 8·16 per cent). Table 8 shows how your money builds up at various rates.

Table 8  **Growth of Savings in a Building-Society Ordinary-Share Account**
How a £100 investment grows at different ordinary-share rates

| Term (years) | Rate of interest | | | | | |
|---|---|---|---|---|---|---|
| | 5·5% | 6·0% | 6·5% | 7·0% | 7·5% | 8·0% |
| 1 | 105·58 | 106·09 | 106·61 | 107·12 | 107·64 | 108·16 |
| 2 | 111·46 | 112·55 | 113·65 | 114·75 | 115·87 | 116·99 |
| 3 | 117·68 | 119·41 | 121·15 | 122·93 | 124·72 | 126·53 |
| 4 | 124·24 | 126·68 | 129·16 | 131·68 | 134·25 | 136·86 |
| 5 | 131·17 | 134·39 | 137·69 | 141·06 | 144·50 | 148·02 |

| Term (years) | Rate of interest | | | | |
|---|---|---|---|---|---|
| | 8·5% | 9·0% | 9·5% | 10·0% | 10·5% |
| 1 | 108·68 | 109·20 | 109·73 | 110·25 | 111·30 |
| 2 | 118·11 | 119·25 | 120·40 | 121·55 | 123·88 |
| 3 | 128·37 | 130·23 | 132·11 | 134·01 | 137·87 |
| 4 | 139·51 | 142·21 | 144·95 | 147·74 | 153·45 |
| 5 | 151·62 | 155·30 | 159·05 | 162·89 | 170·81 |

The ordinary-share rate changes often. Most societies follow the Building Societies Association's recommended ordinary share rate, but some smaller societies pay higher rates.

*Term shares.* These offer extra interest to investors who can tie up their money for an agreed period. Most societies pay an extra ¾ per cent above the industry's ordinary-share rate for two-year money. The differential is 1 per cent for three-year, $1\frac{1}{2}$ per cent for four-year and 2 per cent for five-year money. Many savers think that the return they get at the start from a term share continues for the rest of the investment period: in fact the rate floats up and down in line with the ordinary-share rate. Building societies do not normally allow early withdrawals from term-share accounts except in cases of death. Interest is normally paid each half-year – but pensioners and others depending on investment income can often arrange to have interest monthly. With many societies, the minimum investment in term shares is £100 but some have a minimum of £1,000.

*Deposit accounts*. The word 'deposit' has a special legal significance in the building-society industry. If a society hits trouble all savers with deposit accounts have to be paid in full before anything can be done about share-account savers. Deposit accounts are, therefore, even safer than share accounts – but the risk of loss due to a collapse is so small for well-established societies that there is little point in having a deposit account, particularly as most societies' deposit-account interest rate is $\frac{1}{4}$ per cent less than the ordinary share-account rate. Nowadays, deposit accounts are used mainly by companies and other organizations which are outside the special tax arrangements the societies have with the Inland Revenue.

*Escalator bonds*. These are a recent hybrid which reward investors for long-term saving but give them limited rights to withdraw their money sooner than they had planned. With a typical escalator bond, the interest you get is on a rising scale. Usually the interest rates are based on fixed differentials above the ordinary-share rate and the longer you save the higher the differentials. For example, with the Alliance's Bond Shares version of the escalator idea you get a differential of $\frac{1}{2}$ per cent for the first year, $\frac{3}{4}$ per cent for the second, $1\frac{1}{4}$ per cent for the third, 2 per cent for the fourth and 3 per cent for the fifth. The differential is paid as a bonus at the end of each year and you are locked in for the whole of the first year. After that you can get out on three months' notice.

In a variant from the Abbey National you can choose between different lengths of fixed initial period – either one, two, three, four or five years. The longer the initial period, the higher the initial interest rate and it continues for the rest of the period. If you choose a three-year initial period, for instance, you get 1 per cent on top of the ordinary-share rate. After the fixed period, your interest rate rises in steps to a maximum of 2 per cent above the ordinary-share rate. You can continue getting this rate for as long as you leave your money in – a feature which compares well with most other societies' escalator schemes. In all cases, once the initial period is up, you can withdraw your money on three months' notice.

Although there is little to choose between the major societies on their ordinary-share and term-share rates, escalator-bond arrangements vary widely. For further information on term-share and ordinary-share rates, the most convenient source is the *Financial Times*, which each Saturday publishes an advertisement tabulating the rates of the major societies and of many of the smaller ones. The table usually appears in the last few pages of the paper.

With escalator bonds, you need to compare the leaflets of the societies concerned – preferably with a sharp eye for small print and a working knowledge of the strange effects of compound interest. One point to watch for is that if you leave your interest with the society, you may not get a truly compound rate. This is because the differentials usually apply only to the original capital.

Subscription-share accounts and other ways of saving regularly with a building society are discussed in the section on regular saving later in this chapter.

## Bank and Finance-House Deposits

Bank-deposit rates fluctuate even more widely than building-society rates. In most of the recent past, banks' ordinary deposit rates have been higher than the tax-paid savers' rates at the building societies, so banks have been a better bet than building societies for non-taxpayers. But after tax is deducted at the basic rate, bank interest rates have generally worked out lower than building-society rates.

Ordinary-deposit money at the banks is usually technically on seven days' notice. In practice, the big banks repay such money on demand – but they treat the preceding seven days as the notice period. Interest ceases to build up from the beginning of the notional notice period.

The banks have recently been developing a wide range of special savings schemes to meet building-society competition. In the autumn of 1980, the National Westminster Bank, for instance, launched a plan offering higher than usual interest to people who can invest at least £2,500 on a minimum of at least three months' notice of withdrawal. The initial interest rates were 14¾ per cent for three months' notice money and 15¼ per cent for money on six months' notice.

NatWest reserves the right to vary the interest rates at any time but pledges to keep them above its rate on standard seven-day-notice deposits, which were paying 14 per cent at the time of the launch. By comparison, the building societies' standard deposit rate at the time was 10·5 per cent tax-paid – worth 15 per cent gross.

At about the same time, Lloyds Bank launched a scheme for deposits of at least £2,500 invested for terms of between two and seven years. The interest rates are variable and are determined by a formula involving Lloyds' own 'base' rate for lending purposes. The starting rates for the scheme ranged between 15 and 16 per cent.

A feature of both the NatWest and Lloyds schemes is that investors can get at their money quickly in a financial emergency. At NatWest, the arrangement is that you can withdraw your money as quickly as you like but at the expense of a penalty of ¼ per cent for each month of notice period that you want waived. If, for instance, you want to withdraw £1,000 from a six months account at only two months' notice you will be charged a penalty of £10 (¼ per cent of £1,000 multiplied by 4). Lloyds's arrangement is that you can borrow back up to 90 per cent of your investment – at an interest rate of 2½ per cent above the bank's base lending rate.

Finance houses often pay higher rates than the big banks. But the problem is they are not usually so well-established as the banks, so your money may not be as secure. Several big finance companies failed in the 1974 crash and, though few small investors lost money, they had a nail-biting time waiting for rescue arrangements to be mounted. Some of the soundest finance companies are part of larger groups, often banking groups. Lombard North Central, for instance, is part of National Westminster. UDT and Mercantile Credit are linked to Barclays and Forward Trust is owned by Midland. And the Royal Bank of Canada owns the Plymouth-based finance company, Western Trust.

Before placing a deposit with a finance company, it is worth getting professional advice – from a bank manager, accountant or solicitor. As elsewhere in the investment world, a good general rule with finance companies is that the more tempting the proposition looks, the more risky it is likely to be: risky borrowers have to pay high interest rates.

## Local-Authority Loan Offers

Local authorities are heavy borrowers and advertise regularly for savings from the public. Terms vary widely at any one time between different authorities and interest rates move up and down rapidly in line with general economic conditions. Usually local authorities borrow for a fixed period – typically between two and five years – and the interest rate is guaranteed throughout the term. They tend to borrow for longer periods when interest rates generally are expected to rise. And they borrow for shorter periods if they expect interest rates to fall.

Latest local-authority loan offers are usually advertised in the financial section of the *Sunday Express*, the 'Money Mail' section of the Wednesday issue of the *Daily Mail* and in the City pages of many other newspapers. You can get a full list of current offers from the Loans Bureau of the Chartered Institute of Public Finance and Accountancy, 232 Vauxhall Bridge Road, London sw1. Enclose a stamped addressed foolscap envelope.

One problem with local-authority loans is that income tax is usually deducted at source from the interest – but if you are a non-taxpayer you can claim a refund later from the Inland Revenue. For non-taxpayers who can put up with the inconvenience, the total return is usually better than they can get almost anywhere else. For taxpayers, too, local authorities can often be a good bet, because in times of keen competition for funds local authorities have to pitch their rates so that the return net of basic-rate tax compares well with building-society rates. Smaller authorities often have to pay higher interest rates than better-known ones. But all local authorities are equally secure, being backed by government guarantees.

Many local authorities insist on a minimum investment of £1,000 but some accept as little as £100.

Local authorities are, therefore, a useful alternative to building societies for fixed-term investments and the returns are particularly attractive for non-taxpayers. The snag is that it is virtually impossible to get your money out early – a point that may be particularly important for pensioners with little other savings. Local Authorities return money early only in cases of extreme hardship or death.

### National Savings

The National Savings Department's range of investments has grown up over the years with little overall planning. Many National Savings investments have outlived their function and have little to offer today's savers. But National Savings Certificates, the National Savings Bank's Investment Account and the inflation-proofed Save As You Earn scheme (which is discussed under 'Regular Savings' later in this chapter) are excellent bargains.

*National Savings Certificates.* The returns from these are free of all tax so they are a particularly good investment for high-rate taxpayers. The main version of Savings Certificates, which is open to all investors, promises guaranteed interest on a rising scale over four or five years. And you can withdraw your money at any time on less than a fortnight's notice. The combination of a guaranteed interest rate and early withdrawal arrangements is a major plus compared to the nearest rivals of the certificates – building-society term shares.

The Nineteenth Issue of National Savings Certificates, which was launched in February 1980, runs for five years. Each £10 unit grows to £10·50 after one year, £11·40 after two, £12·45 after three, £14·10 after four and £16·35 after five. You get the benefit of the growth only when you cash in. The increments represent a tax-free return of 5 per cent in the first year, 8·6 per cent in the second, 9·2 per cent in the third, 13·2 per cent in the fourth and

16·0 per cent in the fifth. If you hold on for five years, the bonuses represent an average compound interest rate of 10·3 per cent. The maximum holding is £1,500 for each individual.

You have to wait until the end of the first year for any bonus – if you cash in earlier you get just your original investment back. In the following years, each year's increment is divided into three equal bonuses, one paid after each four-month period. When you have held National Savings Certificates for the full term originally planned, you usually have the option to continue for a further period. The interest rates offered on these extension periods vary widely and unless you are a high-rate taxpayer you will probably be better off cashing in.

The Retirement Issue of National Savings Certificates is a special, inflation-proofed version for pensioners and other investors who have reached state retirement age: sixty-five for men and sixty for women. The bonuses are calculated by reference to the cost-of-living index and the idea is to compensate pensioners for the fall in the value of their money in the time it has been invested. Before the issue was withdrawn from sale in the autumn of 1980, you could invest up to £1,200 in units of £10. If you hold them for a term of five years you get an extra tax-free 4 per cent on top of the inflation-proofing bonuses. The first bonus is attached at the end of the first year and after that bonuses are added each month. If you hold for longer than five years you continue to earn monthly inflation-proofing bonuses and the 4 per cent bonus is also inflation-proofed.

The second Index-Linked Issue of Savings Certificates was launched in 1980 to replace the Retirement Issue. It works in much the same way except that the maximum holding for each person has been raised to £3,000 and it is open to both men and women from age sixty. Investors can hold the maximum in both issues.

Savings certificates can be left in a will but in the case of the Retirement Issue the beneficiary is allowed to continue holding them only if he or she is also of retirement age. Both Nineteenth Issue and Retirement Issue certificates can be bought over the counter at most Post Offices. For the Retirement Issue, no proof of age is normally needed but you have to sign a declaration that you meet the age requirements.

Savings Certificates can be cashed in by writing to the National

Savings Department at Durham DH99 1NS enclosing a completed form obtainable from most Post Offices. You have the choice of getting either cash from the Post Office or a warrant you can pay into your bank account.

*National Savings Bank Investment Account.* This is an ideal savings vehicle for many pensioners and others on low incomes. The interest rate is high and is paid without deduction of tax. Withdrawals can be made on one month's notice. The interest rate was raised to a record 15 per cent in January 1980, giving a net return of 10·5 per cent to anyone paying 30 per cent tax.

One snag is that interest starts clocking up only from the first day of the month after you invested the money and it ends on the last day of the month preceding withdrawal. The National Savings Bank is operated through most Post Offices.

*National Savings Bank Ordinary Account.* The major advantage of the ordinary account is that you can withdraw up to £100 on demand and the rest of your money quickly by post. But the interest rate is only 5 per cent before tax. The first £70 of each year's interest is tax-free.

*Premium Bonds.* These are probably the best-known National Savings investment and they were held by more than 25 million people at the last count. They pay no interest but a sum equivalent to interest of 7 per cent a year goes into a lottery to pay out prizes ranging from £50 to £250,000. Prizes are paid out each month but the chances of any particular £1 bond winning a prize in any one month are only one in 18,400. The maximum holding is £10,000 per investor.

There is a waiting period of three months before a newly purchased bond becomes eligible for prizes. Prizes are tax-free, so Premium Bonds are a relatively better investment for high-rate taxpayers than other investors.

**Certificates of Tax Deposit**

If you expect soon to have to meet a tax demand, the Inland Revenue's interest-bearing Certificates of Tax Deposit may be a good investment. Normally the proceeds are used later to pay tax bills, but you can get your money back if you want. In that case, however, you earn a lower rate of interest.

The interest rates are adjusted occasionally in line with competing investments – and they are usually pitched so that the return on money used to pay off tax bills compares well with other short-term investments. In the autumn of 1980, for instance, the interest on tax-bill money worked out at a yearly rate of 17 per cent for the first three months and fell to 15 per cent thereafter. By comparison, the standard building-society deposit rate at the time was 10·5 per cent tax-paid, equal to a gross rate of 15 per cent. For money withdrawn as cash, the certificates paid only 11 per cent.

Interest on the certificates is subject to income tax in the normal way. The minimum investment is £2,000 and top-ups thereafter have to be at least £500.

## Government Securities

Government securities differ from most other savings instruments in that they can be bought and sold on the Stock Exchange. They are usually known as gilts and they are issued in units of £100. The interest rate is fixed at the outset and – usually – the date by which the government will have to repay them. But several of the best-known gilts are 'undated' – that is, there is no obligation on the government ever to repay and it can just go on paying interest for ever. Consols and War Loan are examples.

Where the government has to redeem a gilt, it usually has to repay 'at par' – that is, to pay investors £100 for each £100 stock unit irrespective of what price they may have bought at.

The rate of interest you get per £100 unit is known as the 'coupon'. This is not the same as the 'yield' because if you buy on the stock market the price of each unit may be well below or above £100 depending on general investment conditions. The coupon on War Loan is $3\frac{1}{2}$ per cent – that is, the government pays £3·50 interest before tax each year on each £100 unit. But the yield is usually much higher. In 1974 when War Loan's price crashed below £20, for instance, the yield shot above 17·5 per cent (£3·50 is $17\frac{1}{2}$ per cent of £20). A gilt's coupon reflects investment conditions at the time of issue – and the yield reflects them today.

Most recently issued gilts carry coupons of more than 10 per cent and a few have ones of more than 15 per cent.

The main influences on gilt prices on the stock market are the level of the Bank of England's minimum lending rate and the outlook for inflation. Generally, if interest rates on other investments rise, the price of gilts will fall. Undated stock are usually worst-hit. Short-dated stocks (that is, those within five years of redemption) stand up much better to rises in the Bank of England's minimum lending rate and other bad news: the prospect of early repayment acts as an anchor. It is wise to get expert advice before investing in undated and long-dated gilts, because they are so much of a gamble on the prospects for the economy. But short-dated gilts can be compared directly to National Savings Certificates and other investments discussed in this chapter and can often be a useful alternative. Most short-dated gilts carry low coupons and their prices stand well below the redemption price. This gives the investor a certain capital gain if he can hold until redemption – and this is particularly attractive to high-rate tax-payers, especially as there is no capital gains tax to pay on profits from gilts held for more than a year.

Take Exchequer 3 % 1983. In 1979, its price fell as low as £76. So with just four years to go to redemption, buyers could look forward to a gain of £24 for every £76 they invested – a capital profit of $31\frac{1}{2}$ per cent by 1983. In the meantime, there was a yield before tax of 3·9 per cent (£3 as a percentage of £76).

The normal way of buying gilts is through a stockbroker. But most gilts can also be bought through the National Savings Department and charges compare well with those of a stockbroker, particularly for small investments. You can buy up to £5,000-worth of each individual stock in any one transaction through the National Savings Department. The procedure is to fill out form GS1, available from most Post Offices, and send it in a special supplied envelope to the Blackpool National Savings office. One problem is that there is a gap of at least a day before the transaction is carried out – so you do not know the price you are buying at. If you are paying by cheque, you can either leave the amount blank or make it out for rather more than you expect to pay (you will get a refund later). Your cheque should be enclosed with Form GS1.

The National Savings Department's charge for both buying and selling deals is usually £1 per £250-worth of stock. For purchases the minimum charge is £1 but for sales which bring in less than £100 the rate is 10p per £10 of the proceeds.

Government securities you can buy through the National Savings Department, using a form available from the Post Office, are listed in Table 9.

Table 9 **Post Office Gilts**

| Name of stock | Dates of half-yearly interest payments* | |
| --- | --- | --- |
| 2¼% Consols | 5 January | 5 April |
| | 5 July | 5 October |
| 2½% Annuities | 5 January | 5 April |
| | 5 July | 5 October |
| 2½% Treasury Stock 1975 or after | 1 April | 1 October |
| 3% British Transport Stock 1978–88 | 1 January | 1 July |
| 3% Redemption Stock 1986–96 | 1 April | 1 October |
| 3% Treasury Stock 1982 | 15 February | 15 August |
| 3% Exchequer Stock 1983 | 21 February | 21 August |
| 3½% War Stock | 1 June | 1 December |
| 3½% Conversion Stock | 1 April | 1 October |
| 3½% Treasury Stock 1979–81 | 15 February | 15 August |
| 3½% Funding Stock 1999–2004 | 14 January | 14 July |
| 4% Consols | 1 February | 1 August |
| 5% Treasury Stock 1986–9 | 15 April | 15 October |
| 5½% Funding Stock 1982–4 | 15 January | 15 July |
| 5½% Treasury Stock 2008–12 | 10 March | 10 September |
| 5¾% Funding Loan 1987–91 | 5 April | 5 October |
| 6% Funding Loan 1993 | 15 March | 15 September |
| 6½% Funding Loan 1985–7 | 1 May | 1 November |
| 6¾% Treasury Loan 1995–8 | 1 May | 1 November |
| 7¾% Treasury Loan 1985–8 | 26 January | 26 July |
| 7¾% Treasury Stock 2012–15 | 26 January | 26 July |
| 8% Treasury Stock 2002–6 | 5 April | 5 October |
| 8¼% Treasury Stock 1987–90 | 15 June | 15 December |
| 8½% Treasury Loan 1980–82 | 15 January | 15 July |

Table 9 – *continued*

| Name of stock | | Dates of half-yearly interest payments* | |
| --- | --- | --- | --- |
| $8\frac{1}{2}\%$ | Treasury Loan 1984–6 | 10 January | 10 July |
| $8\frac{3}{4}\%$ | Treasury Loan 1997 | 1 March | 1 September |
| $9\%$ | Treasury Loan 1994 | 17 May | 17 November |
| $9\%$ | Treasury Loan 1992–6 | 15 March | 15 September |
| $9\frac{1}{4}\%$ | Treasury Stock 1983 | 18 January | 18 July |
| $9\frac{1}{2}\%$ | Treasury Stock 1999 | 15 January | 15 July |
| $9\frac{3}{4}\%$ | Treasury Stock 1981 | 1 April | 1 October |
| $11\frac{3}{4}\%$ | Treasury Stock 1991 | 10 January | 10 July |
| $12\%$ | Treasury Stock 1983 | 17 March | 17 September |
| $12\frac{1}{4}\%$ | Exchequer Stock 1992 | 25 February | 25 August |
| $12\frac{3}{4}\%$ | Exchequer Stock 1981 | 23 May | 23 November |
| $12\frac{3}{4}\%$ | Treasury Stock 1995 | 15 May | 15 November |
| $13\%$ | Treasury Stock 1990 | 15 January | 15 July |
| $13\frac{1}{4}\%$ | Treasury Stock 1996 | 15 May | 15 November |
| $13\frac{1}{4}\%$ | Treasury Stock 1997 | 22 January | 22 July |
| $13\frac{3}{4}\%$ | Treasury Stock 1993 | 23 May | 23 November |
| $14\%$ | Treasury Stock 1982 | 16 March | 16 September |
| $14\frac{1}{2}\%$ | Treasury Loan 1994 | 1 March | 1 September |
| $15\frac{1}{4}\%$ | Treasury Stock 1996 | 3 May | 3 November |
| $15\frac{1}{2}\%$ | Treasury Loan 1998 | 30 March | 30 September |

*When stocks are bought within five weeks of a forthcoming interest payment, this normally goes to the previous holder.

## Regular Saving

If you can commit yourself to saving a set amount regularly, there are several ways in which you can get a better return on your money. If you do not want to be tied to a particular saving period, building-society subscription-share accounts are probably the best form of regular saving. Insurance-linked building-society plans and the government's inflation-proofed Save As You Earn scheme are not as flexible but offer even higher returns. (The building-society Save As You Earn scheme, which is not inflation-proofed but offers guaranteed tax-free bonuses, is described later.)

*National Savings Save As You Earn.* This inflation-proofed scheme is run by the National Savings Department and application forms are available from most Post Offices and banks. Investors have to contribute each month for five years and their money earns tax-free bonuses to compensate fully for the fall in its value since it was invested. You have to complete the term to get the bonuses, which are calculated using a complicated formula based on the government's monthly Retail Price Index. You can stop the contract at any time. If you cash in during the first year, you get only your contributions back, but after that tax-free interest of 6 per cent a year is added to the proceeds from early cash-ins.

The minimum monthly investment is £4. The maximum was originally £20 but, as this book went to press, it was due to be raised to £50 early in 1981.

Because the rate of inflation varies so much it is difficult to make exact comparisons with other regular savings options. But if, for instance, inflation is 15 per cent a year and you save £20 a month, you will get a pay-out after five years of £1,747 – a profit of £547 on your total investment of £1,200. With inflation at 12½ per cent, the pay-out is £1,642, giving a profit of £442; and inflation at 10 per cent gives a pay-out of £1,543 and a profit of £343. What happens if the cost of living actually falls? That is highly unlikely but it is reassuring to know that the government guarantees at least to pay you your money back in all circumstances. It would, however, then make sense to cash in before maturity so that you get the 6 per cent interest.

After the five-year contribution period is completed, you have the option of leaving your money for a further two years – making no further contributions. After seven years you will get a further bonus, to compensate for the rise in the cost of living in the two years, plus an amount equal to two months' contributions. If you cash in during the two-year period you get only what you were entitled to after five years. If you want to make full use of the scheme but are worried that you might not be able to complete the course, it is better to take out a series of small contracts than one large one. This enables you if need be to cash in part of your saving without affecting the cost-of-living bonuses on the rest.

If you want to make your contributions by bank standing order, fill out the red version of the application form, which is available at banks. The green version available from Post Offices enables you to pay by National Girobank or by cash each month across the Post Office counter. Many employers deduct your contributions to the SAYE scheme from your salary upon request.

Anyone over sixteen can invest in the scheme.

*Building-society subscription-share accounts.* Most building societies offer higher interest rates to savers who save a set amount each month in what are usually called 'subscription share' accounts. Your money usually earns an extra 1¼ per cent above the normal ordinary-share rate.

You can usually withdraw your money at short notice but, if you make a partial withdrawal, the interest on the rest of your balance is cut to the ordinary share-account rate.

Many societies have a minimum saving rate of £5 a month, but some will accept as little as £1. The maximum is often as little as £20, but many societies will accept as much as £100. Table 10 shows how your money builds up at various subscription-share rates.

*Building-society Save-As-You-Earn.* This is a government-sponsored scheme and the interest is free of all tax. To get the interest you have to save between £1 and £20 a month for five years. Interest is equal to fourteen months' savings payable in one go at the end of the term. This represents a tax-free interest rate of 8·3 per cent a year.

You have the option of leaving the contributions and interest for a further two years and after seven years you get total interest equal to twenty-eight months' saving. This represents an interest rate of 8·6 per cent. The scheme is useful mainly to high-rate taxpayers who are already making full use of the inflation-proofed National Savings SAYE scheme and insurance-linked investments.

**Table 10 How Your Money Grows in a Subscription-Share Account**
The balance you will have at the end of each year if you are a basic rate taxpayer and save £20 a month

| | Rate of interest | | | | | | | |
| --- | --- | --- | --- | --- | --- | --- | --- | --- |
| Year | $6\frac{3}{4}\%$ | $7\frac{1}{2}\%$ | $8\frac{1}{4}\%$ | $9\%$ | $9\frac{1}{4}\%$ | $9\frac{1}{2}\%$ | $9\frac{3}{4}\%$ | $10\%$ |
| 1 | 249 | 250 | 251 | 252 | 252 | 253 | 253 | 253 |
| 2 | 515 | 519 | 523 | 527 | 528 | 530 | 531 | 532 |
| 3 | 799 | 808 | 818 | 828 | 830 | 834 | 837 | 840 |
| 4 | 1,106 | 1,120 | 1,137 | 1,154 | 1,161 | 1,167 | 1,173 | 1,179 |

| | Rate of interest | | | | | | |
| --- | --- | --- | --- | --- | --- | --- | --- |
| Year | $10\frac{1}{4}\%$ | $10\frac{1}{2}\%$ | $10\frac{3}{4}\%$ | $11\%$ | $11\frac{1}{4}\%$ | $11\frac{1}{2}\%$ | $11\frac{3}{4}\%$ |
| 1 | 253 | 254 | 254 | 254 | 255 | 255 | 255 |
| 2 | 534 | 535 | 536 | 538 | 539 | 540 | 542 |
| 3 | 843 | 846 | 850 | 853 | 856 | 859 | 863 |
| 4 | 1,185 | 1,191 | 1,198 | 1,204 | 1,210 | 1,216 | 1,223 |

*Insurance-linked building-society saving.* Several building societies run regular savings schemes in association with life-insurance companies. The insurance link means that each monthly payment gets the usual tax subsidy for life insurance – worth $17\frac{1}{2}$ per cent in 1980/81 and 15 per cent in 1981/2 of the gross premiums. The result is an extremely high return.

Technically the plans are ten-year endowment policies, but they are usually designed to be cashed in after four years. Investors pay their money to the building society, which passes it on to the insurance company. The company in turn makes a deduction for its administrative expenses and life-cover costs and passes the rest back to the building society, where it is invested in a special account.

Once the plan has been running four years, basic-rate taxpayers can cash in without tax liability. The net return to younger investors can be as much as 15 per cent. If you invest £20 a month, for instance, you may collect as much as £1,294 after total contributions of £960. High-rate taxpayers usually have some tax to pay if they cash in before maturity – but the bill will probably be small if the policy has been running at least four years. For an investor liable to tax at 45 per cent, for instance, the tax payable will reduce the net annual return over four years by less than 1 per cent. The maximum amount you can invest is governed by the usual rules for life-insurance premiums (see Chapter 2).

Among the best-known societies which offer these plans are the Bradford & Bingley, linked with Eagle Star, and the Bristol & West, linked with Equitable Life and Windsor Life. Returns from two smaller societies, the Cheshire and the Marsden, are usually better. Both societies' plans are linked with the Royal insurance group. The Bradford & Bingley also runs a variant for lump-sum investors. The Alliance runs a similar lump-sum scheme linked to a friendly society and designed to run for ten years.

If you want to save regularly for no more than a year or two, building-society subscription shares are probably the best bet. The returns are better on insurance-linked building-society plans but you have to save for at least four years. The inflation-proofed National Savings Department S A Y E scheme is excellent if you can save for five years.

# 8. Tax

Tax can bedevil people's lives. In one or two cases the sight of a tax form has the same effect as a stoat on a rabbit when it comes too close. Rabbit and taxpayer close their eyes in terror, and pray that the beast will disappear. But it does not. Yet, for all the fear it induces, tax is not as complicated as it looks. People who work for the government, for local authorities, companies or, indeed, an employer of any kind – and that is nine taxpayers out of ten – have what they owe deducted week by week or month by month through the Pay As You Earn system before any money reaches them. The crucial point is to ensure that the tax office knows about any changes in your personal circumstances immediately they happen, so that you are getting all the allowances to which you are entitled. If you get married or take out a mortgage for instance, you should get in touch with them fast.

## Tax Allowances and Reliefs

There are a whole series of allowances which just postpone the point at which you start paying tax and they usually change each year. Parliament has laid down that the Chancellor of the Exchequer should raise the main allowances, which affect everyone, in line with the cost of living, unless the House of Commons specifically decides otherwise. The rule makes it far harder for government to leave allowances where they are in money terms or to go only part of the way in maintaining their real value, after allowing for rising prices over the year.

Each tax year runs from the 6th of April to the 5th of April in the following year. In the year beginning 6 April 1980 and ending a year later (the tax year 1980/81) the main allowances were as shown in Table 11 (we have left a space so that you can fill in those for the next tax year). A new widow's bereavement allowance has appeared, though it applies only in the year the husband dies. The

widow can claim the married man's allowance which he would
have received, to cover the months after he has died. Assume that
he dies half-way through the tax year. She can claim the half of the
tax allowance which he has not had. The rule, incidentally does
not apply to widowers.

Table 11 **Main Tax Allowances**

|  | Tax year 1980/81 | Tax year 1981/2* |
| --- | --- | --- |
| Single person's allowance | £1,375 | .......... |
| Married man's allowance | £2,145 | .......... |
| Wife's earned-income allowance | £1,375 | .......... |
| Single person age allowance | £1,820 | .......... |
| Married man's age allowance | £2,895 | .......... |
| Additional personal allowance (for bringing up children on your own) | £770 | .......... |
| Dependent relative allowance | £145 | .......... |
| Son's or daughter's services allowance | £55 | .......... |
| Blind person's allowance | £180 | .......... |

* Figures for 1981/2 may be added when the 1981 Budget details are
known.

You can also deduct from your taxable income money that you
use in certain ways. If you buy your home on a mortgage, for
instance, or borrow money to make permanent improvements to
it, you will get tax relief on the interest you pay, at least on the first
£25,000 of any loan. The one proviso is that it is 'your main or
principal residence'. (You can, incidentally, get relief on the same
basis if you have a dependent relative – perhaps a mother or
mother in law – who lives in a house you own and does not pay
you rent.) You collect tax relief whoever provides you with the
loan, though not, as a matter of curiosity, if you finance your
borrowing via an overdraft. But that is hardly a real worry. Your
chances of getting an overdraft to buy a house are infinitesimal.

What are permanent improvements? The crucial point is that
they should become a permanent part of the house. A loan to
install a central-heating system, for instance, would qualify for

tax relief, whereas a loan for free-standing storage heaters which you could take with you when you moved would not.

With mortgage interest, and also with any contributions you make towards a pension scheme, you get relief at your top rate of tax. Assume that you pay 50 per cent on the highest £300 of your income and are providing the building society with £600 of interest. The first £300 of the interest will attract relief at 50 per cent, while the other half will ensure that you get tax relief at 45 per cent which is the next tax band down. If you are just paying tax at the basic 30 per cent rate, relief comes at 30 per cent. The one proviso on pension contributions – though not on mortgage interest – is that you cannot set off any tax you have paid on savings through the Investment Income Surcharge, which is explained below. You can collect tax relief, too, on part of the cost of a life-insurance policy. This relief is granted directly so that your payments to the life company are lower than they would be otherwise, as we explained in Chapter 2.

## The Tax You Pay

It is only when your income is higher than your allowances and tax reliefs combined that you start paying tax – or, in the Inland Revenue's jargon, have taxable income. When the system takes its levy it does so at the rates shown in Table 12. So if you are

Table 12 **Income-Tax Rates**

| Rates of tax | Band of taxable income | |
| --- | --- | --- |
| | *1980/81* | *1981/2\** |
| 30% | £1 to £11,250 | ........... |
| 40% | £11,251 to £13,250 | ........... |
| 45% | £13,251 to £16,750 | ........... |
| 50% | £16,751 to £22,250 | ........... |
| 55% | £22,251 to £27,750 | ........... |
| 60% | £27,751 and upwards | ........... |

*Figures for 1981/2 may be added when the 1981 Budget details are known.

relatively affluent, you will pay a different rate of tax on each band of your income.

*The investment-income surcharge* is an added levy, which appears if the income you get from dividends, building-society interest, and so on breaks through a particular tripwire. In 1980/ 81 the surcharge does not apply to the first £5,500 of what you receive. Once your tax office has done the various calculations, you have to pay an extra 15 per cent on any investment income which is over £5,500.

A lot of money from investments comes with allowances for tax which has been paid already. The building-society interest comes tax-paid – at least at basic rate – for instance. If you have dividends from a company, they will usually come with a tax credit showing that the group has paid some of the tax bill. In most cases that will cut back the total tax you have to pay. The rules do not apply when it comes to working out whether you have to pay investment-income surcharge or indeed higher-rate tax on the interest you receive on investments. Tax inspectors 'gross up' income which comes tax-paid, to assess what figure you would have needed before tax to end up with what you actually receive. Assume that you get £70 of interest tax-paid from a building society, for instance. Normally you would have to collect £100 before tax to end up with your £70. But the inspectors will add the full £100 to your income to assess if you are liable for either the surcharge or a higher-rate tax. This 'grossing up' rule can also hit pensioners, (for details, see later in the chapter).

The government has now decided to index-link the starting-point both for higher-rate tax and investment-income surcharge. They will move up in line with rising prices year by year, unless the House of Commons specifically decides otherwise: the move will ensure that what are rich men's taxes in one year do not become the scourge of middle management two years later because of the fall in the value of money in between.

If you sell shares, or units in a unit trust, you do not get 'income', at least as the Inland Revenue understands it. If you have made profits on your investment, there will be 'capital gains', on which you may or may not have to pay tax. For details see the section on capital-gains tax later in this chapter.

The tax rates and advantages change as people go through life. First comes life as a child and student. Marriage will change the pattern, and there will be further alterations if both husband and wife become high earners. People shift from working for an employer to striking out on their own, where again different rules apply. There may be complications on divorce and maintenance. Finally there is retirement and life as a pensioner.

*Children* in Britain count as adults for tax purposes. They have the usual personal allowances, so that in 1980/81 the first £1,375 of any income they receive is tax-free. The state only regards their income as belonging to their parents, and taxes them on it, when the parents themselves provide them with the money – in a lump sum or in instalments year by year – in the first place. This rule only applies to children who are both unmarried and under eighteen. Presents from other people and grandparents do not come into the parents' tax picture at all. (These rules have not always applied. At one time, governments added money children received in this way to the parents' income and taxed it as such.) Any son or daughter over eighteen does not need to worry about this aggregation at all. Even what parents provide belongs to the child outright.

*Vacation work* is what students usually look for. Many find themselves on an emergency tax coding, even though their earnings over the year are never large enough to bring them into the tax net. The result is that week by week they pay tax – or, rather, have it deducted from their pay – and then have to go through the rigmarole of claiming it back. Avoiding the problem is not difficult. They can ask their employers to get authority from the tax office to give them their money without any tax deductions, though, of course, they will still have to pay for National Insurance contributions.

*The seven-year covenant* is the way that parents, godparents or others can provide children, at a university or poly, for example, with regular funds in such a way that the children actually collect more than they are given. The trick is done through tax relief. It will only work for as long as the children, who must be over eighteen, do not get so much from jobs, savings and everything else that they become taxpayers themselves. The covenant does not have to last for seven years, but it must be capable of continuing for more than six. The parents sign a formal agreement to give the child a fixed sum each year for seven years or for as long as his or her further-education course continues, whichever is the shorter. But parents have to be careful to include both possibilities in their covenants.

The money is paid from income which has already been taxed. If the person getting it is not a taxpayer, he or she can claim back the basic-rate tax which the parents provided in the first place. There is a vital proviso. If parents insist that they have the right to stop the covenant at any time they want, their child cannot get the relief. Covenants can only end when the original conditions no longer apply – in many cases, when the children leave university.

Four-year covenants apply to charities. If you are prepared to commit yourself for no less than three years, the charity can collect its basic-rate tax relief in the same way. But if you are a higher-rate taxpayer – and do not contribute more than £3,000 to charities over the year – extra help is available, though you collect it, not the charity. Assume that you pay 50 per cent tax on the top £400 of your salary, and decide to give £400 to Oxfam. With a basic rate of tax of 30 per cent, you hand over £280. Meanwhile, the treasurer can collect back the basic-rate tax you have paid on the money – or £120, in this case. At the same time, you can reclaim the extra 20 per cent, when the tax inspector sorts out your affairs after you have sent in your tax return. The system may seem convoluted, but as you get more relief so you can afford to be more generous – at least in theory. It starts in April 1981.

*Child benefit*, which comes tax-free from the Post Office in cash and goes to wives each week, has replaced the old tax allowances which fathers used to claim and so reduce their tax bill. The benefit – technically a social-security benefit – was adjusted sharply upwards as the tax allowances disappeared. (Or almost disappeared. Child allowance still exists for some parents who cannot claim child benefit.) One problem now is that the child benefit stops when children reach the age of eighteen or leave school, whereas the old tax allowances used to continue for as long as the children were getting full-time education. However, there are arrangements, complicated admittedly, designed to make up the difference, organized through the student grant system.

*Additional personal allowance* is the main form of tax allowance related to children that is left; it goes to people bringing up children on their own, mothers, fathers, or anyone else. If this additional allowance is combined with the normal single-person allowance that is payable anyway, it produces the same amount of tax-free income that a married man claims.

*Marriage* brings special tax rules for the tax year in which you take the plunge. In the tax year in which you marry, both husband and wife are responsible for their own tax bills and fill in their own tax forms. A wife can claim the single person's allowance for the whole year – and any other allowances to which she is entitled – even though she may only be single for a few days of it. But once the year in which she has married is over, the allowance gets rechristened the wife's earned-income allowance. But it only applies to earnings, so that no one can claim the allowance against income from shares or other investments.

Husbands used to do better in the past than they do today. Originally they could could claim the married man's allowance for the whole of the tax year in which they were brought to the altar or registry office, even if they were only married for a couple of days of it. Alas, no more. The state will only give a man the standard proportion of the allowance you might expect. If he marries in mid-July, three months into the tax year, he will get nine-twelfths, or three-quarters, of the difference between the single man's and the married man's allowance, as well as the single man's allowance for the whole year.

What is he taking on financially? He is responsible for sending back full information on his wife's earnings and her other income to his tax inspector. By one of those curious quirks of the law, she does not have to give him the information, even so. Men usually have to pay the cheque for the joint tax bill. Even if they go for separate taxation of wife's earnings, the husband has to settle the bill for her income from investments and savings, as well as his own. There is one other way of being taxed – separate assessment – but more of that later.

Once the tax year in which they marry is over, men can claim the full married man's allowance and, if their wives are working, they can claim the wife's earned-income allowance on her behalf. Men may do the claiming. But the code will be fitted in against their wives' earnings through the Pay As You Earn system – so that women get the allowance. That, at least, is the pattern in the great majority of cases. The couple can choose otherwise. But unless they let the tax office know that they want to organize matters differently, they will be treated as a unit automatically. But what are the other choices?

*Separate assessment* will not save any couple which opts for it money overall. What it will do is ensure that the overall tax bill is split between them, with each paying their respective share of the total. The tax office works out their total income, from investment as well as from their jobs, and then sets the standard allowances against it. In general these reliefs are split between them, each getting the same proportion of reliefs as they would have done, assuming that they had paid tax on their whole income.

There are a couple of caveats. If the man pays the mortgage in full, he gets the tax relief in full. The other problem concerns the size of his wife's allowances. The reliefs attributed to her must not be less than the earned-income allowance that she collects anyway. If they fall below that magic figure, the tax office channels over enough of her husband's reliefs to her to bring her up to the necessary level.

Salary increases and bonus payments during the course of a year can make even the most careful calculations on the balance between the two incomes go awry. A husband may end up earning only one and a half times his wife's salary, rather than twice as much, as he had forecast. Clearly, no one is going to know how everything has worked out until the end of the year. If their estimates turn out wrong and the man has had too much of the allowances, he has to pay the extra tax. His wife, meanwhile, will collect a tax rebate. Each makes a separate tax return and they are treated as two separate beings, unless they both ask the local tax office to ensure that the overpayments and underpayment cancel each other out, so that he does not pay the extra tax and she does not get a rebate.

Separate assessment makes particular sense if there are family rows about money or one partner is careful whereas the other is always getting into financial muddles. A husband does not need to get his wife's agreement if he wants to be assessed in this way, and she is equally free to opt for it without consulting him. In any case, it does not alter their overall tax bill, but merely divides it differently. Whoever applies has to do so in the six months up to the 6th of July in the year they want their tax separately assessed. That may seem a bit of a mouthful. But if men or women want to choose it for the tax year 1981/2, for instance, they have to put in their request between January 1981, which ironically is in the previous tax year, and 5 July 1981.

*Separate taxation of wife's earnings* – or wife's earned-income election in the jargon – is very different. This time both husband and wife have to agree to the idea, because it alters their overall bill. It only makes sense, anyway, if both are getting relatively high salaries. The law will treat the couple as two single people who happen to be living together, at least on their earned income, so that the husband will lose the married man's allowance. He will, in addition, still be responsible for tax on any income of his wife's from investments.

The difference between the single and married man's allowance stood at £770 in the tax year 1980/81. With the basic rate at 30 per cent, that meant that the average married couple would have saved £231 in tax by getting the higher, married man's allowance. If higher-rate tax does not come into the picture, that is all gain. But if you are both fairly high earners, joining your two incomes will mean that you hit the point at which higher-rate tax begins considerably faster than you would if husband's income and wife's income were each considered separately. However, you need to be sure that you save more on the higher-tax-rate swings than you lose in the tax-allowance roundabouts before you commit yourself.

The point at which wife's earned-income election makes economic sense will change with the tax allowances. But in 1980/81 it would not be wise for any couple with a joint income of less than £17,000 between them to think of it, and even then the wife should be earning a substantial proportion of the total. If other tax allowances or reliefs come into the picture – perhaps for a mortgage – the level at which the earned-income election will save money is higher still. Figures and circumstances will vary enormously. If you are thinking of going for separate taxation in this way, it would make sense to consult an expert before you finally commit yourself.

*Pay As You Earn* (PAYE) takes much of the pain out of tax-paying by making the process automatic. Instead of presenting you with a vast bill at the end of the tax year, the system takes the money from your salary week by week or month by month before you get your cheque or pay packet. The tax office should have all your personal details: whether you are married or single, if you pay a mortgage and so on. If you delay sending them in, the odds are that you will be paying too much tax, but it could be too little, which will involve extra payment later on. Officials supply your employer with a code number which indicates how much the accounts department should deduct before the money reaches you.

You can learn something from the numbers and letters in your code. If the letter L appears, the code contains a single personal allowance. An H indicates the married man's allowance or the higher personal allowance and D shows that you contribute higher-rate tax. You have the right to ask the tax office not to use the code, perhaps to conceal a failed marriage, a second job or whatever. If you do that, the letter T will appear, with a new problem in that the firm will then be aware that you have something you want to hide. A further problem is that you would not get the benefit of any changes in personal allowances immediately. The employer would have to wait for the tax office to provide them with the new T coding.

The numbers on the code, incidentally, will be the same as the total allowances you are getting, minus the last figure. So if your allowances come to £1,683 and you are single, your code will be 168L. Your employer does not know everything that has gone into the code, but you will get a notice giving a breakdown in detail. If you do not understand it or think it inaccurate, you should get in touch with the tax office or one of the PAYE inquiry offices.

If you are starting your first job, the company will probably put you on 'emergency coding', which means that you will only be credited with the single person's allowance. You will get one-fifty-secondth of it weekly if you are paid by the week, or one-twelfth of it monthly if you are paid by the month. You remain on emergency coding until the firm receives notice of the proper code, when the odds are that you will get a rebate. The tax office will only issue a proper code when you have filled in a tax form claiming your allowances.

Those at least were the rules in 1980. Details of plans to simplify the system by giving employers more right to decide what the first coding should be had not been announced when this book went to press.

It is all too easy to find that complications occur every time you leave a job, but there is one simple way of avoiding trouble. When you move, the company you are leaving should always present you with the form P45 which will show, not just your current coding, but the total pay and tax deductions that have been made since the beginning of that tax year. If you give it to your new employer, you will be taxed on the right basis immediately, for he can carry on where your last boss left off. Another form – the P60 – should arrive from your employer at the end of each tax year. It will show how much you have earned in the year and how much tax you have paid on it – and it is well worth keeping. It would be invaluable if there were some dispute on the figures later.

*PAYE expenses and perks.* If you pay tax through PAYE you are certainly working for someone else, which means that, in tax terms, you come under a series of rules known as Schedule E. There are special tax rules to treat the perks that come your way through the firm, like using a company car for your own purposes or joining a private health scheme. They are considerably tighter than the rules covering the expenses of people who are self-employed. If you work for a boss, you can claim expenses only if they are 'wholly, exclusively and necessarily' incurred in doing your job. So you have to show, for instance, that you cannot do your work without what you have bought, and that you bought it for that reason. Above all, you should not have the cheek to claim for expenses which the firm has paid anyway.

Companies provide far more perks than they did in the past, though how the tax office will treat them depends on what you earn from the job overall. It is not just pay which comes into the figures for earnings. The rules depend on your 'remuneration': the whole financial package you receive including commission, certain expenses, a company car for your own use and so on. If the package brings in less than £8,500 in 1980/81, you do not have to pay tax on most of the benefits you receive, though as always there are exceptions. If your company gives you a voucher entitling you to clothes, hampers, holidays or anything else for which you yourself would normally have to pay, you will have to pay tax on its value. What happens if you earn £8,500 or more from the total package of benefits you receive? The answer is that you will have to pay tax on all the extras you get.

*Company cars* are a case in point. If your total earnings with extras are over the £8,500 limit, you will have to pay something, but the penalties depend on how much you use the car on company business. From the tax year 1981/2, which begins on 6 April 1981, the rules on cars change. The scale charge, the amount which the tax inspector will add to your tax bill to allow for private benefits you have had from the car, will depend partly on the amount of your business use, though the original price, the age and the engine size of vehicle all come into it. Assume that you have a three-year-old Ford Cortina. As it is in the middle engine range, you will come into the middle of the Inland Revenue table, with a scale charge of £300 as can be seen from Table 13.

Table 13 **Tax on Use of a Company Car (1981/2)**
The amount (£) added to your income for tax purposes (drivers doing between 1,000 and 18,000 miles a year on business)

| Value of car when new and engine size | Under four years | Over four years |
| --- | --- | --- |
| *Up to £9,600* | | |
| Less than 1,300 cc | 230 | 155 |
| 1,301 to 1,800 cc | 300 | 200 |
| 1,801 cc and upwards | 450 | 300 |
| *£9,601 to £14,400* | 660 | 440 |
| *£14,401 and upwards* | 1,050 | 700 |

What happens if you do not fall within those boundaries? If you do less than 1,000 miles a year on business use, the tax office will bump up the figures by half as much again. If you travel more than 18,000 miles a year on work, you only have to pay half the rates listed. These rates do not cover 1980/81, for which the rules are very different.

*Cheap loans*, in most forms, are taxable. Mortgages, the most-usual form of loans that companies provide, are the shining exception. People who receive them to buy their homes on special terms because they work for banks, building societies or insurance companies do nicely with cheap interest and full tax relief. Problems can appear, however, if you want to change jobs, for then your former employers may ask you for speedy repayment. If you receive some other form of loan, you will be taxed on the difference between the special cheap rate at which you borrow and what the Inland Revenue calls the official rate, which happened to be 15 per cent in 1980. Assume that you get your funds at 4 per cent, so that there is a gap between the two of 11 per cent. You will have to pay tax on the sum you have saved by not paying that extra 11 per cent. If the difference comes to less than £200, though, the tax inspector will ignore it.

*Health schemes,* which provide the cost or some of the cost of private medical treatment – like those run by BUPA or Private Patients Plan, for instance – are treated differently from other benefits. If the company has paid the cost of premiums, everyone is taxable, whether the employee earns £8,500 or not. The tax inspector adds the cost of the company's contributions for each person to their income and taxes them at whatever their top rate of tax happens to be.


## The Self-Employed

People working on their own, taxed under Schedule D, have mixed fortunes. It is true that they have far more scope for claiming expenses and in effect they are taxed in arrears, both of which can give them advantages. But tax inspectors may seem to be tougher on them than other people because they have to show that they are not fiddling tax; and the social-security benefits they can collect are minimal. Unemployment benefit is completely out; they will only get the basic rate of sickness benefit (without any earnings-related extra); and they are also stuck with the basic retirement pension. People often talk of the joy of succeeding by your own efforts. But if you work on your own, you take the risk of failing, not necessarily through your own fault, but because big outside events go wrong.

Assume you are self-employed with your own furniture business, which specializes in supplying hotels and offices. You should be well aware – although many people in the same position are not – that a lot of small businesses go bust through bad book-keeping. So it makes sense to have an accountant keep your books in order, and fight your tax battles for you. You obviously have to pay the accountant fees, but you can claim them as expenses and hence get tax relief on them. Effectively, then, the fees are cut-rate.

General tax treatment is good. For a start – and at the start – you, or your accountant, can choose the date to which your own private accounting year should run. Once the business is in full swing, the inspector will usually assess tax on one year on the basis of profits made in your accounting year, which ended in the previous tax year. If the business is doing well and profits are rising, that is a considerable bonus, for you have the use of the money which will eventually go to pay your tax bill. Special rules apply when you begin, admittedly, but they do not affect you if you have been going for some time.

Bills may be put off for a while in this way, and clever but perfectly legitimate timing can postpone them still further. The tax year in which you have to pay your bills to the Inland Revenue is the one after the tax year in which your own accounting year has ended. The starting-point for the twelve months for which your personal accounting year should run is up to you and your accountant. You may decide that your own year should start just after the new tax year begins. Day One might be May the 1st, three weeks into the new tax year. Assume that your accounting year ends on 30 April 1981. That date will fall into the tax year 1981/2, so these profits are taxed in 1982/3. You pay the bill in two halves, the first on 1 January 1983 and the second on 1 July 1983.

Meanwhile, if you make losses in the early years of a business there may be a chance of collecting back at least some of the tax you paid in the three years before you decided to strike out on your own. Assume that you make a loss of £5,000 in the first year of business in 1981/2. You have to go back to the furthest of the three years – in this case 1978/9 – and can claim not the full £5,000, but the tax you paid on £5,000 three years ago. How much that will be depends on your tax rate. The higher it was, the more you can claim back. You may come to a point at which you have used up all the tax you paid in 1978/9. If that happens you can move on to claim some of the tax you paid in 1979/80 on exactly the same basis, and then, if that is not enough, shift further forward to 1980/81.

The odds are that you will not use up all your losses in one year. You can go on using this procedure, claiming back funds you paid – for the first four years of running a business – provided you have made your losses and have not used up all the back tax you paid. The figures are not easy: once again, unless you are a genius with figures and want to spend your time on them, the work entailed makes it worth while to have someone who is professionally qualified to help you.

*Expenses* are also treated more leniently if you are on Schedule D. You can claim them if you have incurred them 'wholly and exclusively for the purpose of your business'. The point is that they do not have to be necessary. Advertising, for instance, can be wholly and exclusively to promote your business. But there is no way of judging whether it is necessary. For example, in the furniture business we cited, you may advertise furniture locally and make plenty of visits to prospective customers, for which you can claim all the costs of printing, paper, hoardings and transport, setting them against the pre-tax profits of your business.

Many people also make a point of working from home, claiming part of the cost of heating and lighting against taxable profits, because their own home counts as their office. If you take that course, you or your accountant should be canny enough not to tie you down to claiming for one particular room as an office, because there can be capital-gains-tax complications, described below. Meanwhile, you may employ your wife to act as your secretary, and can deduct the salary you pay her from your own tax bill. (This is a sensitive point with the Inland Revenue. Tax inspectors take a lot of care to see that she does genuinely work for you, that the pay is reasonable for what she does, and that you actually provide her with the money.) You can set some of your telephone bill against tax, and can also claim the cost of business postage. Meanwhile, your accountant has a whole army of other items that can appear, ranging from professional magazines in the trade to the cost of writing-paper, depreciation on typewriters and a great deal more.

The effect of being able to set expenses against the pre-tax profits you make from the business is considerable. If you pay at the 50 per cent tax rate on the top part of your income, and get nothing from outside, expenses are effectively costing you only half of what you have paid.

*Lodgers* are another possible source of income. If you are thinking of the idea, you should be careful to look not only at the rules on tax, but also at the law on security of tenure. The last thing you want is to be stuck with someone for life. You have to declare the income you collect each year, but you can put numerous expenses against it. Here again, you can claim for the cost of lighting and heating (in this case, for the lodger's room) and set the cost of a charlady and the cleaning materials she uses against the rent the lodger provides. The furniture used by the lodger loses its value as it gets older and the inspector will allow you to claim for some of the depreciation or often suggest an allowance of 10 per cent of the rent you take in. So, effectively, only 90 per cent of the rent is taxable. What worries people letting rooms is capital gains tax rather than income tax. As we show later in this chapter, in the capital-gains-tax section, it is very unlikely to come up.

The timing of your tax demand is curious. It comes, or should come, in November, half-way through the tax year, and is based on the previous year's profit. To add insult to injury, you will be taxed on money that you have not received. At the end of the year, you work out your figures, and if the original estimate was wrong, you will either have to pay more tax, or get a rebate.

## Separation and Divorce

Separation and divorce hit an ever-increasing number of people. Indeed, one in four of marriages in Britain ends in the divorce courts. The tax rules in the year of separation are relatively easy. From the moment that husband and wife split, they are each responsible for their own affairs. Men can claim the married man's allowance for the whole of the year in which they separate.

If their wives are at work until they part, they can set the wife's earned-income allowance against their pay, up to the date of separation. But once they separate, wives have the right to the single person's allowance in full, even if only a small part of the tax year remains. Once couples are divorced, both are two separate people again, and are treated as such in tax terms.

*Other allowances* depend on the circumstances. If, voluntarily, the husband maintained his wife completely for the period between separation and divorce he could perhaps qualify for the married man's allowance throughout. The mortgage is the biggest problem. Usually the tax relief on the interest will go to the husband, unless special arrangements are made. If there was a joint mortgage and each partner had paid part of the building society's bill, the inspector will split the relief in proportion to the respective contributions.

What if there are children to bring up? If the wife looks after them, she claims the additional personal allowance as the head of a single-parent family, which will provide, together with the single person's allowance, the same total tax-free income as a married man. This extra allowance does not only go to divorced people. It is available to widows, and unmarried mothers – or fathers – or anyone else who is actually bringing up children on her or his own.

*Maintenance payments* to a former wife and children may bring tax concessions, though that depends on the way in which they are organized. No help will appear unless the payments are regular and come under some agreement which is legally binding on the ex-husband. If the payments qualify for relief, the way in which the tax inspector treats them depends on whether they come under a court order, and on how large they are. Take payments under court order first of all.

One set of rules covers 'small maintenance payments', defined in 1979 as coming to less than £21 for the former wife, and under £12 a week for each child. The monthly equivalents, by the way, are £91 for a former wife – or even husband occasionally – and £52 a month for each child. With smaller payments of this kind, men give the money in full, but they have to make a point of telling the tax office that they are doing so. Officials can then adjust the PAYE coding to ensure that the men get tax relief on what they have provided. Meanwhile, ex-wives who get this help will have to pay tax on the money, assuming that they are taxpayers in the first place. Many of them may not be. In the rarer cases where funds flow from ex-wives to ex-husbands, the treatment is, of course, exactly the same.

If there is a legal agreement to provide the ex-wife with regular funds, the regulations are different from those which would apply under a court order. Whatever the size of the payments, they are treated as though they were maintenance payments that are over the small-payments limits. The ex-husband has, in effect, to deduct tax at basic rate before he makes the payments, though he has to let both his ex-wife and his tax office know that he is doing so. This is not so complicated as it seems. Assume that he wants to provide her with £2,000 a year pre-tax. On a basic rate of 30 per cent, he actually hands over £1,400 but, as it comes from his income, which has been taxed already, his ex-wife has in turn no tax liability on these payments. The one exception would come if she paid higher-rate tax. If that happened, the rules would make her pay the difference between the basic rate and her top rate of tax. If her top rate happened to be 45 per cent, for instance, she would have to pay tax at 15 per cent on the full £2,000 she received from her ex-husband.

### 'Golden Handshakes'

*'Golden Handshakes'* (usually, rewards for long service) can be one of the big preoccupations in the months before retirement. The 'handshakes' come into two categories as far as tax goes. First come the 'gratuitous payments' which the employer does not have to provide but which come as a mark of esteem. If you are going to receive one of them, tax treatment is relatively easy. The first £10,000 of what you receive is tax-free anyway, and it may well be more depending on what you earn and how long you have been with the company. Whatever is left over is subject to tax.

*Top-slicing* is the magic term which describes how the system copes with the extra, taxable part of a 'gratuitous payment'. It is a complex formula and worth going through in stages.

1. You work out all the other income you have received in your final, 'golden-handshake' year, *excluding* the job and

the 'handshake' itself. You then assess how much tax you will have to pay on this other income, which may come from dividends or consultancy fees, etc.

2. You add one-sixth of the taxable part of the 'handshake' you have received to this figure and work out what tax would be payable on the lot.

3. You take away the first answer from the second. Finally, you multiply the result of that subtraction by six and end up with the tax payable on the golden handshake itself.

One difficulty is that you cannot spread your payment at all, because the money has to come in one lump sum.

Redundancy money is treated in the same way.

*Service contracts* are treated differently. People who have been engaged to work for a fixed term of perhaps five years, only to discover that they do not get on with new management, perhaps, and are pushed out after two, can demand compensation. They will get some benefit from top-slicing, though it does not usually provide as much help on service-contract payments as it does with the alternative form of redundancy money we have just described. In tax terms, it makes far more sense to go for the kind of *ex gratia* payment we have just looked at, if you have the choice. One reason for getting an accountant to look at your service agreement before you start is to keep that kind of option open. The distinction between the two kinds of compensation is difficult and may not survive for much longer. Whitehall is already talking of abolition, though any changes in the law would have to go through Parliament.

## Retirement

*Pensions* are a big worry. Many people start on the completely false assumption that they will never have to pay tax on them. The truth is very different. Pensions, including the retirement pension, are almost all taxable. Admittedly, if you receive the basic retirement pension and no more, you do not have to pay tax on it, whether you are single or married. But that is only because it is smaller than the age allowances, which go to most people of sixty-five or over, so that with only a basic retirement pension you do not come into the tax bracket in the first place.

The ordinary state widow's pension is taxable, assuming, of course, that you are rich enough to pay tax at all, and the same goes for any pension which you collect from a former employer. The argument is that it is a form of deferred pay. The saving grace is that pensions are taxed as 'earned income' and not subject to the investment-income surcharge. War widows and disabled ex-servicemen are virtually the only exceptions to the general rule. Their pensions are completely tax-free.

Most pensioners, though, may have a tax bill. Its size, assuming you are a couple, depends not just on how much income you receive, but also on the wife's decisions in the past on National-Insurance contributions. Some women made a point of contributing to the higher-priced, 'big' NI stamp. They earned a pension in their own right, and so did not have to depend on their husband's contributions for their pension. That sounds like a technicality, but there are two points to remember – one on National Insurance, the other on tax. If a husband has fallen down on contributions – or has a bad record – it will affect not only his pension, but his wife's pension if she has to rely on his record. If she has made her own contributions via the 'big' stamp that is not a worry. What is more, if you are a pensioner with a wife who has earned her pension via her own NI contributions, you can claim an extra tax allowance – the wife's earned-income allowance – against your joint tax bill that postpones the point at which you come into the tax net. That would not be possible if she had paid for the 'small' stamp. Those two stamps are a matter of history now. Now everyone who starts work has to pay NI in full. What happens if she goes on working full time? Her employer then deducts both the tax on her earnings and the tax on her pension through the PAYE system before any money reaches her.

*The earnings rule* may be a problem, at least for a time. If you earn more than a certain sum each week – £52 at the moment – you start to lose your pension at the rate of 5p for every 10p that you are over the limit for the first £4. After that, you lose 5p of your pension for every extra 5p you earn. Once you receive £77·30 a week, the pension disappears completely. One comfort is that the rule does not go on for ever. It applies only to the first five years after normal retirement age, so that it runs out at sixty-five for women and seventy for men. Meanwhile, the government is committed to abolishing the earnings rule completely in due course.

*The age allowance* does not appear until the tax year in which you are sixty-five, even when you will usually retire at sixty as a woman. It will apply for a couple together if either husband or wife are past the age limit and as it is always higher than the normal personal allowance, it means that pensioners have a bigger band of tax-free income than other people, provided that they do not have a relatively high income, from savings for example. Once they receive more than a certain total, the age allowance gradually starts to fall.

Assume your income breaks through the tripwire, which stands at £5,900 in the tax year 1980/81. You will then find the age allowance dropping. It falls by £2 for every £3 that your income is over the limit. The extra part of the age allowance would have disappeared completely, leaving a couple with the personal allowances which normally apply to younger people only, if they had received more than £7,025 between them in 1980/81. There are building-society complications, too, which are described in the next section.

*Pensioners' savings* are always bedevilled by tax considerations. Most people in Britain have a building-society account, where the interest comes tax-paid, at least at basic rate. But the combination of high allowances and low incomes ensures that many of the elderly do not pay tax. The problem is that they cannot claim back the tax which the building society has paid before the money reaches them. The same reasons, incidentally, make a building-society account a poor proposition for a child. A bank deposit account, which pays interest without any deductions, is usually a better bargain.

Some elderly couples have a problem at the other end of the scale. Their building-society investment comes tax-paid all right. But because they are getting the age allowance, the inspector 'grosses up' what they have received to see what they would have needed to get before tax to receive the same return as the building society provides after it. Take an example in figures. Assume that a couple had got £300 in interest from the building society, and that the basic tax rate is 30 per cent. The inspector multiplies that £300 by 100 over 70 to discover the 'grossed up' figure. In fact the answer comes to £428·57. He then adds £428·57 to their joint income to see if they still qualify for age relief and, if so, whether they get it in part or in full. One point to remember is that it is his job to do the sums, and so you should only put down on the tax form what you actually receive. In fact, the instructions that go out with it make the point clear.

## Advice for Everyone

Many people find themselves in trouble on tax, particularly if they are self-employed, when they can all too easily sink into their own private whirlpool of panic. The essential point if you are filling in any tax form is to read the instructions which go with it, though apparently many people do not bother to do so. If you find the instructions incomprehensible, you can call in at your own tax office, or indeed at the PAYE inquiry office in your area, for it can summon your tax papers from the office dealing with them. PAYE local offices are listed in the telephone book under Inland Revenue. What the tax office cannot do is give you any advice on where you should invest money to avoid tax. The office will stock many of the simply written booklets which the Inland Revenue produces on the way in which particular groups of people are taxed, and is the place to get advice if you are in doubt about how income from savings or moonlighting should be taxed. If your worry is that too much tax is being deducted on your main job, you should probably check with the accounts department there first.

*Tax avoidance*, by the way, is perfectly legal. It merely means that you are using all the rules inside the system to ensure that you pay as little tax as you need to. *Tax evasion* means that you actually break the law in attempting to cut down tax bills. Tax inspectors examine about 3 or 4 per cent of the business accounts in Britain in great detail each year, and find that extra tax is due in the great majority of cases. Certainly the process of full investigation is disagreeable. Inspectors can go back for up to six years normally, but can indeed go as far back as 1937 if they suspect you of either fraud or almost bloody-minded neglect of your own affairs. If they suspect fraud on freelance earnings, for instance, you may well have to write for corroboration to everyone who has paid you for such work. On top of the back tax itself, there may well be penalties. The inspectors can demand the tax due, and interest on it – and then up to twice as much as the tax bill on top. Generally, though, the scale of penalties depends on how much they believe that your concealment was deliberate, how much co-operation you provide after the investigation begins, and whether you have been caught doing the same before.

Inspectors will not tell you what they know about your un-declared income. Instead, they will wait for you or perhaps your accountant to divulge the details in an interview with them.

*Appeals and payments* cause problems. Many people disagree with their tax inspectors about how much they should pay. If that applies to you on what you earn through your main job, the starting-point for inquiry is probably your accounts department, to ensure that they have got the right code. If they have not, write to the tax office which deals with your employer's accounts. Appeals against assessments on other income from savings or a second job should go straight to the tax inspector. It makes sense to send a carbon of the letter to the inspector to the tax collector, whose offices are elsewhere, so that he knows what is happening.

The Inland Revenue provides a form for setting out your objections, on which you have to state why you think that the inspector's demand is excessive and what proportion of the total you accept is accurate. You have to pay a proportion of the bill in advance if you are appealing, or at least it is prudent to do so. If you win your point on the tax in dispute, all is well. But if you lose, you have to pay interest at 9 per cent (in 1980, at any rate) on any money you have kept back, starting from the date when you were liable to settle it. If you and the inspector do not agree, the case will go up to the General Commissioners, who are local laymen with specialist knowledge, appointed to decide on disputes of the kind. It makes sense to check with a professional, like an account-ant or a solicitor, to see what chances you have before you start.

If the point on which you are disputing is particularly abstruse you can appeal to the Special Commissioners, who are profes-sionals. But, again, that only makes sense if you have consulted some financial specialist beforehand and got some idea of your chances. You cannot appeal beyond either group on the facts of the case, but only on the finer points of law, which would mean your going to law itself. That would not come cheap.

*Tax-office delays and interest.* The interest that you may have to pay on tax that is overdue will be backdated to the original payment date. But, for the tax office which has taken too much money from you, the rules are very different. Interest on any rebate does not appear until after the latter of two dates. The office will wait until the end of the tax year in which you actually made the overpayment – or twelve months after the end of the year to which the overpaid tax bill refers. So far so bad. What makes matters worse is that the interest at 9 per cent will only apply from then on, for there is no backdating. The one consolation is that it is, at least, tax-free.

*Saving for tax and calculating bills.* Certificates of tax deposit are one way in which you can save to pay your tax. They pay interest at rates which vary, generally moving up and down in line with what is happening elsewhere. You get a slightly lower return if you withdraw the deposits for cash, rather than using them to settle your tax bill. Whichever you do, the interest is taxable. If you have freelance earnings in addition to a regular job, a special account through which all such earnings and perhaps expenses can go also makes a lot of sense, for you then know how much of your income, outside the main job, is taxable.

Advice from the tax offices is usually good. Alternatively you can go to the local Citizens' Advice Bureau. Some of them in big cities have accountants who can help people whose figures have gone badly awry.

**Capital-Gains Tax**

Capital-Gains Tax is a levy not on income but on the profits you make on selling shares, pictures and certain other kinds of possessions and investments. The Inland Revenue charges you on the difference between the price at which you bought them and the higher price at which you sell them later. There is no allowance for any fall in the value of money in between, so that some of the gains it taxes are not real gains at all. If your gains are taxable (and there are many exemptions), the rates go as follows:

| Total gains in year of assessment | Tax chargeable |
|---|---|
| Up to £3,000 | None |
| Over £3,000 | 30% (of gains over £3,000) |

These rates only apply to your overall taxable gains. You can certainly deduct any losses you may have had as well as all the costs you have incurred, like dealing expenses for selling stocks and shares, auctioneers' fees, and so on, in the same year. If you have had tax losses in the previous year, you will be able to set them off against this year's gains.

You do not have to pay tax on:

The first £3,000 of gain each year.

The proceeds from selling your house (or 'main or principal residence' if you have more than one).

Proceeds of life-insurance policies.

Winnings from the football pools or windfalls from any other gambling.

Gains on gilt-edged stock (government securities) if you have held them for more than a year.

Profits from selling your car, if you are just a private individual.

All gifts are free of CGT – at least, if giver and receiver agree they should be. If your overall gains are under £3,000 a year, there can be a case for wanting gifts of private shares, for instance, to be taxable – when you know that you will not actually pay tax, because they are under the limit at which tax is actually chargeable. It can cut back tax-liability rates; but you should check with an accountant before making your commitment. But do not forget you may have to pay capital-transfer tax (see below) on them.

*Unit-trust and investment-trust gains* are taxable under this heading. Remember that gains mean the profits from the sale of the units. They have nothing to do with the payments from the units, which are taxed as income. The managers of the trusts now do not have to pay any tax on the gains that they make within their funds, which used to be the rule. If you are a small investor the change should leave you better off, assuming that there are any gains in the first place.

*Property rules* are not as ferocious as many people think. If you have lodgers in your own house, and claim some of the expenses which you incur, as a result, against the income-tax bill you have to pay on the rent, you may be worried that if the lodgers occupy one-third of the house, one-third of the profits you make when you come to sell the house will be liable to CGT. That will not happen, provided you share the same entrance and the same kitchen, and if you can always go into their rooms at any time. If your paying guest is part of the household, you do not have to pay CGT on any gain you make on the house when you come to sell it.

There are concessions, too, for people who own their own house, but have a sitting tenant living there who leads an independent life on one floor of the place with his own front door. If permanent tenants occupy less than half the house and your overall profit on the proportion they live in does not come to more than £10,000, you do not have to pay CGT. What is more, even if the profit goes over the limit, you can claim an exemption on the first £10,000 anyway.

The same fear of CGT can afflict people who work at home and claim part of the costs of heating and lighting as business expenses. If they make a claim for rooms comprising one-sixth of the area of the house, they could have to pay CGT on one-sixth of their profit when they come to sell it. Accountants can avoid that risk and get expenses all the same by ensuring that the claim is not made for the same room year after year. Even if you have to pay the levy, you may be able to postpone the evil day for some while. *Roll-over relief* may be the answer. If you move to another house, continue to work at home and claim expenses as you did before, you can defer paying the tax bill until the process ceases. Postponing bills in times of inflation is the same as cutting their cost. If you continue freelancing, or letting rooms for that matter, until you retire, you may never have to pay at all. The operation of retirement relief may come to your rescue anyway. It starts at sixty, and by the time you are sixty-one, you can claim relief on £10,000 of gains. By sixty-two, it moves up to an overall total of £20,000, and it rises in stages to a full £50,000 by the time you are sixty-five.

CGT first appeared in 1965, so that it does not apply to any gains before that. If you bought a house in 1950 and finally moved in 1980, you only have to pay tax on half the gains you have made over that time. Admittedly, you can work out your figures on the proportion of the increase in value which took place before 1965, as against the increase which came later, if you wanted. But you would be a financial masochist if you did.

## Capital-Transfer Tax

Capital-transfer tax is a levy on transfers of wealth – money, shares, property, or anything else – from one person to another. The great difference between CTT and the old death-duties system, which it replaced, is that the new tax does not just apply to what you leave after your death or to gifts you made in the seven years before it. It covers the whole of your life. CTT can penalize transfers of funds you make in your lifetime, though it contains an incentive to early generosity. The rate on lifetime gifts is only half that on what you leave on death, at least for the first £110,000, though you have to survive for three years after making your present for it to qualify as made in your lifetime. After that point, the rates progressively narrow.

There are many exemptions. CTT does not apply to:

Gifts from husband to wife, or vice versa, whatever their size.
Presents worth up to £2,000 in any one year.
Transfers of up to £250 a year to as many people as you want.
Gifts which are part of your normal spending, are made out of your income, not your capital *and* leave you with enough to keep up your normal standard of living.
Presents of up to £5,000 to your children when they get married.
Presents of up to £2,500 to grandchildren getting married.
Gifts of £1,000 to anyone else getting married.
All gifts to charities, provided you survive for twelve months.
Presentations of pictures to the National Gallery or other gifts to the nation.

There are other specialized exemptions, but they only apply to the very rich, who should know of them through their accountants.

Once your gifts become taxable, the Inland Revenue starts its list, and your transfers start to be recorded. You are not charged for them as you go along, but the list ensures that when you die and your estate is finally distributed, the inspectors know what rates to apply at that point. The first £50,000 of taxable gains are 'zero rated', so that you have to pay nothing on them. But making them starts you moving up the escalator towards the point at which there will be a levy. The exemptions, by contrast, do not affect your future liability at all. The rates in 'chargeable gifts' run as shown in Table 14. The point at which rates start to bite may seem high, but it may come earlier than you think. Assume that your affluence ensures that you have to pay CTT on what you have to hand over. The tax is based on what you give and not on what the recipient actually receives, so that you have to make some account of the tax due before making your transfer. If you want to provide some recipient with £1,000 on that 50 per cent rate, you will have to take £2,000 from your resources, giving half to him and half to the Inland Revenue.

Table 14 **Capital Transfer Tax Rates on 'Chargeable Gifts'**

| Slice of funds | Rate on gifts in your lifetime | Rate on gifts on death |
|---|---|---|
| £50,000 to £60,000 | 15 | 30 |
| £60,000 to £70,000 | 17½ | 35 |
| £70,000 to £90,000 | 20 | 40 |
| £90,000 to £110,000 | 22½ | 45 |
| £110,000 to £130,000 | 27½ | 50 |
| £130,000 to £160,000 | 35 | 55 |

and so on as the difference between the two rates narrows to, finally:

| £2,010,000 and upwards | 75 | 75 |

The system does something to soften the impact if one man dies and his immediate heir does so soon afterwards so that the family has to pay a second CTT bill soon after the first. If the second death occurs within a year of the first, you can credit 80 per cent of what you have paid on the first bill against the second levy. The proportion falls rapidly, and if the second death takes place three to four years later, the credit is down to 20 per cent, and it disappears completely thereafter.

There are various life-insurance schemes – based on whole-life policies – which you can use to cut back the bills your heirs may face. They are designed to mature as you die, paying for some or all of the CTT due on your estate.

# 9. Planning for Retirement

Your pension rights can easily be by far your greatest asset – worth more even than your home. Yet, as far as most people are concerned, pensions are a Black Hole in their financial planning – a mysterious area they do not even try to understand, let alone do anything about. It need not be so. Pensions admittedly take some understanding, but all that is needed is patience. And the exercise can be very worth while given the amount of money at stake – and the fact that most people actually have some scope to improve their pension lot.

Just how large the sums involved can be was illustrated recently by one of the big clearing banks in a staff booklet explaining its pension scheme. It calculated that a married man retiring, after full service, on pay of £6,000 a year is in line for pension benefits worth a total of at least £40,000. This was the figure that it would cost to put together a package of similar benefits bought from insurance companies. It was, if anything, on the low side because the pension included in the insurance-company package was geared to rise by just 8½ per cent a year, whereas the bank had given its pensioners rises averaging 11 per cent a year in the previous fifteen years.

This chapter outlines important points to bear in mind in planning for retirement. Here in summary are some of the main ones:

1. If you find you are in line for an inadequate pension, you may well have scope to increase it at little cost. This is because savings you channel into boosting your pension can qualify for enormous – if little-understood – tax subsidies. These are open to people in company schemes, the self-employed and private-sector employees depending solely on the state for their pension.

2. Your eventual pension from a company scheme may turn out

to be a good deal less than it looks on paper if you change jobs before retirement. Few private employers do anything to top up the pension rights of early leavers to compensate for inflation.

3. People working for private employers who depend on the state for their earnings-related pension have to contribute for at least twenty years before they get the full benefit. Even then their earnings-related pension is unlikely to be more than one-fifth of their pay at retirement. The saving grace of the state's arrangements is that they are fully inflation-proofed.

4. Many employers' schemes provide life insurance and sometimes a form of permanent health insurance. Watch the small print. You may not be covered for months or even years after you join the company and there may be other limitations on cover.

5. Millions of working wives paying the lower National Insurance stamp would be better off paying the full stamp.

6. You may be able to harness the value of your home to boost your retirement income. But the best schemes will not accept you until you are in your seventies.

7. The widows' benefits provided by the state earnings-related scheme are grossly inadequate.

## The Importance of Planning Ahead

A pound invested at an interest rate of 10 per cent should grow to about £45 in forty years if no tax is deducted along the way. That in a nutshell is the case for making the most of your pension opportunities.

Money invested for your pension builds up free of almost all tax. This almost unique privilege applies not only to anything invested for you in an employer's scheme but may also apply to extra saving you make off your own bat to add to your existing pension entitlements. If you are in an employer's scheme, you will have to route your extra savings through it to get the tax benefits. If you are self-employed or work for a firm without a private pension scheme, you can choose from a vast range of individual pension plans sold by insurance companies. The returns you get from investing in extra pension arrangements should far outshine what you would get from the alternative vehicle, an endowment policy.

Among the disadvantages you suffer if you save through an endowment policy rather than through pension arrangements are that:

1. The money invested for you in an insurance company's endowment fund pays tax of $37\frac{1}{2}$ per cent on income and 30 per cent on capital gains. Money invested for you in pension arrangements usually pays no tax on the income it accumulates or on capital gains. As Table 15 shows, a pound invested to earn an income of 10 per cent a year before tax in an endowment fund will grow to only £11 after forty years – less than a quarter of what it would come to in a tax-free pension fund.

2. The tax relief you get on insurance-policy premiums is usually far less than you get on pension contributions. The tax relief on endowment policies is $17\frac{1}{2}$ per cent of gross premiums at present – and falls to 15 per cent in April 1981. Pension contributions are usually deductible in full from your income for tax purposes, which means that for most people each £1 you contribute saves you 30p in tax (at current tax rates) and for people paying top rates the saving can be as much as 60p.

Saving through the pension route involves a few snags which should not matter to most people. The main disadvantages of pension-oriented saving are that:

1. Usually you cannot get at your money until age sixty at the earliest. The Inland Revenue, however, allows for retirement at earlier ages in one or two special cases such as airline pilots and foreign-currency dealers.

2. Only about a quarter of the capital accumulated for you in pension arrangements can be drawn as a lump sum – the rest has to be taken as pension. Lump sums are free of all tax; pension income is subject to income tax but, unlike most forms of investment income, it escapes investment-income surcharge.

3. If you die before retirement you may lose most or even all of what you invested.

If you are in a very good pension scheme, the benefits may be so large that you have little scope to top up your pension with voluntary contributions. But few schemes are this good.

Table 15 **Pension Plans versus Endowment Policies**
What a £1 investment grows to if it earns interest of 10 per cent
a year before tax

| Investment period | Endowment fund* | Pension fund |
| --- | --- | --- |
| 10 years | £1·83 | £2·59 |
| 20 years | £3·36 | £6·73 |
| 30 years | £6·16 | £17·45 |
| 40 years | £11·30 | £45·26 |

* An endowment fund normally pays income tax at a special rate of
37½ per cent. Pension funds pay no tax.

## What the State Provides

The basic element in almost everyone's retirement income is the
flat-rate state Old Age Pension. This is inflation-proofed, increasing every November in line with the latest rise in the cost of living.
The basic Old Age Pension rate in the year to November 1981 is
£27·15 a week and the allowance for a wife claiming on her
husband's contributions is £16·30. Generally you need to have
paid full National Insurance stamps for at least nine-tenths of
your working life to qualify for the full basic Old Age Pension.
Women usually get the pension at sixty, men at sixty-five.

A wife due an Old Age Pension on both her own contributions
and her husband's may claim on whichever record gives the higher
pension. Unless she has paid full stamps all her life, the allowance
from her husband's contributions will probably be higher but she
has to wait until he retires for the benefits. If she retires before him
she can in the meantime claim on her own record.

Apart from paying the Old Age Pension, the role of the state in
pensions is to:

1. Provide a national earnings-related pension scheme which
employers can put their workers into (as an alternative to running
a full-scale private scheme).

2. Make sure that schemes run by private employers as an
alternative to the state earnings-related arrangements meet certain standards.

3. Supplement pensions from such schemes where their real value has been badly eroded by inflation.

Since 1978, employers either have had to run an officially recognized private scheme for all grades of their workforce or have had to put their workers into the state scheme, that is, they have had to 'contract in'. For an employer to 'contract out' of the state earnings-related scheme, he or she has to provide benefits at least as good. So for employees who want to understand their pension entitlements, the starting-point must be to look at the state's arrangements.

*State earnings-related pensions.* For the purposes of the state's pension arrangements, a worker's pay is divided into three bands:

The first band is that part of pay up to about the level of the basic Old Age Pension: the limit is £23·00 a week in the tax year 1980–81 and will probably be £27·00 a week in 1981–82.

The second band runs from where the first band leaves off and goes up to about seven times the Old Age Pension rate. In 1980–81, for instance, the upper limit is £165 a week, well above the national average wage. In effect, for most workers, second-band pay is anything they earn above the Old Age Pension rate. If you are 'contracted in' to the state earnings-related arrangements your second-band earnings are your 'pensionable' pay and the pension you eventually get will be based effectively on them.

The third band is any pay a worker may have above the upper limit of the second band. There are no state contributions to pay on this part and it does not count towards state earnings-related pensions.

The boundaries of the bands change each April to reflect the increase in the previous November in the Old Age Pension rate. As the Old Age Pension rises in line with the cost-of-living index, this means that the whole band structure is automatically adjusted each year to compensate for inflation. Each element of pension is in effect revalued in each later year to maintain its real purchasing power in the face of inflation. When you retire, your revalued pension entitlements will be added up to calculate your pension. If you have been in the scheme more than twenty years your pension will be the total of your best twenty years' revalued entitlements. And in the case of people with twenty or fewer years' contributions, all their entitlements will be counted.

Before retirement, the revaluation of your pension entitlements will be based on increases in national pay averages; afterwards, your pension will rise in line with the cost-of-living index. For a worker with a full contribution record, the formula should mean an earnings-related pension equal to about one-quarter (twenty-eightieths) of his or her pensionable pay in the final year at work. In terms of total pay before tax in the final year, the proportion will probably be about one-fifth. These sums are based on the assumption, realistic in most cases, that the worker's final pay will be about the same as the real value of the pay earned in the best twenty working years.

*(In the rest of this chapter, we assume that the 1981/2 second-band boundaries, which had not been announced when this book went to press, will be £27 and £200 a week.)*

To see how the sums work in practice, take, for instance, a man earning £100 a week in the 1981–2 tax year. His pensionable pay is £73 a week (£100 less £27). So each year he is building up a pension entitlement of 91p a week (£73 divided by eighty). Multiply by twenty to get the total pension entitlement he will build up over twenty years or more: £18·20 in today's money.

The maximum earnings-related pension anyone can hope for from the state is about £43 a week in 1981–2 money. This is because the 1981–2 cut-off point in calculating pensionable pay is £200 a week. The maximum pensionable pay is, therefore, £173 a week (£200 less £27). One-eightieth of this is £2·16 a week and twenty-eightieths are £43·25. Adding in the single person's Old Age Pension, this gives a total retirement income of about £70 a week in 1981–2 money – about half today's average industrial worker's earnings.

## Company Pension Schemes

To contract out of the state scheme, a company pension scheme must promise a pension of at least one-eightieth of a worker's final pay for each year of service up to forty years. This means that someone who stays all their life in the same scheme should get a pension of at least half (forty-eightieths) of their final pay. Definitions of final pay vary between schemes but often it is the average of a worker's total basic pay before tax in the last three years. Overtime and other extras are often excluded. Many good schemes credit you with one-sixtieth of pay for each year of service. They, therefore, provide a lifetime member with a pension of two-thirds (forty-sixtieths) of final pay. As the contracting-out rules did not take effect until 1978, employers are not required to give credit for service before that date. In practice, however, most contracted-out employers had occupational pension schemes before 1978 and so will pay pensions in respect of service before the contracting-out rules came in.

The rules mean that most workers should be far better off in a contracted-out scheme than in the state scheme. Take, for instance, a worker earning £75 a week in 1981–2. After a lifetime in an 'eightieths' scheme he or she will retire on half pay – about £37·50 a week in today's money. That compares with the around £12 a week that can be expected from the state earnings-related arrangements. A worker earning £140 a week could be in line for a pension of nearly £93 a week (two-thirds of £140) from a company with a sixtieth scheme but would get only £28 a week from the state earnings-related scheme.

One snag about private pension schemes is that there is no obligation to increase pensions once they are in payment. The state, however, provides supplementary bonuses to protect contracted-out pensions partially from inflation. The state bonuses are linked to that part of your pension which you would have received in any case if you had been, instead, in the state earnings-related scheme. This is called your 'guaranteed minimum pension'. The state's bonuses are geared to maintaining the real purchasing power of guaranteed minimum pensions. To see how this works in practice, suppose, for instance, you retire on a pension of £60 a week from your employer and £20 of this is your guaranteed minimum pension. If after your first year in retirement the cost of living has risen 10 per cent you will then get a state bonus of £2 a week (10 per cent of £20). And if after ten years the cost of living has doubled your state bonus will rise to £20 a week.

The state inflation-proofing is provided in addition to any

increase you may get from your employer. Some employers provide almost complete inflation-proofing for their pensioners. Others provide occasional rises which only partly compensate for inflation. But many employers still provide no pension increases.

*How changing jobs can hit your pension rights.* If you move from one contracted-out firm to another you stand to lose out on your pension rights.

You may have a choice of:

1. Accepting a 'frozen' pension. This is a pension preserved for you by your old employer and normally linked to your pay when you left him.

2. Transferring your pension rights to your new employer. Your old employer will pay a transfer value to buy you rights in the new scheme but usually these will be far less than you had in the old one.

3. Extinguishing part of your pension rights in return for a refund of some of your contributions. Under legislation which took effect in 1980 refunds are available only for contributions you made before April 1975 or for short periods of service. Usually you cannot reclaim contributions made on your behalf by your employer so you have to wave goodbye to them for ever.

In its most basic form a frozen pension offers no protection against inflation: if pay levels rise in the meantime, a pension linked to your pay years ago will look minute when you come to claim it.

The frozen-pensions formula has been modified by the state earnings-related arrangements: now at least part of your entitlement is inflation-proofed under the guaranteed-minimum-pension arrangements. Every year you work in a contracted-out job your guaranteed minimum pension (GMP) increases. The GMP you can expect from a lifetime of contracted-out work should be about the same as the earnings-related pension you would have had if you were in the state scheme. For those who had fewer than twenty years to go to retirement in 1978, GMPs are calculated in exactly the same way as state earnings-related pensions, that is, the total entitlement is built up from eightieths of your revalued pay in each year.

For those who had more than twenty years to go, every year's revalued earnings are included, not just the twenty best years used for the state scheme. But the fraction of each year's earnings you are credited with is less than one-eightieth: the more years involved the smaller the fraction. The formula means that if, for instance, you clock up forty years in contracted-out jobs the fraction of each year's earnings that is counted is half of one-eightieth, that is, one one-hundred-and-sixtieth (1/160th). The idea is that the total of the fractions in each case should add up to one-quarter.

In some cases the burden of preserving your GMP entitlements may be transferred to your new employer, but in view of the inflation-proofing required few employers choose to take them over.

The rest of your pension rights – the part not covered by the GMP provisions – will usually remain with your former employer to be paid eventually when the time comes. Your old employer can in theory transfer the bill to your new employer, but this now rarely happens. In any case the pension-fund managers usually calculate the transfer value so that it just matches the cost of preserving a frozen pension for you. GMPs are also preserved for you if you move from a contracted-out job to a contracted-in one. In this case the total amount of your GMP from both contracted-in and contracted-out work will be exactly what you would have had if you had been in the state scheme all the time. Your private scheme employers will have to make arrangements for that part of your GMP clocked up in their service; the state then makes up the balance.

## What Your Pension Costs

The common element in most people's National Insurance contributions is a levy of $6\frac{3}{4}$ per cent on the first band of pay and this goes towards paying for your Old Age Pension and other basic National Insurance benefits. In the tax year 1980–81, the levy worked out at £1·55 a week ($6\frac{3}{4}$ per cent of £23·00). Contracted-in workers pay $6\frac{3}{4}$ per cent on their second-band earnings as well. Contracted-out workers pay National Insurance contributions of $4\frac{1}{4}$ per cent on their second-band pay. They also usually have to contribute to their employers' schemes – a typical employer with a contributory scheme charges about 5 per cent of pay.

Contributions to the state earnings-related scheme, like other National Insurance contributions, do not qualify for tax relief. Contributions to employers' schemes do: within generous limits anything you pay is counted as a deduction from your income for tax purposes.

Many women who were married before 1978 have the right to stay out of the state's earnings-related arrangements. They pay the 'lower stamp', 2 per cent on both their first- and second-band earnings.

The self-employed pay contributions in two parts: the first is a flat rate, which is £2·50 a week for most people in the year to April 1981. They also have to pay 5 per cent of any net earnings they have between £2,650 and £8,300 a year. Their payments buy only the basic Old Age Pension plus basic state widow's pension and a few other small benefits.

*The false economy of the lower stamp.* Wives who pay the lower-rate stamp can stay on it indefinitely provided they remain at work and remain married. But they have the option to change to higher stamps at the beginning of each tax year; and if they analyse the figures, they will probably find that the switch is worth making. Paying the lower stamp means a saving of 4·75p in every £1 of earnings for wives working for contracted-in employers; wives with employers who run contracted-out pension schemes save 4·75p for every £1 they earn up to the Old Age Pension rate and 2·25p for every £1 of second-band earnings. These savings are tempting, but they are put in the shade by the size of the benefits most wives are in line for if they pay the full stamp.

Broadly, women who are not in company schemes have most to gain from paying higher stamps because otherwise they will have no pension in their own right. Take, for instance, the case of a woman currently earning £50 a week who has five years to go to retirement age. To switch from the lower stamp to the full contracted-in stamp, she has to raise her contributions from £1·00 a week to £3·37 a week. Her extra payments will add up to an investment of £620 over the remaining years of her working life.

This will buy pension of £1·44 a week measured in today's money – £75 a year. So if she lives for nineteen years after retirement – the average life expectancy for a woman at retirement age – she will collect pension with a purchasing power of £1,420 in real terms over the years. Assuming a realistic inflation rate, the total she will actually collect will be many times this – in fact, the higher inflation is the better the full stamp will prove compared to other investments. But even with no inflation, she stands to get back more than twice what she paid in.

The more a woman earns the more it makes sense for her to pay the full stamp. These examples show how much better an investment the higher contributions are for well-paid women than for the lower-paid:

*Case 1:* A wife with five years to go to retirement earning £100 a week with a contracted-in employer. To change up to the full stamp will cost her £4·75 a week (4·75 per cent of £100). So her total investment over five years will be £1,235. For this she is promised an earnings-related pension of five-eightieths of her pensionable pay, so she gets about £4·56 a week in real terms for the rest of her life. With average life expectancy of nineteen years from age sixty, she can, therefore, look forward to a total return of about £4,500 in real money – more than three and a half times her investment.

*Case 2:* A wife of the same age earning £40 a week with a contracted-in employer. To change up to the full stamp will cost her £1·90 a week. Her total investment over five years will come to about £500. Her earnings-related pension of five-eightieths of pensionable pay comes to only 81p a week. That amounts to a return of about £800 over nineteen years – little more than 1½ times her investment.

For wives in line for a pension from a contracted-out employer, the main benefit of paying the higher stamp is that it will provide them with an element of inflation-proofing. This results from the state's undertaking to provide cost-of-living bonuses to maintain the real value of the guaranteed-minimum-pension element of contracted-out pensions. If inflation is low, this benefit will be worth little; but even at a relatively modest rate of inflation of 10 per cent, inflation-proofing protection will be worth buying, particularly in the case of better-paid wives.

Take the case of a contracted-out wife earning £100 a week with the chance of paying one full year's higher National Insurance contributions before retirement. The contracted-out stamp will cost her £2·92 a week extra over her present contributions, making a total investment of £152 over the year. This buys her inflation-proofing for 91p a week of her employer's pension under the guaranteed-minimum-pension arrangements. If prices double every seven years (equivalent to an annual inflation rate of about 10 per cent), after seven years she will be getting a state inflation-proofing bonus equivalent to 91·25p a week. After fourteen years (when prices will have quadrupled) she will be getting an inflation-proofing bonus of £2·74 (£2·7375 to be precise) a week – equal to approximately £142 in a year.

Contracted-in wives in their twenties and thirties may find it makes sense to put off paying the full stamp until they reach forty: as only a maximum of twenty years is counted in the state scheme, a forty-year-old woman will still have enough time to clock up a full contribution record. Contracted-out wives, however, must pay full stamps every year they work if they are to build up a full guaranteed minimum pension.

As a result of the complexity of the sums involved, many wives who remain on the lower stamp are not aware of what a false economy this is. Part of the problem is that even experts like solicitors, accountants, personnel officers and Citizens' Advice Bureau staff do not appreciate how good the benefits from the state earnings-related scheme can be. They advise against the higher stamp simply because once a wife has been paying the lower stamp for a few years she has cut herself off from getting a basic Old Age Pension in her own right: it does not occur to many advisers that the earnings-related benefits on their own are worth paying for.

A further incentive to wives to pay the full stamp is that if they later give up work to have children or look after elderly relatives the state will, for no charge, continue to credit them with contributions towards their basic Old Age Pension. They can earn credits in this way for up to twenty years provided they can show their presence at home was needed to see to family responsibilities. Women who paid the lower stamp before they gave up work have in any case no choice but to pay the full stamp if they return to work after more than two complete tax years' absence.

Paying the full stamp can be a hedge against divorce. After a divorce, a woman may have to rely mainly on her own contributions for her state-pension entitlements. Her claim on her ex-husband's record is limited to contributions he made when he was married to her.

## Taking a Cash Sum at Retirement

Many private pension schemes give you the option at retirement to exchange part of your pension rights for a large tax-free lump sum. If the fund managers have calculated the cash sum to be a fair swop, there is a strong case on tax grounds for taking it: this is because you can buy an annuity – an annual income for the rest of your life – with it and annuity income is taxed more favourably than pension. The maximum cash sum you can take under Inland Revenue rules is one and a half times your annual pay and for that you need to have had at least twenty years' service. Every year by which your service falls short of twenty years will mean a major reduction in your lump-sum entitlement. With fourteen years' service, for instance, your lump sum should be no more than nine months' pay. With nine years' service, you get just four and a half months' pay.

In most schemes, the cut you have to take in your yearly pension will be equal to one-ninth of the lump sum in the case of sixty-five-year-old men and one-eleventh in the case of sixty-year-old women. For a man retiring on a salary of £6,000 a year who takes a lump sum of £9,000, the rules mean he will lose pension of £1,000 a year: so if his full uncommuted pension would have been £4,000 a year he will end up with £3,000 a year.

At most times in the recent past, a sixty-five-year-old man has been able to get an annuity income well above £1,000 for a £9,000 lump sum, so taking cash has made sense. The figures look even better after tax because a large part of an annuity income is treated as a repayment of capital to the annuitant, so it is exempt from tax. One snag of annuity income, however, is that it may be subject to investment-income surcharge where you have a large income, whereas pension counts as earned income. Anyone in line for automatic pension increases after retirement has less to gain from commuting their pension, because it takes a very large sum to compensate for the loss of a rising income.

## Buying Extra Pension

Most people have scope to increase their pensions by making extra payments off their own bat, and usually these payments qualify for full tax relief. Employed people get tax relief on total contributions of up to 15 per cent of their salary which they put into their employer's scheme. So a typical company-scheme member already paying 5 per cent in basic contributions, for instance, can claim tax relief on further contributions up to 10 per cent of his or her salary. These voluntary contributions will be treated separately and will add to the employee's eventual pension rights.

If you are relying on the state for the whole of your pension, you have even more headroom for making extra payments towards your pension, since nothing of what you pay to the state counts against the 15 per cent limit. If you are in a company scheme, you have to channel your extra payments through it. If you are not in a company scheme, you are treated as self-employed for pension purposes by the Inland Revenue so you can choose from a vast range of self-employed pension plans on the market.

Until recently only a handful of company schemes were geared to cope with voluntary contributions from members. Now, although they are still only a minority, many more firms recognize what a boon it is for a worker to be able to save in this way. If your employers do not yet have this facility they may well install it if you ask. Some employers are happy to pay the administration charges involved and many insurance companies have ready-made systems to deal efficiently with the extra paperwork entailed.

Usually any voluntary contributions you make to a private scheme share in the fund's full investment performance, so, thanks to the fund's freedom from taxes, they should build up into a handsome capital sum by your retirement. Then, within the overall limits laid down by the Inland Revenue, you can take part of the capital as cash and the rest as pension of one form or another.

Table 16 shows that even if you assume only a conservative growth rate of 10 per cent for the pension fund's investments, the rate of return after taking account of tax relief can be phenomenal. If, for instance, you put aside £500 a year for five years before retirement, you can expect to build up a capital sum of £3,358. The total amount you will have invested is £2,500 but the real cost to you will be only £1,750 after tax relief at, say, 30 per cent. That means that your investment will have nearly doubled. And, if you can take the money in a lump sum at the end, the net rate of return you will have had will be 22·6 per cent a year. For anyone claiming tax relief at 45p in the pound, the net rate of return would be an almost unbelievable 31·4 per cent a year and for people on top rates of tax the figures are astronomic.

Usually the leeway between the pension you are in line for on your compulsory contributions and the maximum the Inland Revenue will allow you to take out of the scheme is so large that it will accommodate all the extra saving you are capable of. In most cases your extra contributions will be fully absorbed in improving

Table 16 **Voluntary Pension Contributions: How Your Money Grows**
Return on £500 invested each year

| Starting age | Cash value at age sixty-five | Net annual yield if you pay | |
|---|---|---|---|
| | | 30 per cent tax | 45 per cent tax |
| 45 | £31,506 | 13·2 per cent | 14·4 per cent |
| 50 | £17,477 | 14·0 per cent | 16.6 per cent |
| 55 | £8,766 | 16·2 per cent | 20·4 per cent |
| 60 | £3,358 | 22·5 per cent | 31·4 per cent |

Figures are based on the assumption that the fund's investments will grow by 10 per cent a year and that the benefits can be taken as a lump sum.

*Source:* Legal & General Assurance Society Ltd.

your pension to the maximum level allowed by the Inland Revenue. But if there is something left over, it can, for instance, be used to build up extra benefits for your dependants or to buy some protection against inflation. If you had enough money you could, for instance, arrange for the whole of your pension to rise by 5 per cent for every year you draw it.

To see how topping up your pension can work in practice take the case of a man earning £6,000 a year who retires at sixty-five after twenty years' service with his present employer.

In a typical good scheme his service would put him in line for a pension of £2,000 a year (twenty-sixtieths of pay): if he commutes this to £1,500 a year he will get a lump sum of three-eightieths for each year of service, i.e. £4,500. But in fact he has enough service to be allowed under Inland Revenue rules to take out up to £3,000 a year from the scheme plus cash of £9,000. There is, therefore, a gap of £1,500 a year pension plus £4,500 cash which can profitably be filled: that will require a capital sum of £18,000, which can be built up by making extra contributions of about £300 a year to the scheme. If the same man retires after just ten years' service he will probably get £750 a year pension plus £2,250 cash from a typical scheme. That compares with up to £3,700 a year in pension and £2,700 in cash which the Inland Revenue would allow him to take out of the scheme. Any level of saving he is likely to be capable of will probably not make full use of the opportunity: £700 a year, for instance, will build up to only £12,272 and provide only £1,450 a year pension and £450 cash.

One of the biggest opportunities for using voluntary contributions is in improving the post-retirement widow's pension. In a typical scheme this will work out at less than half the Inland Revenue maximum.

You can usually leave voluntary contributions in your scheme if you change jobs; normally there is no question of them being frozen and you should benefit as much from them as if you had not moved jobs. In calculating what the Inland Revenue will allow you to take out of your pension scheme, one snag can be the benefits preserved for you by previous employers. Frozen benefits may sometimes have to be deducted first in arriving at the maximum the tax man will allow from your present scheme. Inflation will, however, probably mean that any frozen pension you are due is so small that it will make little difference to the sums. Normally you have to undertake to make contributions for five years to get the tax advantages. But, of course, if you change jobs in the meantime this condition is waived. In fact, for anyone who expects to move jobs before retirement, making additional voluntary contributions is often about the only thing they can do to meet the gap in their pension planning caused by low transfer values.

## The Self-Employed

Anyone who is not covered by a company pension scheme is free to take out an individual pension plan enjoying the usual pension-scheme tax privileges. These plans – sometimes known as 'self-employed deferred annuities' – are provided by the insurance industry and sold in much the same way as endowment policies. Salesmen concentrate on the self-employed, but about 6 million employed people relying solely on the state scheme for earnings-related benefits are also eligible. For anyone who has the choice between a pension plan and an endowment policy as a savings vehicle for retirement, the pension plan's tax advantages usually far outweigh its minor disadvantages. The chief of these is that your money is locked up until age sixty or later and there is not even a surrender value. And on retirement most of the cash value you build up has to go towards buying a pension, which is liable to tax, and only a quarter can be taken as a tax-free lump sum.

Figures supplied in 1979 by Equitable Life show that for the same net cost to you the cash value you can build up in a pension plan over fifteen years works out about half again as much as you would have got from a fifteen-year endowment policy. Equitable Life used for its sums the case of a man of fifty who could afford to save £200 a year net. He could look forward to a pay-out of £6,700 from the endowment at sixty-five and nearly £10,400 from the pension plan. It was assumed he would claim tax relief at a rate of 30p in the pound on the pension contributions. For the endowment, there was a tax subsidy of about £42 to be added to his net premium bringing the total investment for him each year to £242.

The self-employed qualify for full tax relief on pension contributions, totalling up to $17\frac{1}{2}$ per cent of 'net relevant earnings' each year. Net relevant earnings are all earnings from non-pensionable work less deductions for such things as expenses, trading losses, capital allowances and mortgage interest.

Traditional pension plans come on either a with-profits or without-profits basis, as with endowment policies. There is also a unit-linked version, which is discussed in Chapter 10. For most people, a with-profits plan offers the right combination of stability and growth. A without-profits plan guarantees a larger pension at the outset but the bonuses the with-profits plan accumulates over the years mean that, barring a financial disaster, it should be the better performer in the end. The leading firms in the pension-plan field are those which also usually do well with endowment policies. Among companies which have done consistently well for pensioners in the past are National Provident, Prudential, Scottish Provident, Norwich Union and Equitable Life.

Under the recently introduced 'open market option' arrangements, you have the right at retirement to transfer the full capital value built up for you to another company, which will then be responsible for paying your pension. This option may be useful if your company pays lower-than-usual pensions per £1,000 of capital built up for you; but in many cases, in practice, companies by offering special bonuses to those who stay make it unattractive for the option to be exercised.

One major way in which pension plans can differ from endowment policies is that you need not tie yourself down to paying a set premium each year. You can instead buy a series of single-premium contracts, where each year's premium or premiums buy a separate element of your pension. The tax rules do not require you to keep up premiums for any set period – unlike endowment policies, you can claim tax relief no matter how few premiums you pay. Single-premium plans avoid the problems that arise with regular premiums when you suddenly discover you can no longer continue paying. The self-employed never know when they may have to wind up a pension plan prematurely: bad trading or ill-health, for instance, may force them to go into an ordinary job as an employee, when they would no longer qualify for the same tax relief. They may also have to give up their self-employed status if their business is taken over or as a result of a change in company law.

A single-premium arrangement should also be the first choice of employed workers in non-pensionable jobs. They never know how long they can keep up paying, because their employer may unexpectedly introduce a company scheme or they may suddenly find they want to move to a company with its own scheme. In a single-premium plan each year's contributions are invested separately and the amount of pension they buy depends mainly on how far away you are from retirement. A single investment of £500 with Legal & General should buy pension of about £1,272 a year plus a cash sum of £3,816 for a thirty-year-old planning to retire at sixty-five. A forty-year-old can expect only £541 a year plus £1,623 cash. A fifty-year-old is in line for only £201 a year plus £603 cash. In each case the figures are for plans where contributions are returned to your estate if you die early. If you opt for no return of premiums, you get slightly more pension.

Most self-employed pensions in payment cease immediately on the death of the pensioner. If you pay slightly more you can arrange for a pension to be guaranteed up to age seventy, meaning that if you die between sixty-five and seventy, the balance of the benefits you were due up to seventy will be paid to your widow.

If you take out a single-premium contract and then have to stop contributing prematurely, you usually have to accept a 'paid-up' pension. Sometimes the arrangement is that the pension you eventually get will be scaled down in direct proportion to the number of years of the planned term in which you will not be contributing. If, for instance, you stop half-way through the term, you will have to accept just half the pension you would have had with full contributions. This is unfair, because the early premiums of a regular contract buy a much bigger proportion of the total promised pension than the later ones. Even with companies which aim to give fairer paid-up values, someone who has to drop out early from a regular plan will find in most cases he will not do as well as he would have done with single premiums. Paid-up values are often miniscule or non-existent in early years and it takes them a long time to build up into anything.

Take, for instance, the case of a thirty-year-old man who pays £500 a year into a regular premium plan and stops after five years. One major company which prides itself on good paid-up values would provide him with a pension of £5,188 a year plus £15,565 cash at sixty-five. If he had instead paid five single premiums of £500 he would be in line for £5,486 a year plus £16,459. Despite the drawbacks of regular-premium contracts for most savers, it suits salesmen to promote them, because the commission is better. A salesman usually gets 25 per cent of the first two years' premiums when he sells a regular plan to anyone aged forty-five or under. Commission is scaled down for higher ages depending on how close the client is to retirement. The commission on single-premium contracts is just 3 per cent of each year's payments, so the client has to contribute for seventeen years for the salesman to earn as much commission as he would have from a regular contract. In the meantime there is always the danger that the client will drop out early – he may cease to be self-employed or, worse, he may be persuaded to buy another plan by a rival salesman.

The disadvantage of single premiums is that if you pay them all your working life you will end up with a slightly smaller pension than you would get from a regular premium plan. The shortfall, which reflects the insurance company's higher administration costs, should not, however, be more than 1 or 2 per cent in the case of a good plan.

The self-employed and others not in a company pension scheme are entitled to special tax privileges in buying life insurance. Provided the policy is of the pure protection type – that is, that it has no savings element – and provided it meets one or two other criteria, the premiums can be deducted in full from your income for tax purposes. Equitable Life in particular has made a special effort to tailor policies to make the most of the tax concessions. Another way to provide for your family is to take out a separate widow's pension for your wife. Premiums up to 5 per cent of your income earn you full tax relief. But anything you spend on this score counts against your allowance of 17½ per cent of income which you can put into a pension plan for yourself.

The detailed tax rules on self-employed pensions are extremely complicated. Here are some of the more significant points:

*Tax relief.* Tax relief generally takes effect in the year of assessment, rather than the business year concerned.
*'Carry-forward' and 'carry-back'.* The annual limits on qualifying contributions are modified by arrangements to allow for the

fluctuating and unpredictable nature of self-employed people's earnings. The rules were substantially overhauled by the 1980 Finance Act and, as of 1980/81, the main provision is that the self-employed can carry forward unused relief in respect of earnings going back up to six years. Thus, in the case of 1980/81 contributions, the maximum amount allowable can be boosted by unused relief from earnings going back as far as 1974/5. The 1980 Finance Act specified the order in which the various bits of relief are to be used. If the premium paid in the current year exceeds net relevant earnings and if the carry-forward of unused relief from earlier years is available, the earliest year is taken first.

It is also possible to 'carry-back' contributions. Under the 1980 Finance Act, pension contributions paid in a year of assessment may be treated as paid in the previous year – or, in some cases, the one before that. Certain carry-back provisions under earlier legislation also apply in 1980/81 to ease the transition to the new arrangements.

*Restrictions on benefits.* The Inland Revenue insists that pensions should not normally be payable earlier than age sixty or later than seventy-five. Any lump-sum death benefit to the self-employed person's survivors should not exceed the total of his contributions plus reasonable interest. Any pension payable to a surviving spouse should not exceed that payable or being paid to the self-employed person.

*Early retirement.* The Inland Revenue permits a lower-than-normal retirement age for certain occupations – currency dealers and North Sea divers, for instance. The option to take the pension early must be written into the contract from the outset. A self-employed person should think carefully before taking advantage of this concession because if later he changes his mind about early retirement he many find himself circumscribed by a rule requiring him to take his pension not later than ten years after the earliest date allowed in the contract. People who because of illness cannot continue to work in their chosen occupation or a similar one may get Inland Revenue approval to draw their pension early.

*Contribution levels for older people.* People born before 1916 may be allowed rather more generous contribution limits – ranging in 1980/81 from 20½ per cent, for those born in 1914 or 1915, up to 32½ per cent, for those born in 1907 or earlier. These limits, however, only apply where a person has no entitlement to a pension from an employer's scheme.

## Widows' and Widowers' Pensions and Benefits

Here are the main benefits a widow may qualify for on her husband's pension and National Insurance contributions:

*The basic flat-rate state widow's pension.* This is equal to the basic old-age pension. It is aimed mainly at helping widowed mothers (and in this instance is known to officials as the widowed mother's allowance). Other women may qualify for part or all of the pension if they are widowed between forty and sixty. Payments cease at sixty.

*State orphans' benefits.* These work out at a little less than one-third of the old-age pension for each dependent child. In the year to November 1981, the rate is £7·50 per child. Most children cease to be considered dependants soon after they reach sixteen (the official cut-off point is when the child ceases to get child benefits).

*Earnings-related widows' pensions.* In most cases where a widow's husband was an employed worker she gets some earnings-related benefits either from a company scheme or the state. The state benefits, known to officials as additional state widow's pension, are usually small and depend on how much her husband had contributed. Widows of men in company schemes may do much better.

*Old-age pension.* Most women widowed after retirement get the full old-age pension and it is paid also on retirement to women who before were receiving a full or scaled-down flat-rate widow's pension.

*Widow's allowance.* This is paid to all women widowed before they reach sixty or before their husbands reach sixty-five. The benefit rate works out at a little over one-quarter the current national average earnings and payments continue for six months only. In 1980-81, the rate is £38·00 a week.

In most cases, where a woman remarries her state widow's

benefits cease and in theory they also cease if she lives with a man on whom she is deemed to be dependent. Many company-scheme widows' pensions these days continue after a woman remarries.

*Qualifying for a state widow's pension.* A widowed mother gets the full flat-rate state widowed mother's allowance until her last child is off her hands. After that she is treated as if she were a woman of the same age who has just been widowed without dependants.

If a woman without dependants is widowed before forty, she gets no flat-rate widow's pension. If she is widowed between forty and fifty she gets a proportion of the full rate, ranging from 30 per cent for a forty-year-old to 93 per cent for a forty-nine-year-old. Whatever proportion is fixed at the start remains in force subsequently – there are no increases simply because she grows older (so the only rises she can expect are for inflation). If she is widowed between fifty and sixty she gets the full flat-rate widow's pension.

*Earnings-related widows' pensions.* The rules for qualifying for a widow's pension from the earnings-related part of the state scheme follow closely those for the flat-rate widow's pension. Generally, where a widow of a contracted-in worker is entitled to a flat-rate pension she is also entitled to an earnings-related pension from the state. Where a scaled-down flat-rate pension is payable, the earnings-related widows' pensions will be scaled down in proportion. And, as with the flat-rate pension, the earnings-related pension is not paid to women widowed under forty without dependants. Also, it ceases where a widowed mother's children cease to be dependent before she reaches forty.

Except where benefits cease before forty, state earnings-related widow's pensions generally continue until you die or remarry. And where a scaled-down pension was being paid before retirement under rules for women between forty and fifty, the full amount becomes payable afterwards.

A woman widowed after both she and her husband retire usually inherits the whole of his state earnings-related pension. She can continue to collect anything she is due in her own right from the scheme, provided the combined pensions do not exceed the maximum pension that one person can clock up. Measured in

1981–2 money, that means the most a widow can hope for from the combined pensions is about £43 a week.

Where a man dies before retirement and his widow is entitled to state benefits, the full earnings-related entitlement will be simply the pension that would be paid to a person retiring on the same contributions record. If the husband had contributed for only five years, for instance, the full widow's entitlement would be just five-eightieths of his average revalued pensionable pay. For a man who paid the maximum contribution rate – that is, someone who is earning in 1981–2 at least £200 a week – the full widow's pension after five years' contributions will be only £10·81 a week.

The widow of a man in a full company scheme is guaranteed at least as much pension as she would have had if he had been in the state scheme. In the case of men who have not been with the company many years, that may not amount to much; but many good schemes give husbands credit not only for their contributions to date but for years of service they might have completed if they had lived until retirement. In the case of contracted-out workers who die in retirement, a widow may get up to two-thirds of her husband's company pension.

*Widowers' pensions.* A few company pension schemes pay pensions to husbands of women members who die early. Many schemes, however, provide life insurance on the lives of female as well as male members and the cover often ranges up to five times the member's yearly salary.

There is usually no specific provision for children of single women in company pension schemes. The most that a woman's children can usually expect is an *ex gratia* payment, and most schemes allow the trustees discretion in such cases.

The state provides pensions for widowers aged sixty-five or over and whose wives die after reaching sixty. They inherit their wives' earnings-related pension entitlements in the same way that widows inherit their husbands' where both are over pension age.

## Annuities

An annuity is an arrangement which allows a pensioner to swap his capital for a guaranteed income which will continue for the rest of his life. This means that the older you are when you buy an annuity the higher the income you can expect. Some plans provide for increases in the income as the years go by but most pay the same income each year. If you are hard-pressed, an annuity can be a good way of squeezing the last penny out of your capital. Annuities offer you the chance to run down your capital in an orderly way. If instead you dig into your savings as you go along, you risk being left very short at the end: there is always the chance that you will live longer than the average and you would then have very depleted resources for your last years.

Annuity income is taxed on a specially favourable basis, because part of each year's payments is regarded as repayment of the capital you invested. For a man of seventy-five, for instance, more than half his annuity income will usually be tax-free. If he invested £10,000 to buy an annuity of about £2,000 a year, he would have to pay tax on only £875 so his annual tax bill would be only about £260 assuming he was paying tax at 30p in the pound.

Special ready-made plans, sometimes called 'home-income plans', are provided by insurance companies which allow you to borrow against the value of your home to buy an annuity. The best-known plans are run by Hambro Provident and by the Save & Prosper group. The idea is that the insurance company provides a large mortgage secured on the pensioner's home. The loan will buy an annuity large enough not only to cover interest payments to the insurance company but to provide a worthwhile amount of free income for the pensioner. No repayments on the loan are due in the pensioner's lifetime. The loan will be repaid eventually when his or her house or other assets are sold after he or she dies.

Usually you need to be over seventy for the idea to work properly: at younger ages, annuity rates are not high enough to provide enough free income. Where both partners in a marriage are still living, these schemes are usually based on a 'joint life–last survivor' annuity, that is, the annuity income continues until the death of the surviving partner. But this means a much lower income for the size of your borrowing. Usually, therefore, couples are not accepted for a home-income plan until the younger of the partners is seventy-five.

A big part of the idea's attraction is that it can enable you to cut your tax bill on any income you already have. This is because the interest payments you make on the loan count as mortgage interest and qualify for tax relief. To make the most of this concession you need to be paying a substantial amount of tax on your present income. If you are not, a home-income plan probably has too little to offer you to be worth while, unless you choose a variant on the idea which is based on an option mortgage.

It is not usually possible to borrow more than 80 per cent of the value of your home. These schemes are rarely suitable for homes worth less than £15,000. Table 17 shows how a seventy-five-year-old woman with a substantial amount of taxable income can get a net increase in her income of £581 a year by borrowing £10,000. The example illustrates one of the quirks of these schemes: the low rate of annuity paid. This is again for technical reasons and the insurance company makes up for it by charging an interest rate well below market levels on the mortgage.

Table 17 **An Income from the Money Tied Up in Your Home**
The extra annual income a seventy-five-year-old woman taxpayer can secure if she owns a £15,000 home

| | | |
|---|---|---|
| The insurance company lends £10,000 at 6 per cent interest. | | |
| The cash buys an annuity of | £1,034 a year | |
| Tax on this is | £33 | |
| Net annuity income | £1,001 | |
| Interest payments to be met | £600 | |
| Total net payments from insurance company | | £401 |
| Tax relief thanks to mortgage relief on interest payments | | £180 |
| Total net increase in her income | | £581 |

*Note:* Income-tax rate assumed to be 30 per cent.

*Source:* Hambro Provident Assurance.

Many pensioners do not need extra income but simply free capital, perhaps to pay for urgently needed roof repairs, for example. Home-income plans are not the ideal solution here because, for tax reasons, it is possible to take only a small part of the borrowing as an immediate cash sum. At Hambro Provident, for instance, the most you can take immediately is 7 per cent: the rest must be invested in an annuity. A better solution for pensioners who just want a few thousand pounds of immediate cash is to borrow from a well-off relative, perhaps providing their home as security. A solicitor can work out a scheme that will be fair to all parties.

Sometimes families see home-income plans as a way of paying for nursing-home treatment for an elderly relative. The snag is that anyone who needs to go into a nursing home is unlikely to have a long life expectancy. So home-income plans in their basic form are a bad bet. There are, however, variants which return some of the capital to an elderly person's estate if he or she dies soon after taking out the arrangement. These use 'capital-protected' annuities. This sort of each-way bet, however, carries a price – a lower annuity income. What happens if an elderly person loses his or her mind, but looks likely to live for many years to come? The family could consider taking out powers of attorney to arrange a home-income plan to meet medical and other bills.

For pensioners who live longer than expected, home-income plans are of course an unmitigated bonus as the insurance company will have to continue paying out until they drop. And each year a pensioner goes on the house's value will probably rise further, so the mortgage debt which started out looking very large may in the end take proportionately only a small bite from the sale proceeds. The eventual repayment of the mortgage on death will reduce the pensioner's estate for capital-transfer-tax purposes. So there may be a worthwhile tax saving if the estate is sizeable and is subject to high capital-transfer-tax rates.

## Putting Off Retirement

Anybody who works beyond the official retirement age is entitled to a special increased Old Age Pension when they retire. For every extra week they work they build up a little more pension and this works out at an extra $7\frac{1}{2}$ per cent a year. The increase comes on top of any rise due to them through inflation-proofing. Any pension due from the state earnings-related scheme is increased by the same proportion.

The sums work out much better for women than for men: a woman of sixty has on average nineteen years to live, a man of sixty-five about eleven years. A woman who works for one year after official retirement age will have eighteen years to benefit from the extra $7\frac{1}{2}$ per cent. The total gain she gets adds up to 135 per cent of the first year's pension she sacrificed – and that is in real purchasing power. A man expecting to live to seventy-six who works one year after retirement will collect extra pension adding up to $77\frac{1}{2}$ per cent of the first year's pension he sacrifices.

A further bonus of deferring retirement is that you cease paying National Insurance contributions on your salary after you reach state retirement age.

## The State Graduated Scheme

Everyone who worked at any time between 1961 and 1975 is due a pension from the old State Graduated Scheme but in most cases the entitlements are so small that they are hardly worth taking account of in planning for retirement. At most you can expect only a few pounds a week in today's money. The basis of the scheme was that you clocked up a pension of $2\frac{1}{2}$p a week for each unit of contribution. For men a unit cost £7·50 and for women £9. Every member has been notified of the units he has clocked up, and the pension will be paid automatically when they reach official retirement age. The benefits are now inflation-proofed: each unit will buy pension with purchasing power equal to $2\frac{1}{2}$p in 1978 money.

## Captive Pension Schemes

The owners of small companies can use 'captive' pension schemes to invest for their retirement without taking money out of their businesses. Captive schemes are mini company pension schemes for one person or a few people who perform a key role in a small business. In practice they are usually designed for the major shareholder/chief executive of a business. The advantage from his point of view is that he can be a trustee of the pension fund, and so have a great deal of discretion over how the fund's money is invested. He pays the contributions from his company's profits;

but the money can be reinvested back immediately in the company. In certain circumstances the pension fund can buy some of the company's assets – factory premises, for instance – as an investment. Alternatively the fund may provide a loan to the company.

Either way, from the prospective pensioner's point of view the pension payments may amount to no more than transferring money from one pocket to another. But on the way the payments will count as a deduction for corporation-tax purposes in the hands of the company. And if, for instance, the businessman transfers shop premises to his pension fund, the rent his business pays the fund thereafter for the use of the shop will also count as a deduction for corporation tax. The rent will be tax-free in the hands of the pension fund.

The captive-fund idea also has attractions for businessmen who want to pursue a more conventional investment strategy with their savings. The prospective pensioner can invest the money in almost anything he chooses, so he can enjoy the thrill of playing the stock market direct. Under current Inland Revenue rules, captive pension funds can lend back up to half their money to the prospective pensioner's company. The assets the fund invests in, however, have to meet the criteria that they must be realizable at the time the pensioner retires and they must fall within the range of investments that a normal pension fund might consider. That said, the possibilities are enormous. The funding rates the Inland Revenue allows are often astronomic: in the case of a forty-five-year-old man planning to retire at sixty, for instance, his company will be allowed tax relief on transfers each year up to as much as twice his annual salary. The multiple in the case of a fifty-five-year-old may be as much as four times.

The maximum funding rate is based on an actuarial calculation of how much is needed to provide not only a full two-thirds pension for the businessman but also the usual pension benefits for his wife. In each case the projected benefits are related to his final salary, which will probably be much greater than his present earnings. And the sums can allow for an annual rise of up to $8\frac{1}{2}$ per cent in the benefits each year. Several big insurance broking firms now provide ready-made arrangements to run captive pension schemes. Towry Law is one firm which has gone after this market particularly. It charges a few thousand pounds to set up a scheme and get Inland Revenue approval. Afterwards, Towry Law acts as trustee for a charge of a few hundred pounds a year.

Captive pension schemes are subjected to the scrutiny of the Inland Revenue's Superannuation Funds Office, which is empowered to veto their right to the usual pension-scheme tax privileges. The Superannuation Funds Office requires that where the members of a pension scheme are a closely knit group, there should be an independent 'pensioneer' trustee. The pensioneer trustee is usually an actuary, accountant or solicitor and he is vetted by the Superannuation Funds Office. His duty is to make sure that the pension fund is not wound up prematurely and the proceeds distributed to members.

# 10. Unit Trusts and Other Risk Investments

Unit trusts, investment trusts and investment bonds are ways of harnessing the skills of financial experts to enhance the return on your money. Unit trusts and investment trusts aim in the main to make your capital and income grow through investment on the stock market: they, therefore, are particularly useful to high-rate taxpayers for whom capital gains are more attractive than income. They can be useful for many other investors who can afford a flutter, can tie up their money for a long time and want the excitement of following the progress of their investment day by day or week by week. Investment bonds, which are technically single-premium insurance policies, are in most cases geared to property or shares or both and are, therefore, also for risk-takers. In aiming for capital growth they suffer disadvantages compared to unit trusts and investment trusts.

The unit-trust idea has been adapted successfully to serve regular savers. Hundreds of insurance and pension plans are now on the market which invest part of your payments in unit trusts or other unit funds. The criteria for qualifying for tax encouragement for such saving are the same as for ordinary endowment policies and pension plans. Thus you can have the best of both worlds: tax advantages plus the potential for long-term growth that a careful choice of equity investments offers.

Investment is a game of chance as well as skill and it is only over the long term that you determine what part skill has played in an investment house's performance. Almost any investment house can find a period over which its performance has been better than the market average. The only useful guideline in assessing an investment management company's performance claims is that the shorter the period concerned, the less the figures mean. The best a skilful investment company can hope for is consistently to beat the average performance of shares by a small margin and to cushion investors from the worst of stock-market depressions.

The single most important thing you should hope for from a skilful investment management team looking after your money is to spread your risk. If you are investing direct into the stock market you will probably need at least £5,000 for a reasonable spread of risk: to get a well-balanced portfolio you need a minimum of ten well-chosen shares and these days it does not pay to deal in less than £500-worth of one share.

A unit trust will usually spread your money around dozens if not hundreds of shares and the minimum amount of money you need put in may well be as little as £200 or less. Of course, if the trust is one which specializes in a particular type of share, its advantage as a risk spreader will be limited; but even so you will get a much better spread with a £200 unit-trust investment than you would from investing direct in the stock market.

## How Unit Trusts Work

Unit trusts are the nearest thing in the investment world to a co-operative institution. Investors put their money in a common pool and are allocated so many units. The price of the units is usually worked out each day and it depends on the fluctuating values of the underlying investments bought with the pool's money.

Unit trusts are 'open ended': the number of units in a trust fluctuates in line with supply and demand. New units are issued as more investors want to join it and units are extinguished at times when the number of investors wanting to withdraw exceeds new recruits. The fund's administration and its investments are looked after by a management firm which is in most cases authorized by the Department of Trade (if it isn't, the trust cannot be advertised). The management firm is usually paid partly from an initial charge on the money put up by investors and partly from an annual fee which is proportionate to the size of the fund.

Every unit trust has an independent trustee whose main job is to keep an eye on the trust's assets. Usually the trustee is a bank or other large institution which can be relied on to make sure that management companies do not use a trust's funds to their own advantage. The trustee has also to make sure that the managers keep a proper register of unit-holders or delegate that function to reliable agents.

The combination of Department of Trade authorization and guardianship by a responsible trustee has proved its worth over the years and no management group has ever gone bust. Those that have got into difficulties have been quickly rescued by the stronger groups in the industry and in most cases unit-holders have lost little. You can buy a unit-trust holding direct from the managers (whose telephone numbers are listed in the unit-trust prices section of the *Financial Times*) but most investors buy through a bank manager, insurance broker or other adviser.

Unit trusts pay an income just like you would get if you had a direct holding in shares. Most of the dividends a trust receives from its shares are passed straight on to unit-holders. And the advantage for the unit-holders is that it saves them coping with the masses of paperwork involved in running a portfolio of shares. Most trusts pay the income twice a year. It comes after the deduction of basic-rate tax (but if you are a non-taxpayer you can reclaim tax paid on your behalf). And usually the return is close to the average for shares: a typical yield in recent years has been about 4 or 5 per cent a year before tax. Some trusts, particularly trusts offering higher yields, pay their income every quarter or even more often.

Until April 1980, unit trusts in common with investment trusts had to pay capital-gains tax on cashing in profitable investments, but the tax paid within the funds meant that investors in trusts paid tax at a specially low rate on their gains. Now, unit trusts and investment trusts are exempt from capital gains, but investors no longer get special treatment for gains made from holdings in units and investment-trust shares. Such gains are added to any other gains an investor may have in the tax year and, under the rules applying in 1980–81, if the total comes to more than £3,000, capital gains tax at 30 per cent has to be paid on the excess.

Each trust quotes two prices for its units, one, the 'offer' price, for investors buying and the other, the 'bid' price, for investors selling. Under Department of Trade rules, there could be a spread of up to 13 per cent between the offer and bid prices. But if investment management companies actually made full use of this leeway they would scare off many investors: in practice, therefore, they tend to have much narrower gaps. The Department of Trade rules mean that for a trust whose units are each backed by 100p of assets, the offer price can be as much as 110p and the bid price can be as low as 97p. The extra 10p over the basic asset value which the managers are allowed to charge incoming investors is made up of the initial management fee (usually 5 per cent) and the costs of buying shares (stockbrokers' commission, stockjobbers' 'turn' and stamp duty). The justification for a bid value as low as 97p is that that is all the underlying assets are worth after paying stockbrokers' commission and other dealing costs.

In practice, management firms try to pair off buyers and sellers so that units cashed in by a departing investor can be passed on to a new investor without any need either to buy or sell underlying investments. Where buyers and sellers are matched a unit-trust management firm's costs are drastically reduced. Hence management companies can afford to have a much lower gap between bid and offer prices than the full amount officially allowed. The average gap is in fact around 7 per cent.

Most managers charge the highest offer price the rules allow and then pitch their bid price about 7 or 8 per cent below this. Departing investors, therefore, get well above the minimum bid price the managers could in theory quote. In the case of a fund with 100p of assets for every unit, the offer price would be 110p and the bid price about 102p. Some managers prefer to quote prices at the lower end of the range: their bid price will be the lowest they are allowed to charge and their offer will be 7 or 8 per cent above that. For a fund with assets worth 100p per unit, the bid price would be 97p and the offer price around 105p.

Managers who quote prices at the top end of the range are said to be on an 'offer basis'. This is the appropriate stance for an expanding fund, for little is lost by paying a more generous bid price than is needed to investors cashing in (because by definition there will be few of them). Managers who quote prices at the lower end of the range are on a 'bid basis'. This is the appropriate stance for a contracting fund and for one that has been hit by a temporary wave of selling.

Some managers switch around regularly between an offer and a bid basis; others maintain the same stance for years on end.

Ideally you should find out the pricing basis of a trust before deciding to buy. The point is that if a fund switches from an offer to a bid basis soon after you buy, 6 or 7 per cent will be wiped off the value of your holding overnight. Every serious investor should, therefore, know the omens that precede a switch from offer to bid. A more difficult trick – but one that some investors have learned to exploit to great advantage – is to spot a fund that is temporarily down on its luck and is just about to switch from bid to offer.

Until recently most unit-trust managers regarded the pricing basis of a trust as a trade secret and it was up to investors to make intelligent guesses. Now most trust managers are willing to say – privately at least – what basis they are on: they may not discuss the matter with an individual investor, but they will probably talk to his broker or other adviser. To determine whether a trust is likely to make the switch from an offer to bid basis it is useful to know something of its history, the interest among the public in its units and the general stock-market outlook for the type of shares the fund invests in. A fund that has been going several years is more likely to suffer a large flow of selling by unit-holders than a recently launched fund: so it is more likely to have to switch to a bid basis (if it has not done so already). You can determine from a trust's latest accounts, available from the managers, the level of buying and selling interest in its units in the previous year. Sudden changes in the outlook for the type of shares the trust invests in often bring changes in its pricing basis: funds specializing in American shares in particular have often switched from bid to offer and back again with disconcerting speed in recent years, reflecting sharp changes in investors' confidence in Wall Street.

## Choosing a Unit Trust

The basic principles on which the unit-trust industry was founded were to spread the investor's risk widely and to give the managers great discretion about the kind of shares to buy. These principles are still sound and many well-established trusts – often with the word 'general' in their name – operate by them. But most new trusts these days – and the trusts that hog the attention of the press – back a particular type of share, whether shares of a particular country like Japan or America, or shares in business sectors like commodities, banking or North Sea development.

Often a new trust specializes in a sector which happens to enjoy a vogue on the stock market at the time of its launch: in the early 1970s the financial sector – which takes in banks, merchant banks, financial conglomerates and property companies – was one of the most popular on the stock market and several 'financial' unit trusts were launched at this time. In the City crash of 1974, they were among the worst-hit and it took years for them to get back to their original launch prices.

Some trusts have been launched on the back of booms so ephemeral that they now seem ludicrous; a 'motorways' trust, for instance, was launched to cash in on the 1960s road-building boom. A few years later its investment objectives were recognized to be too restrictive and it was taken over by a more broadly based trust. The industry's history is littered with other eye-catching trusts that have failed to pass the test of time: among sectors that had a vogue, but have since proved disappointing, are atomic energy, education and the drinks trade. The evidence of the past is, therefore, a strong warning for anyone tempted to put too much money into a specialist fund. But in providing these funds, the unit-trust industry is appealing to a basic urge among investors to back their own hunches. If you are being level-headed you will recognize that your hunches are no more likely to be right than those of thousands of other investors, so you will delegate decisions about which share sectors your money should be in to managers of a general fund. This, however, will mean that you will miss out on much of the fun of the stock market: a satisfactory compromise might be to back several specialist funds each concentrating on a different sector of the stock market.

Several trusts which have proved outstandingly successful in the last decade go under the 'recovery' or 'special situations' banner. Instead of specializing in a particular sector of the stock market, these trusts seek out all sorts of shares that seem to be temporarily under a cloud. Many of the choices involve a degree of risk which would be hair-raising for an ordinary private investor. Often, for instance, the shares are in companies trapped under a mountain of debt built up over years of poor trading or bad management. Just a little more bad news may cripple the company permanently or even tip it into the hands of a liquidator; but this is just the sort of company whose prospects could be transformed quickly with a little good luck.

The recovery idea demonstrates to the full the advantage unit trusts have in not having to put all their eggs in one basket. By carefully choosing risky shares in different sectors of the stock market, the managers can hope that even if they lose their shirt on one or two investments, other investments will probably make up for this with spectacular gains. The trick is to find shares which have already fallen so far that the chances of reward outweigh the risk of a further fall.

Many unit trusts launched in the 1970s specialize in providing investors with a higher-than-average-dividend income. Some of these trusts have at times advertised income returns as high as 12 per cent or more before tax: that compares with returns on American trusts, for instance, as low as 2 per cent or less and barely 1 per cent from Japanese trusts. The high-income idea has claims to being the ideal solution for a large section of the investing public. It leaves the managers free to pick shares from any stock-market sector: they can, therefore, achieve a good spread of risk. It focuses attention on what City traditionalists regard as the only valid criteria for assessing share values: the level of dividends a company pays and the prospects for their growth. (The high-income idea is partly a reaction to the discredited 'growth stock' philosophy, which ignored the level of dividends and which proved so disastrous for many investors in the 1974 shares crash.)

High-income trusts have their pitfalls for uncritical followers. If you go for the unit trusts promising the highest income, the chances are you are backing a three-legged horse. Prospects of your capital appreciating are probably negligible; worse, your income may not grow either, so you will quickly be left behind by inflation. If you want a high-income trust with a reasonable chance of protecting you against inflation, you will probably have to choose one with a starting dividend return of less than 8 per cent before tax. This is about the highest income available in most of the recent past from shares with reasonable growth prospects (that is, 'ordinary' shares in good companies).

Unit trusts offering a higher income than this may achieve it by investing in 'preference' shares, which take precedence over ordinary shares in the queue for dividends when a company hits hard times. In return for a high, near-guaranteed income, preference shares, however, forgo any chance of participating in the growth of a company's profits. Funds which get their high income largely from preference shares are usually clearly identified as such in their advertising and they are of interest only to low-income pensioners and other investors who do not pay income tax.

Where a unit trust achieves a suspiciously high income from an 'all-equity' share portfolio (that is, it has all its money in ordinary shares), you should check the quality of its investments. In some cases trusts straining to provide a high income have invested in shares with dubious prospects: a mine threatened with nationalization or with political upheaval, for instance, or one which has nearly exhausted its ore. Another short-sighted investment policy which can help produce an artificially high income is to back companies which have hit trouble whose dividend pay-outs are good for the moment but are not expected to continue much longer.

If a high-income trust really wants to cheat it can indulge in 'dividend stripping'. This is the practice of buying a share just before its dividend becomes payable, and selling just afterwards. The money can then be used to do the same thing with another share; and in the course of a year a fund can collect a vast amount of dividends. The trouble is that this policy plays havoc with the value of a share portfolio. For when a trust buys a share just before a dividend is payable the price is inflated by an amount roughly equal to the net value of the pay-out. Immediately the dividend has been assigned to the current holder of the shares, the share price falls. In short, you can't have your cake and eat it.

Unit trusts which invest in high-yielding government securities are an innovation which has been catching on in a big way. Until recently most unit trusts investing in gilts were based in Jersey, for tax reasons: they could pay out income free of almost all tax. The unit-holder was, of course, liable for tax in the usual way, but he was in a much better position than if he invested in a trust based on the mainland. This was because until 1980 unit trusts' gilt income was subject to 52 per cent corporation tax on the mainland. Now, mainland-based unit trusts are not subject to corporation tax on gilt income provided they do not accept companies as unit-holders. Gilt income is taxed at the basic rate within the fund and there is no further tax to pay by a unit-holder paying basic-rate tax. Non-taxpayers can reclaim the tax and high-rate tax-payers have extra tax to pay. The position is almost exactly the same as if the unit-holder invested direct in gilts.

There are two main types of gilt unit trust: income funds and capital funds. Income gilt trusts are managed to produce the highest possible income, so they are a good bet for low-income investors, particularly pensioners, for whom income is more important than the chance of capital growth. Capital funds aim to use the special capital-gains-tax position of gilts to produce capital growth and are aimed particularly at high-rate taxpayers.

The return for gilt unit-trust investors has averaged well over 10 per cent in most of the recent past. A major snag which gilt unit trusts have in common with preference share funds is that they offer no protection against worsening inflation. And gilt prices usually wilt when the general level of interest rates in the economy rises.

### Which Management Group?

A handful of big investment management companies dominate the unit-trust industry. Some groups have more than twenty trusts and dozens of groups have more than ten. The biggest five companies, listed in Table 18, manage more than half of all unit-trust money.

Having decided on which kind of trust to back, you will, therefore, have to choose between several management groups which each have a suitable fund. Here are some points to bear in mind in assessing unit-trust groups:

*Investment expertise.* Investors who want to play safe should make their choice from the major firms, unless they can verify fully the claims of smaller groups. Many small groups can hope to do as well for you as larger ones but they are hard to distinguish from dozens of less successful small groups. Among the major groups M & G, Allied Hambro and Henderson are regarded in the City as reliable investment performers and they show up well not only in one-year performance tables but in longer-term comparisons which are much more convincing evidence of expertise. Other companies which are well-regarded include Gartmore and Britannia and, among smaller groups, Framlington and Perpetual.

Table 18 **The Major Unit-Trust Groups**

| Group | Total under management (£m) | Number of trusts | Number of unit-holders |
| --- | --- | --- | --- |
| Save & Prosper | 705 | 24 | 550,000 |
| M & G | 589 | 24 | 152,000 |
| Barclays Unicorn | 374 | 17 | 251,000 |
| Allied Hambro | 319 | 23 | 98,000 |
| Britannia* | 188 | 24 | 238,000 |

* Excluding Schlesinger.

The most reliable criterion of a group's performance is how its total funds under management have done. Comparisons on this basis are rare but a good substitute is the average of the performances of a group's individual trusts. The limitation of this exercise, however, is that it gives the same weight to a group's large trusts as to its small ones. A group whose major trusts are its best performers may produce the same average performance as another whose best performers are its smaller trusts but it will be doing better by most of its investors. There is also the point that a group can be expected to put more effort into managing its major funds (and the larger a fund is, the harder it is to manage well) so its performance with these is a more reliable guide to its investment expertise.

Among the factors that bedevil short-term performance comparisons is the bid–offer pricing basis of trusts. A group which wants to do well in the performance tables of a particular year may put most of its trusts on a bid basis in December of the previous year: in the course of the next twelve months it can then switch its best-performing funds to an offer basis and so artificially enhance their gains to an extent that may move them up twenty places or more in the performance tables.

*Switching facilities*. If you follow the stock market closely, you can make money by well-timed switching from one investment sector to another: having done well with one sector, you sell and switch into another sector which so far has been in the doldrums but looks set for a rise. Unless you are careful, however, you stand to lose about 7 per cent of your capital every time you switch from one unit trust to another (because you get only the bid price for the units you sell but you will have to pay the full offer price for the new units). This is a weighty handicap for even the most brilliant investment strategy; but you can cut the cost of switching if you pick the right group and stay with it. For most trust groups allow an investor to switch from one of their funds to another on preferential terms: often you get a discount on the usual offer price of the trust you want to switch into. Table 19 shows some of the discounts available to switchers.

Table 19 **Switching: How You Fare with Major Groups**
Percentage discounts on the offer price of the unit trust switched to if switching from another trust within the group

| | |
|---|---|
| Save & Prosper | Nil |
| M & G | 1 |
| Barclays Unicorn | 2 |
| Allied Hambro | 1 |
| Britannia | 2 |
| Hill Samuel | $1\frac{1}{4}$ |

*Note:* The figures apply in the case of investors who hold their units directly, rather than through a bond. Switches are usually cheaper if you invest via a bond.

Active investors may prefer to invest in units via an insurance bond rather than have a direct holding. That way switches can often be effectively free: for the money you get from the sale of one holding will go into the new trust at its bid price. Sometimes there is a small charge for this service but the cost is usually much lower than for making a switch between direct holdings in units.

*Minimum purchases*. The minimum amount you can invest varies considerably between groups and even between different trusts in the same group. The minimum investment in some trusts is as little as £25, but others will accept nothing less than £5,000. A typical minimum figure is £200. The best advice for anyone with a limited amount to invest is to shop around among the groups.

*Share-exchange schemes.* Unit-trust groups often accept shares from investors in exchange for holdings in units. A group has a choice of two courses of action in dealing with shares received under exchange arrangements:

1. It may add the shares to the investments held by its unit trusts. This is the better bet from the point of view of the person exchanging the shares. Usually you have to have a minimum of £500 in each shareholding, but groups like Allied Hambro and Target will accept smaller shareholdings. Most groups prefer shares in large well-known companies. If your shares are accepted for inclusion in a unit-trust group's portfolio, you will usually be credited with the price the managers would have to pay on the stock market for them (which is considerably more than you would get if you were to sell in the normal way, because there is often a difference of up to 5 per cent between buying and selling prices quoted by share dealers). The unit-trust group will also pay the stamp duty on the transfer.

2. The shares may be sold on your behalf. Groups do this where the size of the shareholdings is too small to interest them or where the shares are in obscure companies or are otherwise unacceptable. You will be credited with whatever price the group is bid for them on the stock market (which will be lower than the 'middle' price listed in the newspapers). The one advantage is that the group will usually pay the stamp duty and the stockbroker's commission on the sale. But even for this service your holdings have to have a total sale value of at least £500 if they are to be accepted by most groups.

When an investor disposes of shares through a share-exchange scheme he is liable to capital-gains tax in the normal way. But if the investor disposes of shares when the stock market is depressed he will probably have few gains so he may have only a small capital-gains tax bill or even a capital loss which he can carry forward to set against future gains.

*Withdrawal schemes.* Many groups operate 'withdrawal' schemes, which allow you to supplement the dividend income from your unit-holding by a sale of some of your units. You can arrange for the total pay-out to amount to a sum determined by you in advance or to a fixed proportion of the current value of your holding. A typical withdrawal scheme will give you a net pay-out of 8 per cent of the current value of your units, made up of, say, a net dividend pay-out of 5 per cent and a sale of 3 per cent of your unit-holding.

The snag with these schemes is that they eat into your capital and they can do great damage in times of falling share values.

*Dividend payment dates.* Most trusts make dividend payments twice a year but some pay out more frequently. The Arbuthnot group's high-income trust, for instance, makes four payments a year.

*Management charges.* Most management groups make an initial charge equal to 5 per cent of your investment but several charge just $3\frac{1}{4}$ per cent. Lloyds Bank and a few other groups charge as little as $1\frac{1}{4}$ per cent initially in the case of their gilt unit trusts. A low initial management charge may mean a smaller spread between a trust's bid and offer prices so that it is cheaper for an investor to get in and out.

Management groups also make a small continuing charge each year. Where the initial charge is 5 per cent the standard annual charge is $\frac{3}{8}$ per cent; and where $3\frac{1}{4}$ per cent is taken initially the annual charge is $\frac{1}{2}$ per cent. These combinations were the officially approved ones before groups were freed to set their own charges in 1980. Several groups with a 5 per cent initial charge have since introduced an annual charge of $\frac{1}{2}$ per cent. And some recently formed trusts have gone as high as 1 per cent.

*Membership of the Unit Trust Association.* One of the Unit Trust Association's aims is to uphold standards in the industry. In cases of complaint, therefore, you can take your case to the association, if an offending group is a member. The association lays down the maximum commissions members can pay to insurance brokers and other intermediaries (the top commission is 3 per cent and this should be paid only to better-established intermediaries). Some groups remain outside the association specifically to pay higher-than-usual commissions to agents but the extent to which this benefits the public is highly questionable.

## Investment Trusts

Investment trusts are broadly similar to unit trusts but differ in several ways which make them an interesting alternative for informed investors. They share with unit trusts the aim of making the most of a well-spread portfolio of investments. The main distinction is that investment trusts, despite their name, are not trusts but companies whose shares are quoted on the stock market.

Many practical consequences result from investment trusts' different constitution:

1. To invest in an investment trust you have to go through a stockbroker or, perhaps, through a bank manager who will put you in touch with a stockbroker.

2. Investment trusts are 'closed-ended'. The supply of shares in an investment-trust company is for practical purposes fixed, whereas the number of units in a unit trust is constantly fluctuating in response to supply and demand from the public.

3. Investment trusts can buy investments with borrowed money as well as shareholders' money. Any profits made from borrowing go to shareholders. With a few minor exceptions unit trusts are barred from using borrowed money to buy shares.

4. Investment trusts cannot promote their shares, whereas unit-trust groups can not only advertise for new investors but also pay commission to agents who promote their trusts.

Investment trusts' different constitutions give them several widely publicized disadvantages compared to unit trusts:

Investment-trust shares usually stand well below the net value of the underlying assets concerned. When you are selling you may have to accept a share price that represents as little as 55 per cent of what you would get if the fund was a unit trust. An investment trust's share price is determined by the balance between buyers and sellers of the shares. If there are more buyers than sellers, the share price will rise. If more sellers than buyers, it will fall. Of course, both buyers and sellers will take some account of the underlying asset values; but in most of the recent past, sellers have outnumbered buyers (reflecting the general exodus of private investors from the stock market). Insurance companies and other City institutions which have bought the shares coming on the market have done so only if they thought investment-trust share prices were a bargain compared to underlying assets. The gap between share prices and underlying assets is known as the 'discount' and it varies disconcertingly with market conditions and with the City's view of each trust's management: in the last decade the average discount has swung from a low of 10 per cent in 1972 to a peak of 45 per cent in 1975. Uncertainty about the future of the discount puts many investors off investment-trust shares.

An investment trust may have to foot heavy interest bills on its borrowings, so cutting its capacity to pay dividends. Borrowings are a millstone around a trust's neck when share prices generally are falling. For a major gulf may open up in a trust's balance sheet as shares it bought with borrowed money fall below the cost of repaying the loans.

Investors are almost powerless to influence the managers of a poorly performing investment trust. Investment trusts are not so much in the public eye as unit trusts so their managements are under less pressure to do well. The sanction of voting with your feet is a powerful influence on a bad unit-trust management, which stands to lose most of its money in time if it does not pull its socks up. But short of winding up an investment-trust company, investors can never get their money back from it. All they can do is to sell their shares to other investors. The one straw that investors caught in such a trust can cling on to is that the selling pressure will force the share price down so far that an asset-stripping financier will launch a takeover bid.

Investment trusts also have advantages. Here are some of them:

Investors can profit from the investment-trust discount if they follow the stock market closely. The average discount is usually close to its widest when the stock market is depressed and at its narrowest when the stock market is high. An investor who gets his timing right will, therefore, show a bigger gain if he invests in an investment trust rather than in a unit trust owning the same underlying shares.

Investment-trust managers have more scope to pursue adventurous investment policies. They can invest for the long term without having to look over their shoulder all the time at their showing in one-year performance tables. A unit trust cannot have many unmarketable shares in its portfolio because it has to be in a position to meet unit-holders' demands for their money back at short notice. Investment trusts can invest in companies so small they are not even quoted on the stock market, companies which often in the long term prove the best investments. They can also invest directly in gold, farms, property and other assets which are out of bounds for unit trusts.

You should get a higher income from the same underlying investments if you invest through an investment trust. This is because, thanks to the discount, you buy more underlying assets. Investment trusts, however, suffer the penalty of corporation tax, which they pay on, among other things, overseas dividends. This burden can in practice, however, largely be avoided; in any case the advantage of the discount usually outweighs the corporation-tax drawback.

In the case of larger investment trusts, the yield is improved by low management charges. Many major investment trusts aim to keep their annual management charges to below $\frac{1}{4}$ per cent of funds managed. Most unit-trust management companies take a fee of at least $\frac{3}{8}$ per cent a year.

Dealing costs can be slightly lower for investors in investment trusts. The buying and selling costs include stamp duty of 2 per cent, two lots of stockbrokers' commission of around $1\frac{1}{2}$ per cent and the stockjobbers' turn of around 2 per cent (in the case of a reasonably sized share block). These add up to 7 per cent. Few unit trusts have a spread of less than 7 per cent.

The fund's share-dealing costs tend to be lower for investment trusts than unit trusts. This is because investment-trust managers tend to make fewer changes in their portfolios. They are under less pressure than unit-trust managers to take a short-term view of investment prospects, so are less likely, for instance, to be panicked into selling a good share because of a minor upset at the company. Some unit-trust managements have in the past succumbed to the temptation to tinker too much with their portfolios in the hope of attracting 'reciprocal business' from stockbrokers. The idea is that where they place a large investment deal with a friendly stockbroker he will return the compliment by selling some of their units to his clients. The more a unit trust deals on the stock market, the more business of this sort it will get.

The proof of the pudding is in the eating: in this case the relative performance of the two types of investments. The trouble is that there are two ways of measuring investment-trust performance and, depending on which you choose, you can arrive at very different conclusions. Net asset values are, in the view of investment-trust management companies, the only fair measure for comparisons with unit trusts, but what matters to individual investors is the prices at which they can buy and sell investment-trust shares. Another problem is that the relative positions differ widely depending on what period you choose: partisans on either side can debate endlessly what is a fair period.

Table 20 shows how different the comparisons look depending on the period involved and which investment-trust measure you use. The *Financial Times*-Actuaries (*FT*-A) Investment Trust Index is the standard measure of investment-trust share prices. The Unitholder Index, compiled by *Money Management* magazine, shows the average movement of all unit trusts authorized by the Department of Trade. The period covered – from 1973 to 1979 – saw an epic series of stock market ups and downs but unit trusts on average showed an overall gain of only 6 per cent in the end. That compares with a net gain of about 3 per cent in investment-trust asset values, but because it was a period of widening asset discounts investment-trust share prices lost nearly 14 per cent. Measured by their share prices, investment trusts managed to beat unit trusts in only two years: 1975 and 1977. But measured by assets they beat unit trusts in 1974, 1975, 1976 and 1978. Part of the explanation for the diverging performances in individual years lies with the heavy weighting of investment trusts towards

Wall Street. When Wall Street does well, so does the investment-trust sector. Overall, Wall Street performed disappointingly between 1973 and 1979.

Table 20 **Unit Trusts versus Investment Trusts: Performance Compared**
Performance in each calendar year (%)

| Year | FT-*A* Investment Trust Index | Investment-trust assets | Unitholder Index | FT-*A* All-Share Index |
|---|---|---|---|---|
| 1973 | −34·7 | −27·7 | −27·2 | −31·4 |
| 1974 | −47·5 | −34·7 | −35·6 | −55·3 |
| 1975 | +120·8 | +66·1 | +65·5 | +136·3 |
| 1976 | −7·1 | +7·8 | −4·3 | −3·9 |
| 1977 | +32·7 | +12·5 | +31·3 | +41·2 |
| 1978 | −2·4 | +8·2 | +6·6 | +2·7 |
| 1979 | −5·1 | No change | +2·3 | +4·3 |
| January 1973 to December 1979 | | | | |
|  | −13·6 | +2·9 | +6·3 | +5·3 |

*Source:* Wood, Mackenzie & Co.

In general unit-holders had a less bumpy ride; they were, for instance, better protected from the 1974 shares slump than holders of investment-trust shares, who saw more than one-third wiped off the value of their shares. But unit-holders missed out on much of the 1975 recovery. Investment-trust share prices followed the trend of the stock market generally, as measured by the *FT*-A All-Share Index.

Investment trusts generally enjoy the same treatment for capital-gains tax as unit trusts.

A major problem for private investors in following investment trusts is where to get information. The newspapers report investment-trust affairs only rarely. The best source of regular information is the circulars produced by stockbroking firms which make a special study of the investment-trust sector. Most big stockbroking firms, however, reserve their investment-trust research material almost exclusively for institutional clients. But Wood, Mackenzie of Edinburgh is prepared to send monthly commentaries and asset valuations to private clients. The service is free to clients who deal on a sizeable scale: the rules vary with circumstances but in 1980, for instance, clients whose share deals totalled more than £10,000 in a year would have qualified. Other clients can have the service on a fee basis.

You can get cards summarizing a trust's financial position and history, at very little cost, from Extel Statistical Services, 37–45 Paul Street, London EC2.

## Insurance Bonds

Insurance-linked investment bonds work on similar lines to unit trusts, but are technically life-insurance policies. Many investors assume that life insurance is included in the package to give them special protection from tax. This is not always the case; in fact, often an investor who invests via a bond can face a larger tax bill than if he had a direct holding in shares or in unit trusts.

For marketing men in the savings industry, bonds have several attractions which are no advantage to the investing public. Bonds are single-premium insurance policies where most of your money goes into an investment fund: a small amount is, however, deducted to provide minimal life cover. The whole package is classed as an insurance policy, which means that it can be sold by door-to-door salesmen, whereas doorstep selling of straight unit trusts is banned by law. The insurance status of bonds also means that they can be advertised even where the underlying fund does not have Department of Trade authorization as a unit trust. This means that the fund escapes the DoT's curbs on management charges. And it means that the fund can invest directly in office blocks, shop premises, and other properties – direct property holdings are out of bounds for authorized unit trusts.

If the bondholder dies early, his family get the greater of the cash-in value of the bond or the basic sum insured. The sum insured varies depending on the investor's age: a typical arrangement in the case of a young investor is cover of twice his initial investment. Bonds do not provide an income as such; the income from the underlying investments is reinvested and the investor gets the benefit in a rise in the value of his bond. Investors who need to live off their capital can, however, make special arrangements for annual withdrawals from the investment fund.

Single-premium bonds are not 'qualifying' policies under Inland Revenue rules so there is no tax subsidy on your initial payment. The underlying funds are, however, taxed at the usual insurance-company rate: $37\frac{1}{2}$ per cent on unfranked income from investments such as government securities and 30 per cent on company dividends. They pay tax at the full capital-gains tax rate of 30 per cent on profits they make from cashing in investment holdings.

The taxes paid within the fund absolve the bond-holder from tax in his hands while the bond is in force. When he cashes in, the proceeds are credited with having already borne basic-rate income tax within the fund and so are usually tax-free for basic-rate taxpayers, but irrespective of whether the rise in the value of a bond is due to reinvested income or to capital gains, it may be liable to higher rates of tax in the hands of a well-off saver. Liability to higher rates of tax is calculated on the Inland Revenue's 'top slicing' principle, which has the effect of spreading the gains over the investment period. Your gain is divided by the number of years you hold the bond. The resulting 'slice' is added to your current year's income. If this calculation puts you into higher rates of tax or if you are already paying tax at higher rates, you will have to pay tax on the profit you have made on the bond. The tax rate payable is generally the appropriate rate of higher tax less a credit for basic-rate tax of, currently, 30 per cent. The tax bill on the slice is multiplied by the number of years concerned to give your total bill.

Tax on cash withdrawals is deferred until the bond is cashed in, provided that no more than 5 per cent of the initial investment is withdrawn each year and the cumulative withdrawals do not total more than 100 per cent. On cashing in, the withdrawals will be counted in calculating the total gain for higher-rate tax purposes. Even so, for high-rate taxpayers the deferral of the tax bill can represent a considerable cash-flow advantage.

Bonds are at their best in providing a secure high return for high-rate taxpayers. They are ideal for high-yielding gilts: the high-rate taxpayer can withdraw 5 per cent a year and the balance of any income from the underlying securities is reinvested for him to add to the value of the bond. In many cases a fund can avoid paying capital-gains tax by leaving gains unrealized for as long as possible. In an expanding fund capital gains need never be cashed in because money from new investors will more than cover payments to investors getting out. In pricing bonds an insurance company has, however, to deduct a provision for tax on unrealized gains and this means that the effective capital-gains tax the investor suffers within the fund is between 10 and 20 per cent.

As with unit trusts the underlying funds are divided into units. The unit prices are quoted in the newspapers and usually involve a spread of a little over 5 per cent between bid and offer prices. Most of the spread is accounted for by the initial management charge the insurance company levies, usually 5 per cent. The insurance company also takes an annual management charge, usually $\frac{3}{4}$ per cent, but in some cases up to 1 per cent. By contrast, most established unit trusts which charge 5 per cent initially usually charge no more than $\frac{3}{8}$ or $\frac{1}{2}$ per cent annually.

Bonds have a major advantage for investors who want to back their investment judgement and switch their money rapidly from one specialist fund to another. An investor switching within a bond can often do so free or for a much lower charge than he would have to bear if he invested either in shares or unit trusts direct. Direct investors in unit trusts, for instance, usually lose at least 5 per cent of their capital each time they switch, even where they make the switches between funds in the same group.

Advocates of bonds as a means of avoiding tax point particularly to the opportunities provided for an investor on high tax rates to defer paying tax until a year when his income is low. One example is for a well-paid middle-aged executive to let his investment income roll up in a bond until after he retires, when his top rate of tax may well fall to only the basic rate. To make the most of this strategy in cases where a large investment is involved, the investor should spread his money between several bonds. Then he can cash them in over several years to avoid having to pay unnecessarily high rates of tax from cashing in the whole lot in one tax year.

The tax deferral advantages of bonds also come into their own with people who are planning to emigrate eventually.

Another use of bonds to defer tax is to hold them until death. The bonds will automatically be cashed in at that point and there may, therefore, be a liability to income tax; the bond proceeds will be aggregated with the dead person's other income in the tax year concerned. If, however, death occurs early in the tax year, the dead person's other income may be only a fraction of what it is in a normal year. The tax charge on the bond proceeds should be correspondingly light and there may be no tax to pay at all.

A further use of bonds is in conjunction with arrangements for avoiding capital-transfer tax. Bonds can be assigned to children or grandchildren without any immediate liability to income tax – the beneficiary will have to pay this later when he or she cashes in and the bill will be assessed on his or her income at the cash-in date. While the bond remains in force the income accumulating in it will not be aggregated with that of a child's parents. The sensible course may, therefore, be for the child to keep the bond in force until he or she is independent of his or her parents for tax purposes.

## Managed Funds

Managed funds are run on unit-trust lines but, instead of investing only in shares, they invest in a mixture of shares, property and fixed-interest securities. The idea is that the managers will vary the proportions of the different types of investment to make the most of market opportunities.

Sometimes a managed fund does not invest directly in shares but instead uses unit trusts to make up the shares part of its portfolio.

In practice, it is usually difficult for a managed fund to live up to its promise of actively switching between different types of investment. The costs of switching are usually so high for a fund manager that he can rarely be sure they are worth paying; it is particularly expensive, for instance, to switch into or out of property. Thus most managed funds tend to vary the mix little. Often the proportions are only changed gradually by directing new money into the most promising investment sector. And if the outlook for most investments is choppy the managers may leave new money in cash deposits to await a better time.

As a result of their relatively passive investment policies, managed funds have often in the past performed mediocrely – they usually do less well than the best-performing individual investment sector, but they should do better than the worst.

Managed funds are often linked to insurance bonds, and the package is known as a 'managed bond'.

## Unit-linked Savings Plans

Many insurance groups have special endowment policies where most of the saver's premiums go into a unit trust or other unit fund whose investment performance can be followed from day to day in the unit prices quoted in the newspapers. These 'see-through' endowment policies also have the advantage that the investor can, if he is good at arithmetic, see how much the insurance group is siphoning off for its paperwork costs and insurance cover. Working out what the various charges add up to is a laborious exercise but well worth doing.

Often the insurance group will have a variety of unit funds to choose from – not only unit trusts but property, managed and fixed-interest funds as well. There may be an option to split each premium between several funds. And sometimes the investor has the right to switch between the different funds, so he can back his own hunches about the outlook for investment markets: full switching facilities are, however, confined mainly to plans designed for larger investors. Such plans may require a high minimum investment level, perhaps £25 a month or even £50. Sometimes the minimum premium may be small but small premiums may still be discouraged by a high flat 'policy charge'.

Most unit-linked savings plans are basically ten-year policies, but they often contain an option for the policyholder to extend the term for a further ten years. One option which is sometimes offered is to turn the plan into a paid-up policy after ten years, leaving the investments to continue to build up while enjoying insurance-company tax rules. This arrangement is useful for higher-rate taxpayers because the tax burden on the accumulating investment income will be lower than if the units were held directly.

Paid-up plans can be used to draw a tax-free income by making partial surrenders: provided you do not cash in more each year than the growth and income you get from the underlying investments, your capital will remain intact – in money terms at least. Such surrenders may be made easier if the plan is split up into a 'cluster' of small policies, each of which has a separate life for tax purposes. The investor can then cash in one or more policies without disturbing the rest, and thus get an 'income' without having to go through the tiresome paperwork that a partial surrender normally entails.

Used to give an income in this way, these schemes have become known as 'greenhouse' plans. The name derives from the fact that for higher-rate taxpayers, the fiscal climate inside an insurance-linked plan is much more congenial than investing in unit trusts direct. There is no bill for higher-rate tax as the money builds up within the insurance fund. The investor can watch his money grow and, using the switching facility, tend it occasionally to make the most of current conditions.

There are four important things an investor should check on before buying an insurance-linked plan:

*Charges.* One of the biggest charges the policy-holder pays is concealed in the difference between the bid and offer prices of the units he buys. This will include the 'front-end load' charge which usually works out at 5 per cent. There is also a yearly charge varying between $\frac{3}{8}$ per cent in the case of most unit trusts up to $\frac{3}{4}$ per cent or more for property-bond funds.

Some groups call units allocated in the first year 'capital units' and impose an extra charge on them. A typical charge on capital units is 3 per cent a year and it usually continues for ten years. Hambro Life, Liberty Life and Abbey Life are among well-known firms which impose capital-unit charges.

Many groups have a policy fee, usually a flat charge of around £5 a year irrespective of the size of your premiums.

The charge for switching between different investment funds is usually either $\frac{1}{2}$ or 1 per cent, with a minimum of £10 or in some cases £25. Sometimes the first switch is free. Normally the price you get for the units you are switching out of is the quoted bid value – and you pay the bid price for the units you are switching in to. But some groups may charge the full offer price less a small discount for the new units: such deals need to be scrutinized closely because the real cost of the switch may be larger than it seems.

*Unit allocation.* The rules about 'unit allocation' conceal what is in effect the biggest charge in many cases. The point is that usually not all your premiums are invested for you – and the older you are the lower the proportion will be. The unit-allocation figure is a percentage calculated by setting the value of units bought for you as a proportion of the total of your premiums *plus* the 21 per cent tax subsidy for endowment policies. With some groups the unit allocation is as low as 40 per cent in the first year and 80 per cent in subsequent ones. The balance of your money is creamed off by the insurance company to pay for its paperwork and life cover expenses and to provide its profit.

A good company will normally give almost 100 per cent unit allocation to younger investors and over 90 per cent even for people above retirement age. But where unit allocation is lower insurance companies usually justify it by pointing to higher-than-normal life cover. The question for investors is whether they need the extra cover and if so whether a straight term policy might not be a cheaper way of buying it.

Some life companies offer unit allocation of fractionally more than 100 per cent for younger investors. They are in effect acknowledging that the cost of life cover is lower than the 5 per cent front-end load they get on the sale of units.

*Surrender values.* The surrender values of insurance-linked savings schemes are based on the bid value of the underlying units allocated to you.

The insurance company will usually deduct something for its paperwork costs. The deductions are normally on a sliding scale, varying from as much as 50 per cent or more of one year's premiums in the first year to as little as 5 per cent after four years.

*The company's record.* Many untried groups have entered the insurance-linked savings field. It is often difficult to assess their prospects and credentials. But the choice of company is particularly important to investors in these plans because of the long time span involved and the large total cost. Companies which have done well in the past and have generally reasonable charges include M & G, Barclays Life and Scottish Widows. Other well-established groups with generally low charges and a reputation for investment expertise are Vanbrugh, Equitable Life and Norwich Union.

For latest details of plans on offer it may be worth buying a copy of *Money Management*'s survey, *Unit-Linked Savings Plans*. Among other things, the book calculates the full burden of the various charges and ranks companies in order of competitiveness.

## Unit-linked Pension Plans

Unit-linked pension plans offer the self-employed a chance to participate directly in the ups and downs of a fund whose unit price is quoted regularly in the newspapers. The attraction for the investor is not only the excitement of watching the progress of his units but also the freedom he gets from the traditional bonus system (which is harder to understand and sometimes works rather arbitrarily).

Often there is a choice of investment funds to link the pension plan to. Insurance companies and other investment management groups in the pension field in many cases have a property fund, a gilt fund, a shares fund and a mixed fund, each geared specifically to the needs of pension-plan investors. The mixed fund is usually the cornerstone of the range and its money is divided between property, gilts and shares in varying proportions depending on how the managers see investment markets.

The investor may have the right to switch between the various funds. Often the charge is $\frac{1}{2}$ or 1 per cent of the money switched. Sometimes, however, the right to switch may be heavily restricted: the investor may, for instance, be allowed to switch only new premium money, leaving his existing premiums in the original fund. With a few funds, switches may be possible only once a year, on the policy's anniversary.

Ideally, the unit funds involved should be 'exempt', that is, they should be funds run on unit-trust lines which have special exemption from tax and are therefore able to pass on to the investor the full tax advantages of pension-oriented saving. In fact many groups do not have a complete range of exempt funds and may include ordinary unit trusts among the choice for pension-plan investors. Ordinary unit trusts, however, suffer the handicap that they pay capital-gains tax, albeit at a reduced rate. Over the long term this can be a significant brake on growth.

The charges that insurance companies and other investment groups make for running unit-linked regular-premium pension plans are often complex and confusing. The main charge is an initial levy, of 5 per cent in most cases, which the investor pays on buying the units. In many cases, however, not all his premiums are invested in units in the first place. Companies' rules about 'unit allocation' vary but often as little as 95 per cent of premium money goes into units. By the same token other groups provide unit allocation of slightly more than 100 per cent in some cases: what they add to the investor's premiums comes out of the 5 per cent they get from the unit purchases.

The management company also usually makes an annual charge, often $\frac{1}{2}$ or $\frac{3}{4}$ per cent. But the picture can be further complicated by the use of what are misleadingly known as 'capital units'. These differ from ordinary units only in that they invoke a particularly high annual management charge, typically $3\frac{1}{2}$ per cent a year. Often the rule is that the first year's premiums go into capital units, with the rest going into ordinary units. Sometimes, however, the first two years' premiums may go into capital units. Capital units add a major extra complication to the problem of working out the real cost of a company's charges structure: the cost of the capital-unit charges is much greater than many investors realize, because of the workings of compound interest.

One of the best sources of information on the total effect of companies' charges is *Money Management* magazine's *Self-Employed Pensions Handbook*. This is available from the Books Marketing Department, Money Management, Greystoke Place, London EC4A 1ND.

## Playing the Stock Market

Playing the stock market in your own right must be regarded as a luxury. Not only are the dealing costs usually greater than if you invest through a unit trust or investment trust but unless you are careful about getting a good spread of shares your investment strategy is likely to involve more risk. Even so, following the stock market can be an absorbing hobby and you may decide you can afford the risks, particularly if you are already making the most of life insurance and other investments that enjoy special subsidies.

Share experts usually advise that you need at least ten different shares to have a well-balanced portfolio. And each share should be in a different area of activity: you do not have much protection against the vagaries of chance if, for instance, you invest in ten gold-mining companies.

To buy shares you usually need to deal through a stockbroker. If you do not have a stockbroker, you can get a list of stockbroking firms interested in private clients by writing to the Public Relations Department of the Stock Exchange, Threadneedle Street, London EC2. An alternative is to deal through your bank, which will forward your instructions to its stockbrokers. But this will involve a delay of a day or two.

Stockbrokers on the London Stock Exchange are simply agents. The heart of the stock market is the 'jobbing' system. Stockjobbers are share wholesalers whom stockbrokers deal with on behalf of the public. They hold a supply of shares and when asked to deal by a stockbroker quote two prices: a buying price and a selling price. Usually their selling prices are at least 2 per cent above what they buy at. The prices quoted in newspapers are 'middle' prices, notional prices standing half-way between the jobbers' buying and selling prices.

The fundamental criterion in assessing how much you should pay for a share is the flow of dividends it will produce. You have to establish not only the present level of dividends but guess at how quickly they will rise in the future. Dividends in turn depend on a company's current profits and its scope for profits growth in the future. Newspapers like the *Financial Times*, *The Times*, the *Daily Telegraph* and the *Guardian* quote companies' current dividends as a percentage of the latest share price. This figure is known as the 'yield'. Normally yields are quoted gross, that is, before deduction of tax (even though basic-rate tax, currently 30 per cent, is deducted automatically at source).

Of course, most investors buy not so much for dividend income but in the hope of seeing the shares rise in value. The most important reason that shares rise, however, is that later investors, perhaps big institutions, take a more sanguine view of a company's dividend-paying prospects thanks, for instance, to an unexpectedly large jump in profits. As a general rule, the lower a company's current-dividend yield the more optimistic the stock market is about the prospects for dividend growth: investors, recognizing the jam tomorrow, have pushed up the shares ahead of the event.

Companies have typically had yields of between 5 and 10 per cent in most of the recent past. Those companies on very high yields may be suspect. The stock market may believe that bad trading may soon force a dividend cut. Or a company may operate in a politically unstable area, with its assets in imminent danger of expropriation. The trick is to spot companies on high yields whose prospects are not as bad as the stock market thinks. When the penny drops with other investors, the shares will rise.

The market in government securities – gilts – has for decades been undermined by inflation and they offer less hope of long-term growth. Gilts can, however, be a relatively safe short- to medium-term investment. And, if high inflation is finally cured, long-term fixed-interest stocks will show spectacular growth.

More information on investing in gilts is given in the section on short-term saving in Chapter 7.

**Further Reading**

There are many books on shares and other risk investments. *How the Stock Exchange Works* by Norman Whetnall (Flame Books) is a good general introduction to share investment. And for the more advanced there is *The Stock Exchange and Investment Analysis* by R. J. Briston (Allen & Unwin).

Unit-trust and investment-trust followers may be interested in *Unit Trusts: What Every Investor Should Know* by Christopher Gilchrist and *Investment Trusts Explained* by A. A. Arnaud (both published by the Cambridge firm, Woodhead-Faulkner).

Sophisticated investors will want to analyse balance sheets. Useful reading includes *How to Read a Balance Sheet* (a programmed-learning text available from the International Labour Office in London) and *Understanding Company Financial Statements* by R. H. Parker (Pelican).

# 11. Wills

### How to Go About Making a Will

Few people like making a will for it can be a disagreeable reminder of mortality. Indeed, three of every ten men and women who die in Britain leave no will behind them, and in those cases, the law lays down who is to get their possessions and in what proportions. If no one else is there, the state may finally take the funds itself. So there is every case for steeling yourself to make one.

The first question is whether you consult a solicitor or do it yourself. There is nothing to stop you making a will on your own. But you need to be sure that your plans for disposing of your possessions are straightforward, that there are no complications in the form of family businesses, trusts, settlements or whatever, and that the words you use in the will mean in law what you think they mean. A misused technical term may ensure that at least some of your money goes to the wrong people. Lawyers make infinitely more money out of ambiguous home-made wills than ever they do in drafting ordinary ones.

Finally comes size. If the total value of everything you own is so large that the family may have to pay capital-transfer tax (CTT) on your death, again you should get professional help. Careful arrangements can cut back the size of any tax bill the family or whoever else is going to benefit from your will has to pay eventually. As we explain in the tax chapter, CTT is cumulative and can cover gifts that you make in your lifetime, so it is not straightforward. Doubts on any of these points should send you off to a solicitor.

If you decide to go it alone, you can use the simple will forms which are available at many stationers and cover the standard situations, where husbands leave all their money to their wives, widows divide what they own equally between their children or people make over all their funds to charities. Many of them will contain the standard legal precautions we discuss below. Alternatively you can always draft your own. Whatever you decide, you should first assess what you are worth, or rather what you would be worth if you were dead. There may be a house, car, life-insurance policy, furniture, family pictures, jewellery and so on. On the other side come any of the mortgage you have yet to pay off, any bank loans or hire-purchase commitments you may have, and whatever you owe on credit cards. If there are likely to be major foreseeable changes in the next four or five years – with promotion at work or even expectations under the will of some elderly relation – they are worth taking in too.

Then comes the list of people to whom you want to leave tokens by which to remember you. There may be golf clubs for some enthusiastic nephew, family brooches for your daughters, and legacies of perhaps £200 to godchildren, doctors or devoted secretaries. Usually, though, there is one main beneficiary who will receive the bulk of what you leave after the small presents have been made. The 'residual legatee', to use the legal jargon, comes last in line for payment, and as a result, any tax which is due will usually cut back his share rather than reduce what goes to the most distant people who actually collect the bequests and legacies.

That, at least, is the rule except in the case of a house or land. But you can soon get round the problem, if you want to, by willing that each legacy should bear an appropriate share of tax.

If you draft your own will, you need above all to be precise. The classic problem arises when a father with three girls leaves everything to his favourite daughter, without naming her. There are other less obvious ambiguities. Assume you write a will to say that you leave all your money to be divided among your nephews and nieces. Two questions arise. Do you mean your money in the sense of your cash in the bank and your savings, or do you want them to inherit all your property including the house and car? The second problem is whether you count your wife's sister's children as nephews and nieces. If you leave everything to your children, but have an illegitimate son in the background, you should make clear whether he is included. The general rule is that he will be unless you say otherwise.

When you are dealing with classes of people, children, grandchildren, nephews, or nieces, it is wisest to name them. If you want other people in the group – as yet unborn, like grandchildren – to be included in the ultimate share-out, you should say so.

Other apparently easy questions can create similar difficulties. Many a husband making his own will leaves everything to his wife, but lays down that when she dies, what he has provided should be shared equally among their children. If you make that stipulation, you run the risk that your wife will become 'life tenant' of the estate – able to live on the interest that your money creates, but not to use the capital. In the same way she could live in the house or other property, but would not be free to sell it. Life tenancies used to be a useful way of avoiding death duties, but they are of no use for CTT. Inflation is beginning to make a nonsense of the whole idea except on very large estates. If you are going to leave everything to your wife outright, you must accept it becomes hers, and she must decide how ultimately she wants to dispose of it.

If you are leaving money to people in particular proportions – so that one gets half of what you leave and another gets a quarter, for instance – you should avoid putting any figures in pounds and pence based on the value of your estate at the moment. Inflation will make the figures look foolish when distributions actually take place whereas the shares in terms of percentages will make sense, whatever the estate is worth. What is more, if your final estate is far bigger than what you have left to the beneficiaries you have mentioned, the rest of what you leave will be distributed as though you had not made a will at all.

If you have a wife and young family, it is easy to leave all the money to her knowing she will use the money to bring up the children. But there is always the possibility that you will both be killed together, perhaps in a car crash. Naming a guardian to look after the children, if that happens, is one move. But you should make clear that the funds are to go to your children, assuming that is what you want. It also makes sense to appoint trustees of the will, whose job is to use your money for the children's advantage while they are under age. Trustees, by the way, probably need wider investment powers than those the law gives them normally. It is also as well to give them authority to use the capital and income in full while the children are under eighteen. If you do not, trustees have to hold half the funds back to present them to the children as they become adult.

There are other legal clauses which may be useful. If you leave everything you have to your wife, you should include the proviso that this should happen only if she survives you by at least twenty-eight days. Although this may seem a quibble, there are very good reasons for it. If you die first, all the money will pass to her free of tax, because transfers between spouses do not attract CTT. But if she follows you into the grave a week later, she will not have had the enjoyment of the money. But her estate and yours together – which have all become hers for that week – may attract CTT, or indeed extra CTT, which would not have been payable if you had drafted the will differently.

That is one point. The other covers how the estate will be distributed. If you have no children, and your wife has left no will, everything she owned, including what you left her, will go to her family.

Finally, you need to name an executor, whose job is to wind up the estate, pay any tax which is due from its resources, and finally distribute what is left in line with your wishes. If children are involved, it will not be the usual twelve-month slog. It might last for ten or twelve years, until the children are eighteen. It is not an easy job, as we go on to show, and the worst course you can take is to invite someone who is not good with paperwork to do it, on the grounds that they might be offended otherwise. One candidate if you are leaving everything to your family is your partner, who may well be receiving most of what you are leaving. But detailed administrative work may be the last thing he or she wants to do after a bereavement, so perhaps one of your children could take on the job.

Solicitors and the big high-street banks will always act as executors, and so will a government body – called the Public Trustee (which works on a non-profit-making basis) – whose fees are sometimes slightly lower than those elsewhere. Whichever you choose, their advantage over a friend or member of the family is that in a sense they are immortal, so that there are no worries that the executor will die before you do. If you are making your own will and do not know whom to appoint, you can always add the words, 'I appoint the Public Trustee as Executor (and Trustee) of this my will.'

Outsiders (including the Public Trustee) will charge fees and insist that the will should allow them to do so, though fees are the last things that those you know personally can demand, if you ask one of them to become executor. Normally executors are entitled to their expenses, but nothing for their time and trouble. It may be a nice gesture to make some recognition in the will, in the form of a bequest, of all the work that the executor will have to do.

## The Legal Rules

The rules for making wills in Scotland are different from those in England and Wales, and Northern Ireland's regulations are almost but not quite the same as those across the sea in Lancashire. So what follows applies to England and Wales only.

You have to be over eighteen to make your own will, through a solicitor, on a will form, or on your own. If you make your own will, you must sign it at the end, in front of two witnesses, also over eighteen, who must then sign it themselves in front of you, and add a note of their names, addresses and occupations under their own signatures. Neither of them must be 'beneficiaries' – getting something from the will – nor indeed, be married to people who are going to do so. What happens if they come into these categories? The will itself is valid, except for what you leave to them or their spouses.

You should always date the will so that if there are any previous wills, your executors will know which set of instructions to follow. In fact, it is probably wise to destroy any earlier wills just in case any confusion should arise. Finally, you have to find somewhere safe for it to go – like your bank, for instance – perhaps leaving a note on your private papers about where it is to be found.

Wills can easily date, as you grow more affluent, acquire new possessions or sell off others, and perhaps become subject to taxes which you were too poor to bother with earlier. So it is wise to look at your will every four or five years to see if changes are needed, and to do the same when the government brings in alterations in the way capital is taxed. Marriage, for instance, will invalidate your will automatically and if you do not make another, what you leave is divided according to the intestacy rules described below. Divorce, on the other hand, has no effect at all.

There are plenty of other ways in which wills can become out of date. If you make a bequest leaving the family silver to one daughter as her share of what you leave, and then have to sell it, she will receive nothing at all unless you make some compensation elsewhere.

Once you have made your will, you should leave it as it is. If you want to make small changes, you can add a 'codicil', a separate document setting out your new instructions, though you will need it signed by two independent witnesses just as the will itself was. But you do not need to retrace the original pair. Dating a codicil is crucial, too, and it is also wise to add 'in all other respects, I confirm my will' so that the scope of any changes is absolutely clear.

A major redraft needs a new will. Constant alterations, each signed by two witnesses, are enormously messy and, worse still, will make clear to your family not only who is in, but also who was scratched out to let them in – a process which may keep them at each other's throats for decades. Worse still, there is a risk that they could make the whole will void.

## Executors

If you have agreed to be an executor, the odds are that at some point you will actually be faced with winding up the estate. The job is not as horrific as it looks. The general principle is that when someone died everything they owned is frozen in its tracks. There are one or two exceptions. A joint account where both husband and wife are free to sign on their own authority is one obvious example. Another is a house which husband and wife own between them, in their joint names, at least usually. This freeze will generally remain until you, as the executor, are free to go ahead with distributing what is in the estate.

Specialists suggest that the order in which you should sort things out should be as follows:

Find out what assets the estate contains, and what they are worth.

Work out what debts – bank loans, HP commitment, money due to local tradesmen and so on – are outstanding.

Make detailed estimates of both debts and assets, and make a calculation to determine whether any capital-transfer tax is due, and if it is, how much it is likely to be.

Send details of both to the local probate registry, if you need probate. (For details see 'Probate' below.)

See if the estate needs a temporary overdraft to tide it over from the time you have to pay any CTT to the moment you can sell off what is in the estate. Arrange it, if need be on a separate executor's account.

Pay CTT (except on land and businesses, for which CTT payment comes later).

Collect the grant of probate.

Send official copies of probate (which you will get from the probate registry) to the bank, insurance company, unit trust or companies in which the dead person had shares. They will not accept your own photocopies, usually.

Collect in what they owe the estate.

Decide whether to sell any property and sell it if need be.

Pay the estate's other debts – which may include income tax. You have to sort out the accounts, which is often the worst job the executor has to face.

Send out bequests, where the will has left particular objects to people. Sometimes the word is used for gifts of money which come next.

Pay legacies (which are always money).

Distribute what is left over in the estate, the residue, in the jargon.

In many cases, particularly when the person was in business, it may be worth advertising his death, and asking creditors to come forward. If you do not take this precaution, and distribute the estate only to find a late creditor appears, you could find yourself personally liable for whatever the estate owes him. One way of avoiding the risk is to delay paying out the money, until six months after getting probate. If you delay for that time, there is no risk that you will be responsible for late claims.

You can certainly manage without a solicitor, but if complications arise – perhaps in the form of family business, partnership, or a marriage settlement – it is wise to seek help. The same applies if the will names people of whom you can find no trace.

The fees lawyers charge do not come from your pocket. They come from the estate and will effectively reduce what goes to the last person in line – the residual legatee – who collects what is left over after everything else has been paid. There are no fixed fees. But most solicitors will give you an estimate on how much they will charge, before taking on the work. It is certainly worth getting one.

## Probate

Probate is official recognition of your right to act as executor. It guarantees any third party – like a bank which releases money to you from the dead person's current account, or a company holding the dead person's shares – against any comeback if later complications appear.

Probate is not needed in small, uncomplicated cases. If money in the form of cash, small sums in savings and personal possessions such as furniture and a car are all the estate comprises, then the family can divide them in line with the will's instructions, without getting legal sanction. The one thing which is important is to keep the will itself. While it is there, no one can suggest that it was ignored or concealed to suit one half of the family.

How National Savings will react to a request for someone's money to be released without probate depends on how much is involved. If it is less than £1,500 overall officials may agree to do so. But the decision is up to them, and they are perfectly free to demand a certificate showing probate has been granted before releasing money. The same rules cover funds in Trustee Savings Banks and building societies. Bank managers will occasionally pay over money in a current account to the executor without probate, but at least one of the high-street banks lays down that they can do so only if the whole estate is worth less than £2,000. The same rules often apply to insurance companies. Most executors have to get probate, but the procedure is less complex than it may seem.

When you first register the death with the registrar, he will give you the address of the local probate office, which will supply you with the necessary forms. Those then go back to the office with a copy of the will and death certificate. The office will also want to know the value of what is in the estate – and you have to provide it when they summon you to swear the executor's oath that you are the properly authorized executor, that you will do your duties faithfully and so on. If the figures come to £50,000 or anywhere near it, and the estate is not left to a husband or wife, where no tax is payable, off they will go to the Inland Revenue. Officials there have to assess if capital-transfer tax is due. As the tax covers certain gifts which people make during their lifetimes, the value of the estate may not give you a completely accurate guide to what you have to pay.

The tax assessment will go back to the probate office, and they will ask you for a cheque to cover the sum involved as well as probate fees, which are comparatively small. Once the money has gone to the Inland Revenue and the registry has examined the will, you collect the grant of probate. It then gives you the right to proceed with collecting the assets and finally distributing them.

How do you work out valuation? Property is valued at the price it would go for in the open market, and the same goes for family pictures, furniture and so on. Inevitably probate values tend to be low, but you certainly do not want them so low that the Inland Revenue will regard them as unrealistic. If you want you can always employ valuers, who are skilled in negotiating with the Inland Revenue about what these values should be.

The procedure we have described covers the personal applications' departments in each probate registry. They are simplified and considerably less daunting than those most solicitors have to use. How long probate will take depends on how complex the estate happens to be. But the average period in the registry itself is about six weeks. But it may take six months or more from the date of death to distributing the money finally. If you find yourself having to act as an executor, the Consumer Association's book, *Wills and Probate*, is an extremely useful guide to what to do. It costs £3·95 and you can get it from the association's offices at 14 Buckingham Street, London wc2.

**Intestacy**

If someone dies without leaving a valid will, a member of the family will have to take on the job as executor. They have to apply to the Probate Registry for 'letters of administration', official recognition of their right to do the work. Technically, they are 'administrators', not executors, but what they do is exactly the same. The law lays down who gets first chance to supervise the process. The surviving wife or husband has the right to first refusal, followed by the dead person's children and grand-children. The precedence is long and elaborate, but the problem is often finding someone willing to act.

How the administrator has to distribute the estate depends partly on how much it contains and also on who is there to receive it. A surviving spouse, for instance, can keep all the 'personal chattels', which covers personal possessions like a car, furniture and so on. If no close members of the dead person's family have survived – and the couple are childless – the surviving spouse collects all of the estate. He or she also has an absolute right to the first £55,000 in the estate, if the couple have no surviving children or grandchildren but there are some close members of the family – like parents, a sister or brothers – still alive. If there are children, though, he or she keeps the goods and chattels, but has an absolute right only to the first £25,000.

What happens if the dead person leaves more than that? It depends on the circumstances. Assume a man dies leaving an estate worth £50,000 and a wife and three children survive him. A fourth child has predeceased him, but produced two children of his or her own before doing so. The wife will receive the first £25,000 as before, and she is entitled to half of what is left over – £12,500 in this case – but only as a life tenant. She can use the interest that the £12,500 generates but cannot spend or use any of the capital itself.

The other £12,500 is divided into four. Each of the three surviv-ing children will get a quarter of the money – £3,125 in this case, but it will be outright if they are married or over eighteen. The last quarter is divided equally between the children of the child who has died. When the wife herself dies, the funds in which she had a life interest will be divided among the four families on the same lines. That is what normally happens. But the widow or widower has the legal right to turn that 'life interest' in half the money over £25,000 into a lump sum. What it will be depends on age and obviously on the size of the sum involved. He or she can also buy the family house at whatever the market price happens to be.

Parents have an absolute right to anything left by an unmarried child. Usually they are not alive to take it, so it will be divided equally among the person's brothers and sisters, but if one of them has died and left a family, the children will divide the share their parent would have received. So the process goes on, and if no one is left to receive the money, the government will use it. The Treasury Solicitor's Department looks after wills of this kind, and will sometimes make distributions to people who look as though they have a moral claim to the money. Someone who had looked after the person for many years or was going to benefit from a will which was not technically valid would be an obvious candidate, but the decision is up to officials.

## Challenging a Will

Wills can often seem unfair. Anyone is free to leave his or her money to a girlfriend or boyfriend or the local cats' home with no provision for the family who have had to cope with the last illness. If that happens, though, the family may have the right to challenge its terms.

Anyone putting in a claim must usually apply for alteration within six months of the grant of probate. Courts will sometimes allow cases which come up after that legal limit. But there is always a risk involved in moving late. Wives, ex-wives, children and people who have been treated as children can all claim. Anyone else, like mistresses or common-law wives (*de facto* spouses, as the Law Commission once elegantly described them), who was financially dependent on the dead man can do so too. But unlike the first group they must show that the person whose will they are disputing made a 'substantial' contribution towards their financial needs. There is one final, common-sense exception. Housekeepers, nurses or anyone else who has been maintained as part of a job cannot make a claim on the grounds that the person who has died kept them.

Husbands have the same legal rights as wives in this context. They can sue – and so can the various other people – if a woman's will seems unfair. Courts have to decide whether the will makes reasonable provision for a husband or wife who is disputing a will. But the test for anyone else is slightly less generous, as the provision must be for their maintenance, or really to keep them going. If the will does not do that, the courts decide what reasonable provision will be in pounds and pence. But they have considerable leeway to decide how people should be treated, and what their entitlement should be.

There are circumstances in which wills can be overturned. They are invalid for instance if the person who made them was of 'unsound mind' when he or she did so; the term covers senility as well as mental illness. Wills do not apply either if it becomes clear that they were made under pressure. The problem if you want to contest a will is showing that what you allege is true. If you plan to take action of this kind it is well worth getting legal advice first.